DATE DUE

GAYLORD   PRINTED IN U.S.A.

Neighborhood Control
of Public Programs

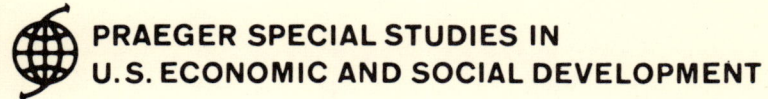

PRAEGER SPECIAL STUDIES IN
U.S. ECONOMIC AND SOCIAL DEVELOPMENT

Neighborhood Control of Public Programs

CASE STUDIES OF COMMUNITY CORPORATIONS AND NEIGHBORHOOD BOARDS

Howard W. Hallman

Foreword by
Royce Hanson

Andrew S. Thomas Memorial Library
MORRIS HARVEY COLLEGE, CHARLESTON, W. VA.

Published in cooperation with the Washington Center for Metropolitan Studies

PRAEGER PUBLISHERS
New York · Washington · London

The purpose of Praeger Special Studies is to make specialized research in U.S. and international economics and politics available to the academic, business, and government communities. For further information, write to the Special Projects Division, Praeger Publishers, Inc., 111 Fourth Avenue, New York, N.Y. 10003.

361.8
H157n

PRAEGER PUBLISHERS
111 Fourth Avenue, New York, N.Y. 10003, U.S.A.
5, Cromwell Place, London S.W.7, England

Published in the United States of America in 1970
by Praeger Publishers, Inc.

All rights reserved

© 1970 by Howard W. Hallman

Library of Congress Catalog Card Number: 73-121713

Printed in the United States of America

FOREWORD

One of the most obvious aspects of the "urban crisis" is that existing systems of local government do not work very well in providing either services or a sense of democratic participation to those who live in cities. Even in rural areas, the poor and minorities often seem apathetic and alienated, in no small part because they regard the institutions that govern them as illegitimate and unresponsive to their needs. In many areas dissatisfaction with existing processes of governance is not confined to the disadvantaged.

In response to the community action-citizen participation thrust of the antipoverty efforts of the past few years, there has been renewed interest in various forms of "grass roots" governing organizations. Borrowing from analogies to town meetings, the ward system, cooperatives, labor unions, and other familiar organizations, a variety of new neighborhood governmental institutions have been spawned. It would now appear that the production of these experiments in participation and control may be among the most important byproducts of the antipoverty programs. An immediate consequence of this activity has been to inject demands for "participation," "community control," and "decentralization" into American political discourse. Quite frequently, these slogans are used with little understanding of the facts of life about community and neighborhood institutions. Idealized word-of-mouth reports of success in some far-off city, based on sketchy news reports or the wish projection of proposal writers, substitute for hard knowledge and clear understanding of the achievements and limitations of these mini-governments.

Howard Hallman's report on neighborhood boards and community corporations should dispel both ignorance and euphoria. By examining the experience of a wide variety of such organizations, he provides practical and comparative information about their strengths and weaknesses. His own commitment to citizen power and his experience in the organization of several attempts to achieve it, give Hallman's judgments a very practical turn. The study is most useful because it avoids ideological blindness and recognizes the problems confronting attempts at community control.

While the community control movement is still in its infancy, it is well to have Howard Hallman's experienced counsel and his perceptive ideas about the future of a significant approach to improving the democratic system and the responsiveness of our public institutions.

>   Royce Hanson
>   The Washington Center
>   for Metropolitan Studies

PREFACE

Demands for neighborhood control of social programs have been growing rapidly during recent years. Today there are both activists and theorists who have made this their cause. And already there are opponents who are resisting the delegation of public programs to organizations controlled by residents of particular neighborhoods. Community control is now a topic of serious public debate and a matter of local contests for power.

The much publicized dispute over neighborhood control of some New York City public schools has aroused great uneasiness among the "establishment" and great despair among the "dispossessed." But this was an atypical situation that occurred while many other communities--including New York itself in other fields of service--were moving more or less harmoniously toward greater citizen involvement in public programs. Yet this other experience is scarcely known. Thus, the debate tends to be a product of hopes and fears, claims and counterclaims.

This study seeks to contribute to public understanding of the issues of community control by analyzing the experiences of a number of fledgling organizations that have sprung up in poverty areas around the country. It is based upon my observation of about 30 community operations in which some degree of control has been given to organizations governed by residents of urban neighborhoods and small rural settlements.

Many of the organizations reviewed can be called community corporations; that is, they have been chartered as private, nonprofit corporations under state law. Others are unincorporated and are commonly known as neighborhood boards in cities and community action groups in rural areas. The common denominator is their governance by a board selected through democratic processes (sometimes through a direct election, sometimes through a pyramid of representation from neighborhood organizations), their control over the appointment and performance of staff, and their authority to make decisions on the allocation of funds within their neighborhoods.

Most of the resident-controlled organizations described here are in some way connected with the Community Action Program and are thus partially financed by funds from the Economic Opportunity Act, which has done more to promote the growth of community control than any other public endeavor. In addition, experiences of projects organized under the Urban Renewal Program and the Model Cities Program are reported.

Much of the material in this volume consists of case studies in a variety of urban and rural areas in the United States. To provide background on the particular communities, each case study presents a brief history leading up to the formation of the community corporation, neighborhood board, or community action group.

To place the subject of community control in a broader historical perspective, citizen participation in public programs during the past two decades is reviewed. This is done in the context of personal experience, primarily in Philadelphia (1952-58) and New Haven (1959-65), where I participated in programs of social reform and civic improvement. In addition, some of my past contacts with the other communities studied are recorded, particularly those made as director of the poverty program study of the Senate Subcommitte on Employment, Manpower, and Poverty in 1967.

Inasmuch as the primary purpose here is to record experience, I have not attempted to develop theoretical models for community control or to make elaborate recommendations to federal, state, and local agencies. However, in the final chapter I present some conclusions which draw upon the case material and suggest issues that need further consideration.

The field work for this study was conducted between April, 1968, and March, 1969. I express my appreciation to the Ford Foundation and the Washington Center for Metropolitan Studies for their support in this work, but I take full responsibility for its findings and recommendations.

        Howard W. Hallman

CONTENTS

	Page
FOREWORD	v
PREFACE	vii
LIST OF ABBREVIATIONS	xiv

Chapter

1 PRELUDE TO PARTICIPATION:
   NEW HAVEN, 1961-65   3

2 COMMUNITY CORPORATIONS IN NEW YORK CITY:
   CITY HALL AND COMMUNITY CONTROL   12

    Antipoverty Organizations   12
    Municipal Reorganization   14
    Organizing Community Corporations   16
       Bedford-Stuyvesant:
         Youth in Action   20
       Ethnic Competition and East Harlem
         Community Corporation   24
       Ethnic Conflict in Three South
         Bronx Corporations   28
       Unity and Competence in
         Brownsville   31
       Other Corporations   36
    Commentary   38

3 THREE CITIES: THREE APPROACHES TO
   COMMUNITY CORPORATIONS   46

    Two Washington, D.C.,
      Community Corporations   46
    Racial Polarization in Newark,
      New Jersey   56
    Columbus, Ohio: East Central
      Citizens Organization   65
    Commentary   73

Chapter		Page
4	COMMUNITY ACTION IN APPALACHIA	75
	Issue Committees in McDowell County, West Virginia	77
	Community Development Volunteers in Raleigh County, West Virginia	79
	Mingo County, West Virginia: Politics and the Community Action Agency	82
	Community Action in Mercer County, West Virginia	85
	Multicounty Agencies in Eastern Kentucky	87
	Commentary	90
5	THREE RURAL AREAS	98
	The Tulare County (Calif.) Community Action Agency	98
	Ten Years' Experience in Guadalupe, Arizona	102
	Rural Mississippi: The Role of Outside Initiative	106
	Commentary	119
6	INDIAN RESERVATIONS	121
	Tribal Administration of OEO Funds	124
	The Zuni Indians	125
	The Northern Pueblo Community Action Program	128
	The Office of Navajo Economic Opportunity	131
	Commentary	136
7	NEIGHBORHOOD CENTERS PILOT PROGRAM	138
	The St. Louis Yeatman District Community Corporation	142
	New York City: The Hunts Point Multi-Service Center Corporation	145
	The People's Involvement Corporation of Washington, D.C.	148
	North Philadelphia's Hartranft Community Corporation	153
	Commentary	157

Chapter	Page
8 CITIZEN PARTICIPATION IN URBAN RENEWAL	163
Limited Resident Involvement: Philadelphia (1952-58)	163
Extensive Resident Involvement: New Haven (1959-65)	166
Hunters Point, San Francisco	168
Collaborative Planning	170
Advocacy Planning	173
Equal-Bargaining Planning in Washington, D.C.	176
Commentary	185
9 NEIGHBORHOOD CONTROL IN TWO MODEL CITIES	187
"Equal Partnership" in Dayton, Ohio	191
Power Struggle in Oakland, California	196
Commentary	202
10 CONCLUSION	205
Standards of Judgment	205
Evaluation Summary	206
Unity, Know-How, and Leadership	211
Representativeness and Accountability	214
The Central Agency	218
Need for a Strategy	221
Neighborhood Government	224
A Final Word	226
ABOUT THE AUTHOR	227

LIST OF ABBREVIATIONS

ACBC	Association of Communities of Bolivar County (Miss.)
AV	Appalachian Volunteers
BIA	Bureau of Indian Affairs (U.S.)
CAA	Tulare County Community Action Agency, Inc. (Calif.)
CAC	Citizens Action Commission (New Haven)
CAP	Community Action Program
CBCC	Central Brooklyn Coordinating Council
CDA	City Demonstration Agencies (HUD)
CDA	Community Development Agency (New York)
CDGM	Mississippi Child Development Group
CHANGE, Inc.	Cardozo Heights Association for Neighborhood Growth and Enrichment (Washington, D.C.)
CIC	Near Northeast Community Improvement Corporation (Washington, D.C.)
CID	Community information depot (LKLP)
CMACAO	Columbus Metropolitan Area Community Action Organization
CPI	Community Progress, Inc. (New Haven)
DNA	DIBEBEIINA NAHIILNA BE AGADITHE, INC. (Navajo legal aid organization)
DOC	Delta Opportunities Corporation
ECCO	East Central Citizens Organization (Columbus)
EOC	Economic Opportunity Committee (New (York)
FCM	Friends of the Children of Mississippi
FDP	Freedom Democratic Party
FHA	Federal Housing Administration
FRT	Federal Review Teams
GO	Guadalupe Organization, Inc. (Ariz.)
HDA	Housing and Development Administration (New York)
HDC	Human Development Corporation (St. Louis)
HEW	Department of Health, Education and Welfare (U.S.)

HITP	Housing Improvement Training Program (Navajo)
HRA	Human Resources Administration (New York)
HUD	Department of Housing and Urban Development (U.S.)
IPA	Institute of Public Administration (New York)
LKLP	Leslie, Knott, Letcher, and Perry Counties Community Action Council (Kentucky)
MACE	Mississippi Action for Community Education, Inc.
MAP	Mississippi Action for Progress
MAT	Moving Ahead Together (Dayton)
MCDA	Manpower and Career Development Agency (New York)
MEND	Massive Economic Neighborhood Development (East Harlem)
MICCO	Model Inner City Community Organization (Washington, D.C.)
NACD	National Association for Community Development
NCPC	National Capital Planning Commission
NDC	Neighborhood Development Center (UPO)
OEDC	Oakland Economic Development Council
OEO	Office of Economic Opportunity (U.S.)
ONEO	Office of Navajo Economic Opportunity
OSTI	Organization for Social and Technical Innovation
PAAC	Philadelphia Anti-Poverty Action Committee
PIC	People's Involvement Corporation (Washington, D.C.)
QUALICA	Community Corporation of Queens Bridge, Astoria, and Long Island City (New York)
RDC	Reconstruction and Development Corporation (Washington, D.C.)
RLA	Redevelopment Land Agency (Washington, D.C.)
SCOPE	Supporting Council on Preventive Effort (Dayton)
SCOUR	Special Committee on Urban Renewal (Dayton)
SNCC	Student Non-Violent Coordinating Committee
TAAC	Target Area Advisory Committees (Oakland)
THAT	Tribal Housing and Training Program (Navajo)

UCC	United Community Corporation (Newark)
UPO	United Planning Organization (Washington, D.C.)
VISTA	Volunteers in Service to America
WAY	Washington Action for Youth
WIRC	Washington Interagency Review Committee
WOPC	West Oakland Planning Committee
YIA	Youth in Action (New York)

Neighborhood Control
of Public Programs

CHAPTER 1 PRELUDE TO PARTICIPATION: NEW HAVEN, 1961-65

The human rights revolution has been a major theme of the domestic history of the United States since the end of World War II. Seeking to put into practice the promise of equality made in the Declaration of Independence, this revolution has taken varied forms. As it sweeps forward toward the 1970's, an emerging trend is the demand for greater control over social institutions by the persons who are involved in these institutions. One aspect of this trend--community control of social programs--is the main topic of this volume.

The effect of this demand for community control is to revolutionize the approach to citizen participation in public programs. For control is much different from participation in neighborhood organizations, advisory committees, informational meetings, and public hearings that have been the characteristic form of citizen involvement in the last several decades.

This recent emphasis upon community control emerged rather suddenly in varied forms in 1966. As an expression of poor-people power, neighborhood control grew under the Community Action Program (CAP), which began in late 1964 under the Economic Opportunity Act. By 1966, CAP had become involved in the issue of neighborhood control in several cities. Community control emerged as a demand of black nationalists as a means of achieving "black power," a slogan that gained popularity during the James Meredith Mississippi Freedom March of June, 1966. As a reaction to the ineffectiveness of programs controlled by stagnant, big-city bureaucracies, neighborhood control became a major interest of Mayor John Lindsay's administration in New York City during this same period.

In a programmatic sense, the concern for community control can be traced to some of the assumptions, though not the organizational forms, of two creative community programs of the early 1960's--the youth development program of the President's Committee on Juvenile Delinquency and Youth Crime and the Gray Area Program supported by the Ford Foundation. Yet these forerunners of the Community Action Program in practice made no provision for true neighborhood control. This is important to recall in order to better understand how far and how fast the forms of resident participation have developed in the last few years.

The requests for funds from Ford and the President's Committee talked about giving poor people more control over their destinies in order to provide for them a greater stake in society and thus reduce their alienation. But in none of the 18 projects created by the two programs did the organizational structure give the persons served a significant voice in formulation of policy, hiring of staff, or control of funds.

In none of the demonstration cities could the programs be called grass-roots in origin. Instead they were the product of socially concerned, progressive leadership: elected officials, staff professionals, and established civic leaders, mostly upper-middle class in background. Except for a project in Harlem, the board members were overwhelmingly white as were most of the staff executives.

The common pattern of organization was a coalition board with members representing the mayor, city departments dealing with social programs, private social welfare agencies, civil rights organizations, religious groups, and sometimes, but not always, the economic "power structure." Neither the Ford Foundation nor the President's Committee required board representation for the neighborhoods being served, and that which the local projects provided was generally token in nature, consisting of middle-class professionals who happened to live, work, or have a constituency in the inner city. This central board held control, although in a number of cases an able and aggressive executive staff was the moving force in policy formulation as well as program administration. This is not at all surprising but is, instead, characteristic of the way social programs were organized and operated prior to the mid-1960's.

PRELUDE TO PARTICIPATION: NEW HAVEN, 1961-65

The case of New Haven, Connecticut, illustrates well the growing interest in the development of community organization programs during this period. New Haven was governed then by what Yale political scientist Robert Dahl described as an "executive-centered coalition." Around each major field of public concern, such as urban renewal, education, economic development, and others, were leadership coalitions with different people involved in each but with dynamic and aggressive Mayor Richard C. Lee at or near the center of all of them. At the staff level, by far the most dominant person was Edward J. Logue, the hard-driving development administrator. Beginning in 1954, the mayor and Logue teamed to make urban renewal the top priority in the Lee administration, and, by 1959, the city had the most far-reaching urban renewal program in the nation. (For New Haven's approach to citizen participation in urban renewal, see Chapter 8.)

One of the things that had long concerned the reformers who held municipal power in New Haven was the need for a deeper approach to the social problems to complement the strong push for physical improvements. Twice Lee had approached Ford Foundation officials without success, and in December, 1959, Logue, another staff member, and I went to New York City in a new attempt to gain Ford support. This time the response was encouraging, but before a proposal was developed Logue switched his attention to Boston, first part-time and then full-time by the end of 1960. In the interim, the planning of a social program was held in abeyance.

After Logue left and staff assignments were shuffled, I renewed the effort to develop a new social program. During the early months of 1961, I gathered together about a dozen staff people from public and private agencies which were part of the executive-centered coalition, and we formulated a tentative proposal which we thought the Ford Foundation might support. At about this time, a huge school building program was proposed, and the Board of Aldermen authorized bond funds for the whole package. By then, the Board of Education was clearly dominated by Lee's appointees. Board President Mitchell Sviridoff and his colleagues began to think how they might improve school curriculum, and naturally they, too, thought of Ford Foundation funds. By June, we merged our respective proposals and had an encouraging meeting with Ford officials.

After further revision, we again submitted the proposal in November, and a month later our contacts at the Ford Foundation were given approval from their trustees to negotiate a grant for New Haven.

Until then, the work had been performed mainly at the staff level, except for two or three lay members of the Board of Education. As the negotiations entered the final stage, Mayor Lee--always informed as things progressed--entered the proceedings in a major way. His concerns were primarily twofold: the composition of the board of Community Progress, Inc. (CPI), the new organization being formed to run the program; and the appointment of the executive director.

The initial CPI board had three persons appointed by the mayor and one each to represent the Redevelopment Agency, the Board of Education, the Citizens Action Commission, Yale University, the United Fund, and the Community Council. In practice, Lee controlled the first six, and the other three were part of the executive-centered coalition. The nine included a Negro, a Jew, a Catholic, and six upper-middle class white Protestants, for Lee wanted an appearance of respectability to protect the program from attack by conservative interests. This need seemed to be particularly important; he selected as executive director Mitchell Sviridoff, who as president of the state AFL-CIO had long been a champion of liberal causes in Connecticut. Similarly, I was appointed deputy director. Lawyers from the Redevelopment Agency quietly got a state charter for the new organization, a meeting was held in the mayor's office, and the new board endorsed the mayor's selections for executive director and deputy director. That done, the program and the $2.5 million Ford Foundation grant were announced to the public.

The new program was developed and announced in this manner because that was the style of New Haven's executive-centered coalition, not because the program itself required secrecy. Indeed, the basic concepts of the program immediately gained widespread public support: provision of new opportunities for poor persons, a multifacet approach to complex social problems, work at the neighborhood level, community schools as an institutional focus for neighborhood activities. The initial programs concentrated on education, employment, leisure-time activities,

PRELUDE TO PARTICIPATION: NEW HAVEN, 1961-65

coordination of social services, and neighborhood organization. A companion planning grant from the President's Committee on Juvenile Delinquency was received for the purpose of designing a fuller youth development program.

As other federal grants were obtained, education and manpower development became the two largest programs, for these were the primary interest of Sviridoff, whose creative leadership dominated the whole CPI program. The task of neighborhood organization by CPI was assigned to neighborhood coordinators, six in the beginning and four later as smaller neighborhoods were combined for administrative purposes. Each of these had a staff of several neighborhood workers, nonprofessionals who lived in the neighborhood served. This team had responsibility for coordination of services and outreach activities, as well as working with neighborhood groups.

CPI's neighborhood organization program was not without strains, for some of the new CPI staff who moved to New Haven from other cities were unaccustomed to working in an alliance with municipal government and instead were much more at home fighting City Hall. Moreover, as is often the case with agencies with decentralized operations, there was tension between headquarters and the field staff, each of which had a different perspective on problems and programs. The first major issue to arise was how far the CPI staff could go in identifying with neighborhood organizations.

After a year's experience the following policy was worked out by a joint committee of CPI's board, headquarters staff, and field staff:

> The neighborhood staff shall not do <u>for</u> people but work <u>with</u> people. They should offer advice, counsel, render assistance of an organizational, technical or generally supportive nature. The neighborhood staff should bring to the attention of the neighborhood those problems which may be of concern to them.
>
> In providing consultation to individuals and neighborhood organizations, members of the neighborhood

> staff shall consistently recognize the right of the organization to establish its own goals and its own methods of attaining these goals. They should encourage the development of self-reliance and initiative. It shall be the role of the consultant to provide technical assistance to the group. To assure effectiveness no member of the neighborhood team shall become a member of a neighborhood organization or act as its spokesman. In the event of conflict between the policy of a neighborhood organization and the policy of CPI, the autonomy and the rights of the neighborhood organization shall be respected.[1]

This policy was in accord with current social work theory, which was no mere coincidence; CPI's director of neighborhood services was Milton Brown, a former staff member of the National Federation of Settlements and Neighborhood Houses.

CPI's neighborhood organization activities tended to focus upon specific neighborhood problems, and for quite a while they were not particularly connected to the broader program development activities of CPI's central staff. The first major planning effort was to develop an action proposal for the President's Committee on Juvenile Delinquency. In the process, the planning staff spent a lot of time with staff from youth-serving agencies. In addition, the youth planning director and I made one round of the neighborhoods to meet with small committees drawn together by the neighborhood coordinators in order to hear the neighborhood's concerns and ideas for youth programs. We intended to have a second round in order to present CPI's tentative proposal, but we became so engrossed in developing a conceptual design that would meet the demands of the research-oriented project-review panel of the President's Committee that we did not find the time for it.

As in planning for the Ford Foundation grant, we performed like most of the cities getting these new

---

[1] Community Progress, Inc., *Policy Statement re Operation of Neighborhood Services Staff* (New Haven: Community Progress, Inc., 1963), p. 1.

funds from Ford and the President's Committee. The truth is that almost all local social planning around the country in the early 1960's was done by staff experts, with lay boards and elected officials scarcely consulted and with persons served rarely meaningfully involved. The only step we took toward greater than usual resident participation was to propose setting aside some leisure-time funds that neighborhood residents could allocate as they determined. This bothered the federal bureaucrats because we could not say exactly what the money would be spent for, but because it was only 5 per cent of the budget they accepted it. However, the plan never materialized because the neighborhood staffs of the Board of Education, the Recreation Department, and participating settlement houses said they had to know precisely how much money would be allocated to them and could not wait for the residents to decide. The need to maintain their cooperation in the difficult task of building interagency community school teams became an overriding consideration, so CPI allocated the money directly to the agencies and dropped the idea of neighborhood determination.

As the youth development project and other federal grants brought more funds to CPI, the neighborhood services division quadrupled its staff of neighborhood workers. By the end of 1964, the division had a director and four professionally trained neighborhood coordinators, two assistant coordinators promoted from the neighborhood workers' staff, twenty neighborhood workers, plus seven secretaries, all recruited from inner-city neighborhoods. Most of the new neighborhood workers were assigned to service programs, such as manpower and community schools, to perform recruitment and follow-up.

Thus, in November, 1964, when New Haven became one of the first cities to receive a grant from the newly established Office of Economic Opportunity (OEO), it was using two principal methods to achieve "maximum feasible participation of residents of the areas and members of the groups served"[2]--hiring indigenous neighborhood workers and engaging in neighborhood organization activities. These are two of the three suggested methods in the preliminary guidelines drafted by OEO. The third was resident

---

[2]Economic Opportunity Act of 1964, P.L. 88-452, sec. 202 (a)(3).

participation upon the policy board, a matter that became crucially important to OEO during the first half of 1965.

CPI was slow to respond to this new federal demand. There were staff discussions on this matter in February, 1965, and in April the board appointed a committee to study the matter. This led to the establishment in June of a city-wide Residents Advisory Committee to devise a plan for board expansion. By November, a year after the first OEO funds were received, representatives from each of the seven neighborhoods with CPI programs were added to the board, raising total membership to 16. In addition to the seven selected by the residents, three were inner-city clergymen who had been appointed previously by the mayor and participating agencies.

In these years, 1961-65, New Haven was considered to be in the vanguard of social reform. So also were most of the other communities with project grants from the Ford Foundation and the President's Committee. Although these projects differed in detail, the main thrust was the same: professional staff and upper-middle class civic leaders took initiative and maintained control.

But this was to change for those projects which came under the Community Action Program (about half of them). Like CPI, these other agencies had to add representatives of the poor to their governing boards. So, too, did newly organized community action agencies.

Soon so many new agencies had been formed that a new interest group emerged: the local staff directors of community action agencies. They banded together and formed the National Association for Community Development (NACD). They had to quickly come to grips with the issue of resident participation, and, in June, 1965, the NACD board of directors adopted a position paper that is considered a landmark document on this topic. This statement accepted board representation but with some skepticism as to its value. The promotion of protest and political action by OEO was resisted, but the biggest concern was over the loss of local initiative which was starting to occur as OEO began to issue national directives. The statement contained a long list of methods for resident participation, and, although this list included "self-managed, indigenous organization carrying out programs,"[3] the notion of what later came to be called "community corporations" was scarcely considered either by NACD or OEO.

Nonetheless, by mid-1965, social programs and their underlying ideology had developed to a stage where soon the idea of community corporations would be cropping up here and there, freshly "invented" by several communities during the next year. The phase of the civil rights movement that emphasized integration and equal participation in the larger society had reached its climax with the passage of the Civil Rights Act of 1964 and the Voting Rights Act of 1965. The next stage would stress black pride, self-determination, and black power. Each year since 1966, demand for community control of social programs has become more widespread and more insistent, and in a number of places around the United States residents of poor communities have gained some measure of control. The experience of operating self-managed social programs in some of these communities is related in the following chapters.

---

[3] National Association for Community Development, <u>The Community Action Agency and Resident Participation</u>, Washington, D.C., 1965, pp. 22-23. (Mimeographed.)

CHAPTER 2 COMMUNITY CORPORATIONS IN NEW YORK CITY: CITY HALL AND COMMUNITY CONTROL

In December, 1965, John Lindsay, who the previous month had been elected mayor of New York City, asked Mitchell Sviridoff, executive director of CPI in New Haven, to join his new administration. Sviridoff agreed to head a study group in New York for six months to examine a cluster of human resources services, including welfare, manpower, community action, youth, and education. I agreed to work part-time on the study.

ANTIPOVERTY ORGANIZATIONS

Because most of the members of the study group were out-of-towners, our first task was to get a quick education on the recent political and administrative history of New York City. Although this briefing covered many topics, this chapter will cover only that phase related to the community action program.

When New York's antipoverty program was set up, the main actors were Mayor Robert Wagner, who in 1965 was nearing the end of a generally adequate but tired 12-year administration; Paul Screvane, president of the city council and heir apparent to Wagner; Adam Clayton Powell, powerful Harlem congressman who presided over the House Education and Labor Committee, which had jurisdiction over the antipoverty program; and Governor Nelson Rockefeller. Outside the government, the most powerful force was the "social welfare establishment," a coalition of professionals and prestigious lay leaders who run multimillion dollar voluntary agencies.

COMMUNITY CORPORATIONS IN NEW YORK CITY

In June, 1964, five months after President Johnson declared "an unconditional war on poverty" and two months before Congress passed the Economic Opportunity Act, Wagner issued an executive order creating the Mayor's Council Against Poverty and the Poverty Operations Board. Both were composed wholly of city officials, and both were chaired by Paul Screvane. A staff was hired with city funds and proceeded to prepare an application for federal funds.

By the following March, a program proposal was ready for submission to the newly founded U.S. Office of Economic Opportunity. The program was to be city controlled and operated mainly through public and large city-wide private agencies. However, Congressman Powell criticized such City Hall domination, and even the private agencies were not satisfied that they had sufficient say in policy decisions. In response, Mayor Wagner issued a new executive order in May, 1965, expanding membership on the Council Against Poverty to include representatives of various interest groups, creating a new Economic Opportunity Corporation to serve as the operating arm of the Council, and reconstituting the Poverty Operations Board (adding the prefix "Anti"). Under this arrangement, the first two bodies would use federal funds, and the latter would handle city money.

But when the Council Against Poverty filed papers with the state government to become a private nonprofit corporation, the secretary of state denied the request on grounds that some of its functions were governmental. To get around this obstacle, legislation was introduced to establish the Council and the Economic Opportunity Corporation as public authorities. The state legislature approved this plan, but Governor Rockefeller vetoed the bill on June 30, 1965. As this was the last day in the federal fiscal year and OEO was holding up its grant pending the establishment of a legal agency to be the recipient, Mayor Wagner hastily issued another executive order continuing the reorganized Council and establishing an Economic Opportunity Committee (EOC) as its operating arm.

The Council increased in size as other interests were added, until it had more than 80 members. As it grew, it became too big to function effectively, and many powers were delegated to an executive committee. However, responsibility to review various local agencies' requests for federal funds was given to a planning and coordinating committee, which consisted mainly of staff from public and private social welfare agencies. This multiplicity of city agencies was bad enough, but the situation at the neighborhood level was even more complicated.

In the early 1960's when juvenile delinquency, rather than poverty, was a major focus of social concern, three major youth development agencies had been established to serve specific areas within the city: HARYOU in Central Harlem, Mobilization for Youth on the Lower East Side, and Youth in Action (YIA) in the Bedford-Stuyvesant section of Brooklyn. The first two received grants from the President's Committee on Juvenile Delinquency, and the third was about to receive funds when the federal emphasis changed; all three immediately got in line to receive antipoverty grants.

Meanwhile, Mayor Wagner's first Council Against Poverty designated 16 parts of the city as antipoverty areas, including the three with existing youth agencies. Then, in the fall of 1964, the Poverty Operations Board, under Screvane's direction, gave grants from city funds to eight local groups to start antipoverty planning. One was to the Central Brooklyn Coordinating Council, which like Youth in Action operated in Bedford-Stuyvesant; three were to existing organizations in other areas; and four were to newly created antipoverty boards. A year later, the newly created Economic Opportunity Committee set about to operate community progress centers in 20 of the poverty areas; these were designed and controlled from central headquarters, although community committees were created through "community conventions" to advise on the operations of the centers. In seven of the ten areas, the grantees of the Anti-Poverty Operations Board were already functioning. But in two of the 16 designated poverty areas, nothing was started.

MUNICIPAL REORGANIZATION

Thus, when John V. Lindsay was inaugurated as mayor in January, 1966, confusion was monumental in the city's antipoverty program. And this was only one small part of the municipal government. Overall, more than 60 agencies reported directly to the mayor, a number well beyond an acceptable span of control. The time was overdue for a reorganization of city government.

Lindsay's solution, in large measure a recommendation developed by the Institute of Public Administration (IPA), was to establish 12 super-agencies, to be called "administrations," modeled somewhat after the major federal departments. One of these was to be the Human Resources Administration (HRA), designed to encompass the antipoverty programs, the widely scattered and separately operated manpower programs, the Welfare Department, and the Youth Board, and to have some kind of relationship to the Board of Education, which by state statute had considerable independence and by practice was accountable only to itself. When Sviridoff hesitated to accept the new mayor's invitation to head the Human Resources Administration, Lindsay persuaded him to direct a study group to determine how this new super-agency should be organized. Henry Cohen from IPA was appointed deputy study director.

To the study group, the basic organizational remedy for the antipoverty program was self-evident: simplify; abolish four of the five major boards and committees and streamline the remaining one--the Council Against Poverty with its fewer members, all of whom were private citizens rather than public officials. For we believed that agency representatives had too many vested interests to be impartial board members. To staff the program, the group recommended that a Community Development Agency be established as an operating department of the Human Resources Administration.

I proposed that the Community Action Program be substantially decentralized, because I believed that it needed to be broken into "New Haven-sized chunks" to be manageable. After some internal debate, the study group accepted my proposal that community corporations should be formed, mainly by converting and merging the plethora of existing organizations. Serving areas of 75,000 to 300,000 people, these community corporations would be miniature umbrella agencies acting primarily as planning and coordinating bodies rather than as operating agencies. They would receive financial allocations from the Council Against Poverty and would have authority to apportion funds within their communities and to subcontract specific programs to other agencies. The community corporations would be governed by boards selected by the residents through some form of democratic procedure, the precise method to be worked out in each community.

In the course of our study, we talked to leaders from most of the poverty areas with active programs. Universally they complained about the cumbersome, centralized operations of the community action program, and they expressed a desire for more community control. When we tried out our formulation of community corporations, they reacted favorably although with some skepticism, having been promised things before.

With some minor adjustments, Mayor Lindsay accepted the recommendations of the study group and in August, 1966, issued an executive order establishing the Human Resources Administration and its constituent agencies, including the reorganized Council Against Poverty. By then Sviridoff had agreed to stay in New York and the mayor appointed him Human Resources administrator. As chairman of the reconstituted Council Against Poverty, Lindsay designated Carl McCall, who was on the staff of the Taconic Foundation and had been a member of the study group. Soon afterward, George Nicolau, who had been with OEO's Northeast Regional Office, was appointed commissioner of the Community Development Agency (CDA), and Frank Espada, formerly a leader of a local welfare rights organization, was selected as director of community organization. To Espada, Nicolau, and McCall fell the primary responsibility for getting the community corporations into operation.

ORGANIZING COMMUNITY CORPORATIONS

Following the recommendations of the study group, the Council Against Poverty designated seven new poverty areas in addition to the previous 16 (later, three more were added). However, the initial thrust in the organization of community corporations concentrated on the 15 with existing organizations: the three with youth development agencies, the 11 with community committees (two of which had been served by a single committee), and East Harlem with two city-funded operations (a special case reviewed in more detail later in this chapter). Under the guidelines adopted by the Council Against Poverty after a public hearing, the community committees and youth agencies were given the first option of forming the planning committees for the development of community corporations. In all cases, they were expected to obtain participation on the planning committee of community interests not represented by the existing organization.

The first required step was a public orientation meeting in each poverty area, to be sponsored by the planning committee. At such meetings, McCall, Nicolau, Espada, and some other representative of the Community Development Agency explained the purpose of a community corporation and the procedures to be followed in the establishment of the new organization. In some instances, the planning committee was reluctant to call such a meeting, because it would lead to its own demise, so CDA had to step in as the meeting's sponsor.

These meetings tended to operate in an atmosphere of suspicion and distrust, for a great credibility gap had developed between neighborhood groups and the city agencies operating the antipoverty program. Some had felt that Paul Screvane had used the program as part of his unsuccessful campaign to become mayor (he was defeated in the Democratic primary). The community committees had come to see that their role in the operation of the community progress centers was quite negligible in that the center staffs were city employees who followed a blueprint drawn downtown. Early in 1966, William Haddad and other members of another post-election task force set up by Mayor Lindsay had gone to all the poverty areas and conducted marathon public hearings at which anyone could speak his piece, and did so far into the night. Shortly thereafter, the Sviridoff study group had made rounds of the same areas, talking mainly to leaders of the community committees and youth development agencies. There had been a second round of meetings to explain the study group's recommendations. By the time the organizing orientation meetings were held in 1966, the neighborhood leaders had grown tired of too much talk and too little action. Local militants were suspicious that they were going to be duped again by the white establishment and its Negro and Puerto Rican stooges.

In spite of this air of local skepticism, the local planning committees went about preparing plans of organization for the community corporations. They were assisted by Frank Espada and his staff, most of whom were from the same type of communities. When a group had agreed upon a plan, it was submitted first to CDA staff review and then to a citizen panel consisting of members of the Council Against Poverty. This panel then conducted a public hearing within the community, heard the proposal explained by the planning committee, received dissenting plans, and listened to other witnesses, pro and con. If the community was divided, the panel attempted to negotiate a plan modification that would satisfy as many as possible. Ultimately the panel made a report to the Council Against Poverty recommending acceptance of either the planning committee's proposal or a modification developed by the panel. When the Council approved the plan, the community corporation could be organized. The time required to get to this point ranged from four to ten months.

The next step was the election of the community corporation's governing board, following procedures specified in the plan of organization. The most common pattern was to have the community divided into districts with all the board members, or at least a majority, chosen from these districts. Any resident was eligible to run, but in a number of communities half the seats were reserved for poor people. Nominations were by petition, and with few exceptions persons ran as individuals rather than allied with others on a slate. There tended to be two or three times as many candidates as positions. All residents over a certain age (usually 16) could vote, and no advance registration was required, except in the South Bronx (which as a result had the poorest turnout). Voting machines were supplied free by the Board of Elections, and the American Arbitration Association, under contract with CDA, supervised the polls. CDA had a staff of 50 workers who went from one community to the next publicizing the election and encouraging residents to vote. Altogether about 55,000 voted in those elections, constituting a turnout of about 10 per cent of those eligible.

After the voting, the American Arbitration Association considered challenges and accusations of irregularity, and where seats were reserved for poor persons, proof of income was obtained for those so selected. When this was done, the results were certified to the Council Against Poverty, which resolved any remaining disputes. Once accomplished, the community corporation could incorporate and begin operation. At this stage, CDA provided some elementary orientation for the new board members.

Although the Council Against Poverty established the general pattern for organizing community corporations, there was considerable variation among the communities, arising from differences in social composition, agency structure, and personalities of the principal participants.

Of the 15 communities where the Council Against Poverty and the Community Development Agency sought initially to establish community corporations, three already had incorporated agencies operating youth development programs. Under the adopted procedures, each was to be given the opportunity to form the planning committee. Each had the possibility of becoming the community corporation, but in the end only one achieved that status.

On the Lower East Side, Mobilization for Youth decided not to get directly involved in the process of setting up a community corporation. Instead, it chose to remain autonomous and somewhat aloof from the reorganized community action program. Well experienced in the art of grantsmanship, it apparently believed that it could stand on its own with funding sources and not be dependent upon a resident-controlled community corporation. Therefore, CDA staff helped residents to set up a separate planning committee, and a fledgling community corporation was formed.

In Harlem, the youth development agency, known as HARYOU-ACT, displayed more interest in the process of establishing a community corporation, but it was not able to take on the exclusive, central role. Harlem, as the longest-established center of Negro life in New York City, has the most experienced and most sophisticated leadership and the most complex array of competing forces of all the poverty areas. Harlem leaders opposed to HARYOU-ACT formed an ad hoc committee and claimed the right to be the organizing group. Representatives of five neighborhood boards, which HARYOU-ACT itself had organized, wanted to have a voice for themselves. To achieve unity and a reasonable balance of power, the Council Against Poverty helped to establish a 90-member committee with

30 representatives from each faction. Although this committee has the responsibility for developing a plan for a community corporation, it has not rushed to complete that task and instead has taken over responsibility for allocating antipoverty funds to Harlem agencies. Consequently, Harlem is the only one of the 15 communities where no election has taken place.

In Bedford-Stuyvesant, however, Youth in Action, the third youth development agency, did form the planning committee and reorganize to become the community corporation. How this change occurred is worth examining in more detail.

Bedford-Stuyvesant: Youth in Action

Forty years ago, the name Bedford-Stuyvesant was unknown in New York City. The section of Brooklyn that is now so identified was essentially a white Protestant area adjacent to a Jewish district. There were a few scattered middle-class Negroes living harmoniously alongside their white neighbors. However, when the Independent subway opened a new line through that section about 1940, there began to be a sizable migration of blacks from Manhattan. They settled primarily between Bedford Street and Stuyvesant Street, which are seven blocks apart, and from these streets the community got its name. By now, though, what is called Bedford-Stuyvesant occupies a far larger area and has 300,000 residents of whom 81 per cent are black, 12 per cent Puerto Rican, and 7 per cent white. Slightly more than one out of four families have incomes under $3,000.

Because the black community in Bedford-Stuyvesant is comparatively new, it has not developed an elaborate institutional structure as has Harlem or the Lower East Side, which for nearly a century has been a receiving area for immigrants. In an attempt to build such a structure, the Central Brooklyn Coordinating Council (CBCC) was formed in the 1950's. Consisting of representatives of various churches, social agencies, and neighborhood organizations, it provided a forum for discussion and an instrument for action. Out of its concern for a rising rate of juvenile delinquency, it formed a youth committee. Following the example of similar groups in Harlem and the Lower East Side, this committee formed a new nonprofit organization, Youth in Action, which was incorporated in July, 1964. But whereas the other two communities had planning funds available from the President's Committee on Juvenile Delinquency, by the time Youth in Action was organized, the federal program emphasis was switching to poverty. Whereas the Economic Opportunity Act had not yet passed Congress, YIA turned to the city's Poverty Operations Board and obtained a $223,000 planning grant in order to develop an antipoverty program for Bedford-Stuyvesant.

In the spring of 1965, YIA had its program planned and sought funds from both the city and the U.S. Office of Economic Opportunity. The city responded with an initial action grant of $400,000 in city funds and an allocation of $40,000 from its share of federal funds for the Neighborhood Youth Corps. In September, the city total was raised to $2.5 million. YIA continued its quest for OEO funds, sometimes negotiating directly with the federal agency, sometimes working through the city's Economic Opportunity Committee. Finally, in the spring of 1966, OEO approved a grant of $3 million. That year the city's share was increased, so that YIA had an annual budget of $6 million by the end of 1966, when the process of establishing community corporations began.

The first two years had been stormy for Youth in Action. The problems of poverty in Bedford-Stuyvesant are enormous, and the staff and board had to overcome a long period of neglect by the established public and voluntary agencies. Both the city and federal antipoverty agencies were new and lacked clarity of goals and the facility for effective administration. The dominant persons in YIA were stronger on militant expression than on program development skills, and often they were frustrated and angry in negotiations for funds.

When the staff from the city's newly established Community Development Agency appeared at the December, 1966, orientation meeting in Bedford-Stuyvesant to explain the procedures for establishing a community corporation, they found the front rows filled with skeptical and demanding young blacks. The situation was not made any easier by struggles for power among community leaders. For example, the Central Brooklyn Coordinating Council, the original parent of YIA, was now in opposition to its rebellious and independent offspring.

In the face of hostility and intra-community competition, the CDA staff stuck to the established procedures, allowed YIA to form the planning committee for the community corporation, but insisted that other elements of the community be included. After several months of negotiation, a plan was ready and aired at a hearing conducted by a panel from the Council Against Poverty. It was then approved by the whole Council.

Essentially, the plan called for YIA to be the community corporation but to change from a closed corporation with a self-perpetuating board to one with an open membership. Any resident age 16 and over could join and vote for members of the board of directors. YIA had previously divided the community into five areas, and from each of these 15 persons were elected to the board. Twelve were held over from the old board, and 12 new members were appointed at large by the elected members, making a total of 99. The election was held in May, 1967, with 6,000 participating, and officers were installed a month later.

Although the Sviridoff study group recommended that community corporations become basically planning and coordinating bodies, leaving program operations to other agencies within the community, Youth in Action has continued to conduct most of the programs it initiated during its first year of operation. These activities include Neighborhood Youth Corps, adult job-skills training, five neighborhood manpower centers (for recruitment, counseling, placement, follow-up), five multipurpose neighborhood services (for varied social services), consumer education and action, homework study centers, Head Start, a youth leadership institute, family counseling, training for young mothers, family planning, family day care, and general community organization.

Much of the community organization effort is channeled through five neighborhood boards, which are elected by the residents of the respective areas. The neighborhood boards are not incorporated, have no funds, do not conduct any programs, and hire no staff, although they receive staff assistance from YIA. Instead, they perform a social action role. Although they do not engage in partisan political activities, they have considerably more freedom of action than if they handled government funds and were subject to governmental regulations.

So far, Youth in Action has spun off only one program, but a board committee is studying whether more functions should be delegated. In the meantime, it has not taken on any new operations for itself, and each of the six new programs started in Bedford-Stuyvesant since the corporation was reorganized are being run by delegate agencies. In addition, the other year-round community programs receiving funds from the city CDA are now required to go through YIA and to be included in the over-all Bedford-Stuyvesant program budget.

Throughout this period, interagency rivalry has been a factor in Bedford-Stuyvesant. As noted earlier, the Central Brooklyn Coordinating Council was the parent of Youth in Action, but the two quarreled. Meanwhile, Senator Robert Kennedy became interested in the possibility of community development corporations with emphasis on economic development. In mid-1966, he and his staff initiated the organization of such an agency in Bedford-Stuyvesant. At first, they worked with the leaders of CBCC, and in the spring of 1967 the Renewal and Rehabilitation Corporation was organized, with Senator Jacob Javits and Mayor Lindsay joining as sponsors. However, this new corporation was immediately attacked as not being representative of the community, and when it failed to expand its board, Kennedy's people organized a new group called the Bedford-Stuyvesant Restoration Corporation; Javits and Lindsay also shifted their support to the new corporation. Soon afterward, it received a $6.9 million federal grant.

The Restoration board is self-selected, but it contains a broad segment of Bedford-Stuyvesant leadership. It works in tandem with another new agency called the Development and Service Corporation, which consists of 11 top white business leaders of New York City, who provide supporting services and contacts with the major financial and business corporations.

In 1967, a separate Model Cities committee was set up in central Brooklyn to work in Bedford-Stuyvesant, Brownsville, and East New York. However, its 30 members include five who are on YIA's staff or board.

Because these several organizations have overlapping interests, it was only natural that competition developed among them. To mitigate the ill effects of intra-community conflict, they devised an arrangement to meet regularly in the presence of an outside mediator, which they did for more than a year. As a result, Youth in Action and the Restoration Corporation have worked out a reasonable division of responsibility. However, the Renewal and Rehabilitation Corporation continues to exist even though it has received no major grant; it is composed primarily of persons from the Central Brooklyn Coordinating Council, and these two agencies are at odds with YIA and the Restoration Corporation. The relationship between YIA and the Model Cities committee has had its ups and downs, and when the Model Cities plan was presented at a public hearing, YIA spokesmen protested that they were not properly involved. So, while mediation has helped, it has not resolved all the interagency disputes.

Ethnic Competition and East Harlem Community Corporation

Mediation procedures were also used to settle disagreements among competing groups in East Harlem, but at a different stage of the process. In that community, there were two major antipoverty agencies --MEND (Massive Economic Neighborhood Development) and the East Harlem Tenants Council--competing for control. As it turned out, neither became the community corporation.

East Harlem is located in Manhattan alongside the East River, north of 96th Street where the Penn Central Railroad emerges from a tunnel under Park Avenue. Its western boundary is Fifth Avenue, the traditional dividing line between East Harlem and Central Harlem.

Historically, East Harlem has been a "melting pot" community. Germans and Irish were the predominant groups at the turn of the century, but today the population is about 40 per cent Puerto Rican, 40 per cent black, and 20 per cent white, of whom Italian-Americans are the largest group. Puerto Ricans tend to concentrate in the southern part, known as El Barrio (The Neighborhood), which is the oldest Puerto Rican settlement in New York City, going back to the 1920's. Blacks are most numerous adjacent to Central Harlem, and the Italian population resides primarily in the northeast segment. Nonetheless, there is ethnic mixture throughout East Harlem.

In her book about East Harlem,[1] Patricia Sexton found that even though four out of five residents were Puerto Ricans or blacks, the major civic and social welfare organizations were dominated by white professionals, particularly social workers employed by local settlement houses (most of whom resided elsewhere) and ministers, such as those from the East Harlem Protestant Parish (who lived in the neighborhood). The long-established East Harlem Council, a civic coordinating body composed of organizational representatives, had 26 board members, and only one or two had been Puerto Rican or black.

When the "war on poverty" began, the East Harlem social welfare establishment brought about the formation of MEND. The board was more representative of the community than the East Harlem Council; of the indigenous ethnic groups, blacks had a larger role than Puerto Ricans. The executive director was Ed Daniels, a black man.

At about the same time, the East Harlem Tenants Council was formed through the initiative of Ted Velez, an articulate and hard-driving Puerto Rican. He had been working for Jesse Grey, who had developed the rent strike in Harlem into an effective tool for social action. The Tenants Council was predominantly Puerto Rican in makeup, and it operated primarily in the southern part of East Harlem, where Puerto Ricans have a majority.

Although neither agency was for one ethnic group exclusively, each tended to represent mostly one group. This was an underlying factor in the contention for control that occurred when the community corporation was formed.

The city's original Poverty Operations Board, not wanting to choose sides, gave a grant to each of these East Harlem agencies, $124,000 to MEND and $140,000 to the Tenants Council. When the Economic Opportunity Committee was established in the summer of 1965, it decreed that East Harlem should have a city-run community progress center and community committee. For once, MEND and the Tenants Council were united. They both opposed the city and fought

---

[1] Patricia Cayo Sexton, *Spanish Harlem, Anatomy of Poverty* (New York: Harper & Row, 1965).

long, hard, and successfully to block a new rival. They also succeeded in enlarging their city anti-poverty grants, so that in the 1966-67 fiscal year MEND received $1,342,000 and the Tenants Council $555,000 plus additional funds under other federal programs. This was where things stood when the Community Development Agency attempted to establish a community corporation in East Harlem.

The process of organizing a planning committee started quietly in the fall of 1966. The two staff directors, Ted Velez and Ed Daniels, met with representatives of CDA. It was agreed that a community meeting would be held, that the names of representatives of 33 organizations would be placed in a hat, that five would be drawn, that the persons so selected would join with representatives of MEND and the Tenants Council, and that these seven would select 12 others to form a planning committee. Thus, the "Committee of 19" was born and was ratified at a community meeting held in December, 1966.

The Committee of 19 consisted of 11 Puerto Ricans, 6 blacks, and 2 white clergymen. As it went about its work, the ethnic competition was ever-present. For example, when the committee attempted to divide the community into districts for the purpose of selecting the board of directors of the community corporation, the committee members favored different boundaries, depending upon which ethnic group would gain. Getting nowhere, they appealed to Mitchell Sviridoff. Drawing upon his previous experience as a labor leader, he suggested mediation and explained how it would work. They agreed to give it a try and set about electing mediators who would be acceptable to both sides. They chose two of Sviridoff's top staff--Cyril Tyson, who was then deputy administrator for community relations, and Marta Valle, who was Tyson's chief assistant. Tyson, a black man, and Mrs. Valle, a Puerto Rican, have long been active in New York civic and social welfare programs and are widely respected for their personal integrity and competence. Once selected, they presided over three long sessions, during which a corporation plan was hammered out.

When the Committee of 19 began meeting, the forces allied with Velez and the Tenants Council had the upper hand, usually winning 12-7 on votes, with the MEND faction on the losing side. On the committee

were representatives of several small groups, some
of which were subcontractors or allies of the Tenants
Council and others of MEND. After a while, these
small-group representatives perceived that they had
more in common with each other than with either of
the two large parent organizations, and a small-group
bloc emerged in the proceedings. Although this made
negotiations more difficult, the fluidity it introduced made an agreement eventually possible.

By May, 1967, a plan was ready for submission to
the Council Against Poverty. It called for two poor
and two nonpoor persons to be elected from each of
seven districts. These 28 then had to appoint at
least 7 additional members, and could appoint as many
as 12 more. The plan was presented at a public hearing in East Harlem attended by 750 people. The session was so stormy that it had to be closed down,
and when it was reconvened later only registered
speakers were heard. After further deliberation, the
Council gave its approval in August.

The election of the community corporation board
was not held until December because other community
elections, and then the general state election, tied
up the election staff and voting machines. MEND and
the Tenants Council still did not want to see a community corporation formed, and their forces vacillated
on whether to participate, ultimately doing so, but
weakly. As a result, the small-group bloc gained
control of the community corporation.

As this organizational process was occurring, the
Committee of 19 also served as an interim community
corporation for East Harlem. However, it had no staff
until midsummer of 1967, and this allowed CDA to deal
directly with neighborhood groups in handing out
summer program funds. In the fall, the upcoming election took all of the staff's attention. It was not
until 1968 that staff time was available to set up
the planning and administrative machinery needed for
an effective community corporation. A permanent
executive director had still not been chosen at the
end of the year.

The first substantive effort of the East Harlem
Community Corporation was developing the summer programs for 1968. A ten-member committee worked 60
hours to put a package together. However, the central
CDA had the upper hand in deciding summer programs,

including approval, veto, and direct contracting with neighborhood groups, with the community corporation signing a tripartite contract as a junior partner. When CDA started changing its submission, the fledgling community corporation balked and decided to boycott the summer program altogether and to stage a protest demonstration. This resistance finally led to some summer funds flowing through the corporation, and it helped to achieve greater unity among the competing groups.

Nonetheless, the community corporation continues to be a fairly weak instrument, and an uneasy truce exists among the major East Harlem organizations. When I last visited East Harlem in October, 1968, the community was in the midst of two more crises, one on youth programs, the other regarding school decentralization. I came away with the feeling that the community leaders were worn out by constant struggle and overcommitment. Not only are they working in the antipoverty programs but also in newer ones, such as Model Cities with its separate system of resident participation. Yet all these programs draw on the same pool of leadership. It is hard enough for a community to cope with the different ways in which federal and city program funds flow into the community, and when the community itself is divided, the problem is compounded.

Ethnic Conflict in
Three South Bronx Corporations

The ethnic competition that occurred in East Harlem also emerged in organizing the community corporation for the Hunts Point section of the Bronx. The southern part of the Bronx, where Hunts Point is located, has experienced an almost complete shift in population during the past three decades. Hunts Point now is approximately 60 per cent Puerto Rican, 35 per cent black, and 5 per cent white. In the two adjacent "poverty areas"--Morrisania and South Bronx --blacks outnumber Puerto Ricans and the white minority is somewhat larger. In all three, there is a notable lack of social service institutions, particularly in comparison to such institution-plentiful places as the Lower East Side and Central Harlem.

When a community committee was organized in Hunts Point in November, 1965, by the Economic Opportunity Committee, it was formed as elsewhere by calling together representatives of established organizations. Because there were apparently more black organizations, the community committee had a black majority, and it recommended to the city that a black person be appointed director of the community progress center. This was protested by Puerto Rican residents, who were a majority in the community, but their protests fell on deaf ears downtown, where blacks held most of the top EOC staff positions.

A year later, the reorganized Council Against Poverty, embarking upon the organization of community corporations, considered the question of ethnic balance in the abstract and adopted the following policy:

> The Council Against Poverty finds approvable a Community Corporation Plan which provides for the broadest most inclusive ethnic representation on the Community Corporation's Board of Directors, but rejects any Community Corporation plan which establishes quotas of ethnic representation.[2]

Working under this and other guidelines, the Hunts Point community committee set about to organize a community corporation. In late January, 1967, the committee submitted to the Council a proposal calling for a corporation board of 55 members: 24 would be members of the existing committee (the entire membership), 24 would be elected from districts, and 7 would be selected at large. The Council rejected this proposal and instead suggested that 24 be elected by districts, who in turn would choose 12 members from the old committee and 5 at large. In March, the community committee accepted the 5 at large and 12 hold-overs but insisted that the old committee choose the 12, not the persons elected from the districts. After months of negotiation, the Council had its way, and an election was held in October. This time the Puerto Rican residents were organized and responsive, and of the 24 chosen by ballot, 21 were Puerto Ricans, 2 white, and 1 black. Then the community committee in its last act arranged that all but 12 of its members would resign so that only those 12 could be

---

[2] Minutes of Council Against Poverty, December 8, 1966.

appointed by the newly elected members; of those left, 10 were Puerto Rican, 2 black, and 1 white. This brought the board to 31 Puerto Ricans, 2 blacks, and 3 whites. Black residents immediately protested to the Council Against Poverty that they were not fairly represented.

The Council was then the only city board or commission with a black majority, and this majority had a feeling of solidarity. Earlier in the fall, only 700 residents of the South Bronx turned out for the community corporation election there, by far the smallest turnout of 15 community elections, and elected 20 blacks, 13 Puerto Ricans, and 7 whites (the community has 22 per cent black, 43 per cent Puerto Rican, and 35 per cent white). No one from the community protested at that time, but CDA Commissioner George Nicolau (who is white) proposed that the election be set aside because the procedures, including a requirement for advance registration, did not achieve an adequate turnout. But the Council Against Poverty allowed the South Bronx election to stand.

In the case of Hunts Point, the Council in January, 1968, ordered the Hunts Point board to add 13 blacks within 30 days to bring about ethnic balance. Immediately, Herman Badillo, Bronx Borough President and a Puerto Rican, accused the Council of creating dissension instead of unity among ethnic groups. He argued that when Puerto Ricans complained about underrepresentation in the South Bronx and Morrisania the Council would not interfere and instead told Puerto Ricans that if they wanted better representation they should have campaigned harder. Puerto Rican pickets surrounded City Hall and got a hearing from Mayor Lindsay, who chose to keep out of the controversy. They also appealed to the regional office of the Office of Economic Opportunity. OEO reviewed the situation and ordered the Council to adopt new rules that would ensure ethnic balance. As its rationale, OEO stated that the Green Amendment to the Economic Opportunity Act required that major community boards be "broadly representative." By May, the Council had complied by requiring that two-thirds of each corporation board be elected directly and that the remaining one-third be appointed by those elected; in doing so, any racial or ethnic imbalance resulting from the elections was to be corrected.

In the meantime, the Hunts Point Community Corporation had acceded to the Council's order and had added 14 blacks. After the Council adopted its new policy, the South Bronx group added some Puerto Ricans, but blacks retained majority control.

The third community corporation in the Bronx was organized in Morrisania, where blacks form the largest group; during its formative stage, it escaped the intergroup struggles of the other two and achieved a board consisting of 20 blacks, 7 Puerto Ricans, and 2 whites. However, ethnic balance is increasingly a troublesome issue there, too.

All three of these Bronx community corporations have built upon the start made in the community progress centers, which they have taken over. The proportion of the budget spent by the corporation directly is about two-thirds in Morrisania, one-half in Hunts Point, and one-third in South Bronx, with the remainder being delegated to other agencies. The programs operated by the Hunts Point Community Corporation, for example, include activities in the fields of manpower, education, housing, health, social services, and neighborhood organization. The delegate agencies in Hunts Point tend either to perform community development work in certain neighborhoods or to be concerned with special issues, such as public education. The corporation itself has several satellite centers, each with an advisory board composed of nearby residents.

Unity and Competence in Brownsville

In many respects, the Brownsville section of Brooklyn has many of the same social and physical characteristics as the lower Bronx, but here the residents are working together and are operating the most successful community corporation in New York City. Developed and settled about 100 years ago, Brownsville was a Jewish community for the first half of this century. But during and after World War II, many of the Jewish residents moved to other neighborhoods with more space and newer homes. Their place was taken by blacks and Puerto Ricans, so that now the population is about 50 per cent black, 40 per cent Puerto Rican, and 10 per cent white (mostly Jewish). This rapid change in population has been accompanied by a sharp decline in building maintenance by the landlords and deterioration of municipal services by the city. Many buildings have been abandoned, vandalized, and torn down, and some streets have the appearance of a bombed-out city. Yet, in spite of a nearly complete change in population in a 20-year period and the resulting replacement of community institutions, the current residents of Brownsville have been effective in launching a new community corporation.

Its origin can be traced to September, 1964, when the Brownsville Community Council was founded. The stimulus to organize was provided by a small group of professional workers from the Youth Board, the Housing Authority, and other agencies with operations in Brownsville, but when the Council was formed, these professionals deferred to lay delegates from a wide variety of neighborhood organizations. Not long after it was established, the Council received a grant from the Poverty Operations Board for the purpose of developing an antipoverty action program. A year later, when the newly formed Economic Opportunity Committee embarked upon its efforts to establish community progress centers and community committees, it decided that Brownsville and adjacent East New York should be combined and have one center between them. The Council for a Better East New York had also previously received a separate planning grant from the Poverty Operations Board. Neither group wanted to be combined, but since the community progress center was essentially a branch office controlled by the central agency, they had little choice.

When the Council Against Poverty was reorganized in the fall of 1966 and embarked upon the organization of community corporations, it respected the wishes of the respective communities and authorized a community corporation for each. The Brownsville Community Council was recognized as the organizing group for Brownsville. It was quick to respond and was the first to hold an election--in January, 1967.

This election was actually the third one held by the Council, and like the other two, participation was limited to organizational representatives. However, the Council Against Poverty required a broader base for representation the next time around, so in January, 1968, 20 board members were elected, four from each of the five "action areas." A month later, the delegate assembly, consisting of representatives of about 100 member organizations, selected nine officers and 21 other board members. These 50 persons then selected five additional members, which were ratified by the delegate assembly.

By then, the majority of the board were also members of the staff, a practice that violated the regulations of the U.S. Office of Economic Opportunity and the policies of the city's Council Against Poverty. This situation arose as community leaders who had been active as volunteers first joined the board and later were hired as staff. To comply with the regulations, the staff members on the board resigned during the summer of 1968, and other residents were appointed by the board to take their places.

The first executive director of the Brownsville Community Council was Major R. Owens, a black resident of Brownsville who previously was a librarian and a member of the professional group that was the catalyst for forming the Council. Writing in The Brownsville Counsellor, a weekly newspaper published by the Council and distributed free, he once observed: "Know-how plus Unity equals Power."[3] In a very real sense, this motto defines the success of the Council.

Unity is displayed in a thoughtful effort to achieve ethnic balance in the composition of the board and staff. A balanced board has been achieved by first electing the 20 members from the five action areas, then selecting 30 members from the delegate assembly, and finally by these 50 appointing five additional members. At the second and third steps, it is possible to consciously select persons who will balance the board. As a result, the ethnic composition of the board approximates that of the community as a whole. This same conscious effort is made in hiring staff. Thus, unlike some of the other New York communities, the black and Puerto Rican leaders in Brownsville understand that by working together they can gain more than by a "winner-take-all" approach.

Know-how is the other prominent attribute of the Brownsville Community Council. In part this is

---

[3] The Brownsville Counsellor, September 1, 1967, p. 2.

attributable to the considerable talents of Owens, who got the program under way. Indeed, his abilities were recognized by Mayor Lindsay, who appointed him to serve as commissioner of the city-wide Community Development Agency after George Nicolau, the first incumbent, resigned. But other members of the staff of the Brownsville corporation are also talented, and, as noted, most of them were previously active as community leaders. Their know-how is seen in the programs sponsored by the corporation.

The foundation for the program is five community action centers, each serving a district or action area of about 25,000 residents. Service to individuals is the primary function of these centers. The center staff provides information on how to go about solving problems, refers persons to other agencies that specialize in the matter at hand, and if necessary acts as an advocate on behalf of the person requesting assistance. Social action and community organization are secondary functions of the centers, for the overwhelming demand for service takes most of the time of the center staff. Furthermore, there are community-wide action groups that focus upon such issues as education, housing, health, and consumer problems. To perform its functions, a typical center has a staff of 16, including a director, an administrative assistant, a welfare specialist, a housing specialist, two clerks, and ten area workers, who perform outreach functions.

Although the community action centers are operated directly by the Brownsville Community Council, they each have an advisory committee, consisting of nearby interested residents co-opted into membership. During 1969, they were to become independent neighborhood boards, and the funds and staff of the action centers were to be turned over to their control. As this happens, a local election will be held to select committee members.

At the community-wide level, there are six board committees, each of which oversees program staff in its functional area. The three most active programs are education, manpower, and consumer activities. There are also embryonic programs in health, housing and physical development, and economic development.

The education committee directs the operation of Head Start and a family day care program, but its major interest is in direct action programs related to public schools. Staff of the education unit have been organizing parents around specific local educational issues, seeking to improve the neighborhood schools. In particular, the committee has sought to influence the way in which funds from the Elementary and Secondary Education Act are spent. The Ocean Hill-Brownsville Demonstration School District, which has received considerable publicity in its attempt to assert community control, includes part of the area served by the Brownsville Community Council. The Council has become involved in this dispute and because of this tense and difficult situation has temporarily put aside its intent to press for community control of other schools in Brownsville.

The manpower committee directs the operation of a community manpower center, under a contract from the city's Manpower and Career Development Agency (MCDA); in addition, two employment counselors are stationed in each community action center. The contract from MCDA represents a victory for the concept of community control, for that agency originally wanted to operate these centers directly. Instead, the community corporations gained control of them, and Brownsville received one of the first contracts to operate its own manpower center.

The consumer committee has sponsored the organization of a credit union and has organized buying clubs. Consumer education takes place through the credit union and the buying clubs.

The other three board committees are in an earlier stage of program development. In May, 1968, the health committee had a one-man staff examining ways in which better medical care could be provided to Brownsville residents; the housing and physical development committee was exploring what types of new housing could be constructed in the community; and the economic development committee was concentrating on small business development.

In addition to these directly operated activities, the Brownsville Community Council supports ten programs conducted by delegate agencies. Five of these are independent inasmuch as they handle their own funds and hire their own staff. Three of them provide services in public housing projects, one provides services to Spanish-speaking residents, and one is an adult education program run by a Black Muslim-oriented group. The other five delegate programs hire their own staff, but finances are handled by the Brownsville Community Council. Two of these are cultural and education programs run by Puerto Ricans, two relate to the performing arts, and the other organizes block groups in one part of the community.

Those close to the Council believe that it has been a distinct advantage for it to operate a number of programs directly, for this has given the Council an important role in the community and has established its credibility as an organization that can deliver. But they also believe that it is now time to reduce its direct operations by delegating functions to other agencies, thus concentrating more on planning and coordination. As already noted, the community action centers are likely to be turned over to neighborhood boards. Separate organizations might be established to conduct Head Start and consumer programs.

The power that has been achieved by unity and know-how has placed the Brownsville Community Council in a good position for dealing with the city-wide agencies that are the source of funds. It has been a constant struggle, but Brownsville has won its own manpower center, has had some limited success in influencing the allocation of elementary and secondary education funds by the Board of Education, and has managed to assert a degree of independence from the Community Development Agency. With the latter, Brownsville's competence has been an influential factor; because CDA has had to be more concerned about the programs run by the less able corporations, it has tolerated the efforts of the Brownsville Community Council to break away from standardized practices.

Other Corporations

East New York, which had previously joined with Brownsville to form a combined community committee, organized its own community corporation. This was done by the Council for a Better East New York, which at one time had been funded separately by the Poverty Operations Board. The new East New York Community Corporation has delegated most of the program operations to seven agencies.

In two other communities--South Jamaica and the Lower West Side--the previous administration had funded two parallel organizations, and in each case one group, the community committee, provided the nucleus for establishing a corporation. They followed the organizing procedures described earlier, and once in operation, the community corporations chose to run most of the programs directly. The South Jamaica Community Corporation works through five satellite centers, each with its own neighborhood council. Because the poverty areas of the Lower West Side are not contiguous but are instead separated by middle-income housing and nonresidential land, the corporation there also works through district operations.

Unique among the 15 communities organizing the first corporations was South Brooklyn, which has one of the few major concentrations of low-income whites in New York City. It also has one of the few remaining older-style political organizations, whose success is founded upon patronage and services to individuals. Because the community corporation threatened the service function and at the same time offered a potential new source of patronage jobs, the political organizations competed unofficially but vigorously in board elections and won in three out of the eight election districts. This was not enough to control, however. The other strong elements in South Brooklyn are the Catholic Church and the settlement houses; and the board, with a white majority, tends to be dominated by persons reflecting the viewpoint of these two institutional forces.

The other two Brooklyn poverty areas organized in the first round were Fort Greene and Williamsburg, both of which grew out of former community committees. The Williamsburg Community Corporation is faced with a three-way ethnic division, with Hasidic Jews, Puerto Ricans, and blacks, and achieving unity is a major task that runs through all proceedings, including the funding of delegate agencies. The Fort Greene Community Corporation has a reputation for being one of the better run of the new corporations.

In Queens, QUALICAP, the Community Corporation of Queens Bridge, Astoria, and Long Island City, was organized by the community committee. This area, like the Lower West Side, has several noncontiguous poverty sections, each with its own identity. Perhaps because of this factor, QUALICAP has experienced considerable in-fighting, and some of the delegate agencies would like to bypass it altogether and be funded directly by the city. Also, it has had more staff turnover than most of the other community corporations.

COMMENTARY

Considered as a whole, these new community corporations have produced mixed results. Some are operating quite successfully, constituting a distinct improvement over the previous city-run operations, whereas others are struggling to stay in existence and are achieving lesser results. Most are still fragile and are so dependent upon community action funds that they probably could not survive if this source of financing were removed.

Although each corporation is different, the most successful ones seem to have two factors in common. One is community unity, achieved through a commitment to working together and to overcoming divisive forces within the community. The other factor is an effective executive director and a competent staff. Both are needed, for the efforts of a capable staff can be thwarted by intra-community disputes, and a unified community cannot achieve significant results without an able staff to carry out its programs.

The now completed organizational stage was exceedingly difficult because it was dealing with the distribution of power and influence outward from the municipal agency to community corporations and within the communities as different groups and individuals gained and lost control. At the city-wide level, delegation of authority from the municipal government was made easier by Mayor Lindsay's acceptance of the recommendation of the Sviridoff study group to reorganize the community action program in this manner. However, some of the private social welfare agencies were apprehensive about the change, which would reduce their influence over the spending of antipoverty funds.

Within the low-income communities, reorganization did not always come so readily. There were the ethnic rivalries that have been detailed, and there was also suspicion and distrust of the city's motivation in the plan for reorganization. In addition, each of these poverty areas already had a set of institutions, such as settlement houses, Protestant missions, Catholic social service agencies, and others, which were accustomed to controlling social welfare programs in the community, and in at least one community (South Brooklyn) the local political organization felt threatened. Moreover, the community committees, only recently formed by the previous administration, were reluctant to face a change even though they had control of the machinery for organizing community corporations. These sets of interests had to be dealt with in 15 communities at once.

When the community committees were originally set up in the fall of 1965, established groups within the community were eligible to send two representatives each to a "community convention," and this delegate body selected members for the community committee. This process tended to give a middle-class cast to the community committees, with under-representation for the poor, who were less organized. In contrast, the community corporation elections in 1967 gave poor people a better chance. In the process, a number of persons who had been on the community committees and had experience in running an organization dropped out. Those chosen were less sophisticated but closer to the problems of poverty.

The top HRA personnel who presided over the organizing process believe that the procedures tended to yield corporation boards that were not sufficiently broad in their representation of a community cross section. There should have been more precise quidelines on what constitutues adequate representation, and a certain proportion of the board seats (but less than half) probably should have been reserved for appointment in order to obtain a more balanced board. However, none of the original organizers would forego the election of a majority of the board, although the electoral process might be improved. Experience with the elections showed that voter turnout was poorest in the one community that required a separate advance registration (South Bronx), and it was best where candidates campaigned actively and competitively. Even if turnout was smaller than for municipal offices, the elections served as a means of arousing interest, publicizing the concept of the community corporation, and providing more experience in the democratic process. Perhaps most important, selection by popular election has given the boards of the community corporations greater legitimacy to act on behalf of the communities' interests than if they had been appointed by city officials or various organizations.

However, it may be that the boards, which range from about 30 to 90 members, are too large for effective operations. Some persons equate board size and breadth of representation, but this is a misunderstanding of the dynamics of boards and committees. When a board becomes too large (perhaps over 30 members), there are too many persons present at a meeting for all to participate in the discussion. This tends to lead to fewer items on the agenda and greater delegation to standing committees and an executive committee. Then the large board works as an assembly, that is, more like a legislative body than a board of directors. Certainly a case can be made for these community corporations being governed by assemblies, but I believe that the nature of their responsibilities is more conducive to a board-style operation.

Those close to the community corporations believe the major shortcomings of the boards are not due to size but rather to the lack of understanding of the full potential of the corporation approach and the relative inexperience of board members with organizational procedures. At first there was a one-shot training program of new board members, but this proved inadequate. Not until most of the boards had operated for a year was an ongoing board training program undertaken. And then it was handled by a training institute without the policy involvement of the corporations.

Indeed, insufficient training and inadequate technical assistance are major deficiencies in New York's program of community corporations. This applies not only to board members but also to the entire staff and participating delegate agencies within the communities. The Community Development Agency has had a small staff providing technical assistance, but it has never been sufficient in size or breadth of program specialities. And for a period, CDA's staff had only community organization specialists working with the corporations, while CDA program specialists gave their attention to other matters. Moreover, the community corporations themselves need their own technical staff to help neighborhood groups develop and operate programs. Part of the problem is the lack of trained personnel available to provide technical assistance, and OEO has not been willing to grant enough funds for this task.

The responsibility for insufficient training is even broader, for it involves the failure of universities and other social institutions to produce an adequate supply of persons with the talents needed as general managers. One of the problems of the community corporations has been finding well-qualified executive directors, and this applies to those corporations who have sought candidates outside their community as well as those recruiting from within.

Some of the community corporations have also had difficulty in internal management. This is partly the result of inexperienced administrators and lack of enough personnel to handle the bookkeeping and auditing. But it is only partly the fault of the corporations, for the entire system of fiscal controls in New York City is cumbersome and archaic. Although this system of check, double-check, and triple-check was not able to prevent the theft of over $1 million from the Neighborhood Youth Corps, it makes payrolls late and keeps internal financial administration in a perpetual state of crisis. Undoubtedly, many of the community corporations could improve their own operations, but the basic deficiency is in the outmoded system prescribed by the state legislature and by City Hall.

One aspect of financial management is the need to define more clearly what responsibilities can be delegated to the community corporations to handle as trustworthy, independent agencies. This question is even more crucial in the matter of determining what programs will be conducted. In talking to staff and officers of community corporations, one hears the same type of complaints that local officials make about federal agencies: "They tell us what programs we have to run and won't let us choose our own." "We send in a budget and they change it." "Priorities are determined downtown, not out here." "They fund another group in our community without telling us."

Indeed, the CDA-community corporation relationship is the OEO-community action agency situation in microcosm.

On the other hand, CDA has had to intervene in the processing of community budget requests because some of the corporations have not followed adequate procedures of due process in dealing with neighborhood groups that have applied through the corporation for city and federal community action funds. For example, a corporation will disapprove a request but will not notify the applicant of its action, much less explain why.

A reasonable balance between the central and decentralized agencies has yet to be achieved. One factor is the lack of clarity on the proper role of the community corporation. The original idea was that it would be an umbrella agency and not necessarily operate a lot of programs directly. However, in the budget for the 1969 fiscal program year, ten of the original 15 community corporations allocated more than half the community action funds to themselves. Over-all, 62 per cent of these funds went to corporations, 25 per cent to their delegate agencies, and 13 per cent to city-wide programs.

The corporations are exercising their control over funds allocated to their communities too much in their own favor and are not delegating enough program operations to other neighborhood agencies. Although they probably need some direct operations to initiate new programs and to engage in creative competition with established institutions, most of them are too heavily engaged in program operations. However, they should have continuing responsiblity for planning, coordination, evaluation, training, and technical assistance. Furthermore, if they concentrated upon these latter tasks, the community corporations might be able to gain a wider role in the constellation of public services. So far, their role has been expanding quite slowly.

At first, the community corporations were accepted within the Human Resources Administration mainly as the local arm of the Council Against Poverty and the Community Development Agency. As a super-agency, HRA is more a federated conglomerate than a unitary department, and its constituent agencies--CDA, the Social Services (formerly Welfare)

Department, the Manpower and Career Development Agency, the Youth Board, and the Addiction Service Agency--tend to act as quasi-sovereigns. Initially, MCDA wanted to operate its own community manpower centers. Although Sviridoff, the Human Resources administrator, tended to favor the corporations for this role, he allowed Samuel Gans, the MCDA commissioner, to make his case at community meetings. George Nicolau, the CDA commissioner, fought for community control of the manpower centers, and Major Owens, then executive director of the Brownsville Community Council, mobilized the corporations on their own behalf. After a short struggle, Sviridoff decided in favor of community-run manpower centers.

At that time, the Welfare Department, headed by Mitchell Ginsberg, also wanted to avoid the corporations. Later Ginsberg succeeded Sviridoff as Human Resources administrator, and since then he has championed the community corporations. It is now the policy of HRA that the community corporations shall be its principal means of resident participation, that all constituent agencies (MCDA, Social Services, Youth Board, Addiction Service) will consult with the corporations before embarking upon programs within their communities, but that the corporations will not be the exclusive agent for all resident involvement nor will they have a veto over all HRA programs.

The issue of the role of the community corporations also arose when the Model Cities Program was organized in New York City. The mayor appointed a Model Cities Policy Committee consisting of the chairman of the Planning Commission, the Housing and Development administrator, the executive director of the Housing Authority, the budget director, the Human Resources administrator, and the chairman of the Council Against Poverty. The Committee began to deal with the question of citizen participation in the Model Cities Program in the fall of 1967, when HRA was still organizing community corporations and had few concrete accomplishments to use as justification for expanding their role. This was also a transitional period between the announcement of Sviridoff's resignation to become a vice-president of the Ford Foundation and the installation of Ginsberg as the new administrator.

Meanwhile, personnel from the housing and physical development agencies had begun to organize a separate structure for community representation, and when the time of decision came for the Model Cities Policy Committee, a de facto apparatus was already in existence. By then, the position of HRA was firm, and Ginsberg and the chairman of the Council Against Poverty proposed that the community corporations select half the members of the three Model Cities boards being established in Southern Bronx, Greater Harlem, and Central Brooklyn. However, they were outvoted as the officials from the physical development agencies took control of Model Cities.

As a result, a completely new and separate Model Cities corporation has been set up in each borough, with its own board-selection process. Although these other city agencies were not willing to accede to a broader role for the community corporations, the struggle helped to enhance the position of the corporations within HRA, leading to the greater recognition previously described.

The other main field where the corporations have a role relates to the allocation of funds under Title I of the Elementary and Seconday Education Act. Thirteen million dollars (about 20 per cent of the available funds) have been set aside for educational projects to be worked out by district school boards in consultation with the community corporations. Among other benefits, this has enabled some of the corporations to shift certain educational programs to the Board of Education and to use the freed funds for other purposes.

As noted earlier, Mayor Lindsay favored the establishment of community corporations in the beginning, and he continues to support them. However, some of the problems arising during the organizational stage, such as the ethnic struggle in Hunts Point, caused him political problems, for he is automatically the target for critics of any and all phases of municipal operations. This factor plus the lack of clearly demonstrated program success seems to have lessened his enthusiasm for the corporations. One evidence of this is the organization by one of his assistants of an Urban Task Force, which is bypassing the corporations and giving out several million dollars to neighborhood groups in the same areas and for the same type of activities as the community action program. A mayor needs program payoff as well as process, and

HRA, CDA, and the community corporations have not delivered as well or as fast as Lindsay would like.

Indeed, this has to be an interim judgment of the community corporations in New York City. They constitute a distinct improvement over the previous arrangement, and on the whole they seem to be doing as well as many city-run operations. They are moving in the right direction, but most of them have not developed the program capacity needed to be the kind of local change agents that are necessary in the largest, most complex, and most troubled of all American cities. The worth of New York's community corporations is slowly emerging, but much of their potential has yet to be fulfilled.

CHAPTER **3** THREE CITIES: THREE APPROACHES TO COMMUNITY CORPORATIONS

While New York City was struggling to create 26 community corporations, a number of other cities were working to develop this form of resident participation in the Community Action Program. The experiences of three of them--Washington, D.C.; Newark, New Jersey; and Columbus, Ohio--illustrate other aspects of the movement for community control. Unlike New York, the municipal government was not directly involved in these three cities.

In Washington, the community action agency turned over four out of ten neighborhood programs to community corporations. Newark's community action program started with eight area boards with considerable influence, then pulled back from giving them so large a role. In Columbus, the East Central Citizens Organization was organized as a special demonstration project apart from the local community action program.

TWO WASHINGTON, D.C., COMMUNITY CORPORATIONS

Washington, D.C. has long been noted for its complex of overlapping and competing agencies. Lacking home rule, its municipal government is headed by presidential appointees, and it is subject to the whims of congressional committees dominated by Southerners and influenced by the wishes of federal agency heads, whose names are scarcely known to District residents. This makes the solution of local problems exceedingly hard to achieve.

In 1960, four private organizations--the Health and Welfare Council, the Washington Center for Metropolitan Studies, the Brookings Institution, and Resources for the Future, Inc.--undertook a joint study to determine better ways to deal with social problems in Washington. Their study recommended "a unified effort to plan for the human needs of the National Capital area, based upon sound research and planning techniques, in partnership with governmental and private interests, to strengthen existing services and design new approaches."[1] After discussions with the District Commissioners and White House staff, they formed the United Planning Organization (UPO) in December, 1962, to be the vehicle for joint planning. UPO then was awarded grants from the Ford Foundation and a local foundation.

During this period, Attorney General Robert Kennedy stimulated the creation of an agency called Washington Action for Youth (WAY) to prepare a youth development project under the President's Committee on Juvenile Delinquency, which the Attorney General chaired. By 1964, when the Economic Opportunity Act was passed, UPO and WAY had both completed their initial planning efforts. UPO then absorbed WAY, and the enlarged organization received program grants from the Ford Foundation, the President's Committee, and the newly established Office of Economic Opportunity.

The foundation of UPO's initial effort was its neighborhood development program, which established service centers and community organization units in ten poor neighborhoods. In the beginning, four of these were contracted to social welfare agencies (three settlements and the Urban League), and the other six were operated directly by UPO. Also, in each of these ten areas, citizen advisory committees were set up. Their role was to advise the administrators of the neighborhood centers and UPO headquarters on neighborhood needs, and not to serve as governing bodies of the centers. When OEO required UPO to add representatives of the poor to its board of directors, a metropolitan citizens advisory council was formed

---

[1]Quoted by Community Action Associates, Inc., in "Community Action Programs in the Middle Atlantic Region," Examination of the War on Poverty, Staff and Consultants Reports (Senate Subcommittee on Employment, Manpower and Poverty, September, 1967), Vol. V, p.1462.

consisting of four representatives from each of the neighborhood committees (and some from the suburbs), and this council chose representatives to the central board. The council was also given authority to review all program proposals prior to consideration by the UPO board. With this instrument for unity and the means of previewing the board agenda, the representatives of the poor soon developed a united bloc at meetings of the board of directors.

In the latter part of 1965 and on into 1966, UPO adopted the tactic of focusing citizen action on specific issues, such as public housing operations, welfare benefits, public education, and recreation facilities. Using the neighborhood advisory committees as a base but adding other citizen leaders, several city-wide, issue-oriented committees were formed. Soon they began to make demands on public agencies, the District Commissioners, and Congress, and the welfare committee even picketed the home of Senator Robert Byrd, a champion of restrictive welfare policies. When this happened, UPO began to get counterpressures from District officials and OEO, which transmitted the feelings of some congressional leaders. As a result, UPO began to de-emphasize the issue committees and to give more attention to the organization of community corporations as an alternative method of achieving resident participation. By the end of 1967, it had contracted with four corporations to be responsible for neighborhood centers and other aspects of the neighborhood development program. Two of these--in the Near Northeast and in Upper Cardozo--illustrate this experience.

The Near Northeast is a densely populated neighborhood of 86,000 people, mostly black, east of Union Station and northeast of the Capitol. About one family out of four is poor, and many of the others are families of blue-collar workers who are just above the government's poverty line. Row houses are the predominant dwelling type, many owner-occupied, and the homeowners form the basis for the many block clubs and other small organizations found in the area. However, until the advent of the "war on poverty," there was no major organization for all of the Near Northeast.

Partly for that reason, UPO decided in the spring of 1965 to take on direct responsibility for the neighborhood development program in that section. In three other sections of Northeast and Southeast Washington, UPO contracted this function to settlement houses, which are supported by the United Givers Fund. No such institution was available in the Near Northeast although there was a small service operation called Hospitality House, with a small budget privately raised and a corps of volunteers. UPO did enter into a contract with Hospitality House to engage in consumer action, to organize a credit union, and to hire ten neighborhood workers for general organizing activities. UPO's own center in the Near Northeast also had ten neighborhood workers, and the two operations divided the area in half for organizing purposes. Hospitality House organized around issues, and the UPO center concentrated on forming block clubs.

In September, 1965, 12 citizens formed the Near Northeast Community Improvement Corporation (CIC), and after a year of negotiations CIC entered into a contract with UPO and took over the Near Northeast center. It was the first resident-controlled organization to operate one of the neighborhood development centers in the District of Columbia.

By then, Hospitality House was no longer operating with UPO funds. However, the citizens advisory committee first organized by UPO stayed in existence, separate from CIC's board of directors, and since it was larger, it had more poor people participating than the 40-man corporation board. So there continued to be division and lack of community cohesiveness. A survey made for the Senate Subcommittee on Employment, Manpower and Poverty in the spring of 1967 found the following:

> Factions have formed to vie for power within the corporation. These have formed around personalities. And one of the issues they fight over is whether to bring in more hard core poor. As poor are brought in leaders of factions compete to win them to their side.[2]

The factional struggle continued throughout 1967. In the summer, a group of residents petitioned UPO to investigate alleged irregularities, and although the UPO board concluded that charges were unfounded,

---

[2] Ibid., p. 1487.

the dispute continued. Finally, in January, 1968, UPO's executive director, Wiley Branton, met with members of the CIC board, delegate assembly, staff, and interested citizens. With the concurrence of those present, Branton placed a temporary freeze on a pending election, took over approval of all hiring and firing, and appointed an ad hoc committee of residents, with himself as chairman, to develop recommendations for improvement within the next 30 days. A month later, the committee reported a new plan for organization which formed the basis for reorganization.

As now constituted, membership in the Near Northeast Community Improvement Corporation is open to any community resident 18 and older who registers. About 500 now belong, and they are all automatically members of the community advisory council, which functions as a general assembly but with weak powers. The council, though, does elect the Near Northeast's representatives to the central UPO board.

Real power in the corporation rests with the board of directors. In June, 1968, ten board members were elected from districts for two-year terms, and in June, 1969, another ten were so selected, replacing ten directors previously chosen by the advisory council. These 20 elected board members select six more, all of whom must be poor. Some of the elected 20 are also poor.

This new structure, however, has not eliminated all factional disputes. The chairman of the community advisory council is Mrs. Nadine Winter, long-time executive director of Hospitality House, who believes that the new board has already usurped some of the powers of the advisory council. She is more interested in organizing residents to foster institutional change than is the CIC board and its executive director, William Michels, who place primary emphasis upon services.

These CIC services, carried out by a staff of 34, are concentrated in four fields: employment, education, consumer protection, and housing. The employment team does a great deal of direct referral to training programs and jobs and to the nearby UPO manpower center. The education unit is initiating a home tutoring project and is developing a consumer education curriculum for junior high school. The consumer protection team performs consumer education and encourages participation in food stamp and commodity distribution programs. The housing group is interested in housing rehabilitation and in street beautification. CIC's headquarters also provides space for staff from other agencies, including a food stamp certification officer, a family and child services worker, a juvenile probation officer, and an aide from the Citizens Information Service (a city-wide information and complaint agency).

The Near Northeast constitutes half of Washington's Model Cities area (the other half is covered by the People's Involvement Corporation and three neighborhood development centers, discussed in Chapter 7). The Model Cities Commission had its own election in December, 1968, with about 5 per cent of those eligible participating. CIC members helped get out the vote, and two CIC board members and two from the staff are on the 29-member Model Cities Commission. The sorting out of respective responsibilities of CIC, a unit of the Community Action Program funded by OEO, and the Model Cities Commission, supported by the Department of Housing and Urban Development (HUD), had not occurred at this writing.

Similar uncertainty of responsibility exists in the rebuilding program along the H Street business strip, which was heavily damaged in two sections of Washington in April, 1968, following the assassination of Dr. Martin Luther King. Mayor Walter Washington set up the Reconstruction and Development Corporation (RDC) and got a Ford Foundation grant to develop plans for rebuilding. This corporation did very little until early March, 1969, when it made arrangements to give planning funds to a new organization run by persons previously active only in another section of the city (see Chapter 8). These "outsiders" were promptly resisted by both the CIC board and the community advisory council, who were in agreement for once. Although pressures from other neighborhoods blocked the consulting contract, RDC itself took on the planning for H Street, N.E., rather than have it done by a neighborhood group. A major reason for this outside intervention was that the organizations in Northeast had not been able to mobilize community resources to speed the task of reconstruction. Thus disunity continues to plague this section of the capital, and the Near Northeast Community Imrovement Corporation continues to struggle for its place in community life.

Doing somewhat better is the second community corporation to organize in the District of Columbia, a group called CHANGE, Inc., for "Cardozo Heights Association for Neighborhood Growth and Enrichment." The corporation evolved from UPO's Neighborhood Development Center (NDC) 3, one of three established in 1964 in a sprawling section north of the central business district. The service area demarcated for NDC 3 has about 55,000 residents of whom about 80 per cent are black, 10 per cent Spanish-speaking, and 10 per cent other whites.

During the Christmas season of 1964-65, meetings were held in five subsections of this area and delegates were chosen to the citizens advisory council set up by NDC 3. Of the 20 persons chosen, about 80 per cent were middle-class residents, and the council chose a clergyman to be its chairman. After that, the role of the citizens advisory council gradually expanded. The UPO-hired neighborhood director consulted the council on where the center should be located, brought members into the final interviewing process for the hiring of neighborhood workers, and turned over the profits of vending machines for the council to use for miscellaneous expenses. The neighborhood workers organized block clubs, which in turn sent representatives to council meetings. In August, 1965, the council, block club members, and neighborhood workers participated in a housing survey which UPO conducted in all poverty areas as a first step toward developing a city-wide housing action committee. In the fall, the council set up a special committee on day care, which incorporated, applied for funds to open day care centers, and was turned down, but did get another day care agency to offer services in the neighborhood.

By this time, members of the citizens advisory council of NDC 3 began talking about gaining greater status and possibly incorporating. In the early months of 1966, a bylaws committee was appointed, and in May it presented a set of bylaws to a general membership meeting of the council. Approval was given, and CHANGE, Inc., was incorporated in the middle of June. The new corporation then entered into negotiations with UPO to take control of the neighborhood center. UPO was basically sympathetic to this idea, but the transfer was slowed down when the CHANGE board hired an executive director who was also an officer in the Young Democrats, a duality of positions in violation of OEO regulations. When he opted for politics, a new executive was hired. CHANGE, Inc., signed a contract with UPO and took over the center and neighborhood organizing program in January, 1967.

CHANGE now has a board of directors consisting of 39 members, of whom one-third are required to be poor persons. The board is selected at an annual membership meeting each November, and anyone from the neighborhood who has participated in one of the CHANGE programs or received its services is eligible to receive a membership card and vote. In November 1968, 300 participated in the election.

CHANGE has organized commissions around its major concerns, including welfare, employment, consumer action, police-community relations, education, health, housing, and senior citizens. A special committee on problemas sociales serves the Spanish community, many of whom are Cubans and South Americans and have language and citizenship difficulties. The chairman of each commission is on the board of directors, but other participants are drawn from the general membership. CHANGE also has staff working in each of these fields.

The housing commission has been concerned with housing code inspection and has gotten the District government to assign three inspectors to work from the CHANGE center. It helped residents of several adjacent buildings owned by the same landlord to form a tenants union. It fought to ensure that Washington's new subway system would serve the area, and it has testified at various congressional and District Council hearings.

The education commission has concentrated on problem solving, particularly matters involving individual pupils, their parents, and school staff. A CHANGE staff member is assigned to each public school in the neighborhood in order to learn what the school needs (such as more books), to build better contacts between parents and teachers, and to be on hand to deal with special problems as they arise.

The consumer commission keeps an eye on prices at neighborhoood stores, conducts consumer education programs, encourages needy residents to buy food stamps, and helps tenants with rent problems. It also relates to CHANGE's separately organized credit union.

The welfare commission has worked for changes in the policies and practices of the District Welfare Department. Its agenda has included the abolition of welfare investigators (notorious in Washington for their disrespect of privacy), an increase in welfare grants, an increase in the number of social workers, improvements in the food stamp program, a requirement for a fair hearing before being cut off welfare, and abolition of the "man-in-the-house" rule. As a result of pressure from this group and other welfare rights organizations, the City Council has required the Welfare Department to provide for fair hearings upon request. In a case brought by a member of CHANGE's welfare commission, the courts have ruled that an investigator cannot enter a home against the will of the occupant. In another court case, the man-in-the-house rule has been abolished.

The health commission has been concerned with the serious deficiency of health services in the CHANGE area. After a long, hard struggle, it served as the catalyst for establishing the Community-Group Health Foundation, Inc., which has opened a comprehensive health center, funded by an OEO grant. The board of this new nonprofit corporation consists of four persons appointed by CHANGE, four by the Group Health Association, Inc., and four by the School of Medicine of Howard University. In addition, there is a 20-member advisory health council, including ten who have received services at the health center and have been elected by those who are on the service rolls.

As this summary of the commission's work indicates, CHANGE is giving considerable attention to utilizing the resources and changing the practices of various public and private agencies. In addition, a number of agencies have stationed personnel at the CHANGE center to provide direct services, including the Welfare Department, Neighborhood Legal Services, U.S. Employment Service, UPO Manpower Division, Family and Child Services, Mental Health Day Care Treatment Program, Department of License and Inspection (housing inspectors), and the Health Department. CHANGE's executive director, Mrs. Ruth Webster, conducts a weekly meeting with the personnel from these agencies, and they seem to have worked out linkages between their various services.

The CHANGE center is located on the third floor of a building on the 14th Street business strip, which was ravaged by rioting, looting, and fire in April, 1968. During the disorders, CHANGE's staff and board served as a calming influence and provided assistance to displaced persons. After order was restored, several of CHANGE's commissions began exploring various aspects of rebuilding the neighborhood. So did two new groups, Build Black and the Columbia Heights Self-Help Association. In December, 1968, they joined efforts and set up the Ad Hoc Committee for Upper Cardozo Redevelopment. With the help of graduate architects from Catholic University, the Ad Hoc Committee prepared plans for renewing the area, including reconstructing the neighborhood business district and converting an old 1,700-seat movie theater into an all-purpose community center. However, like the Near Northeast group, in March, 1969, they were faced with a competing planning organization fostered by the mayor's reconstruction corporation, but they were able to block this outside intrusion.

When CHANGE first took over the operation of the neighborhood development program from UPO, residents could not notice much difference in the way it functioned. Gradually, though, CHANGE has organized more block groups and has developed the commission structure described. Although it has many similarities to other neighborhood centers funded by UPO, it also has distinctive features which make it the neighborhood's own program. The evolution from UPO-controlled to community corporation has made the program more adaptable to neighborhood concerns.

Elsewhere in the District of Columbia there are two other community corporations in charge of neighborhood centers: CHASE, Inc., and Far East Community Services, Inc., both of which also took over UPO operations. Four other centers continue to be run by social agencies: Friendship House, Southeast House, Southwest Community House, and the Urban League. UPO now operates only two directly, NDC 1 and NDC 2. (These last three are discussed in Chapter 7 in considering a pilot neighborhood center established in their service areas.) CHANGE, Inc., appears to be among the best of the ten, whereas CIC ranks in the lower third in terms of accomplishments. The difference between the two seems to be that in Upper Cardozo the neighborhood leadership is united and in the Near Northeast it is not. Neither section is troubled by ethnic disputes, which have been so troublesome in New York City, or even by ideological differences between conservatives and militants.

Rather it seems that in the Near Northeast competing personalities have been more dominant, while a commitment to the community has been stronger in Upper Cardozo. It is these intangibles rather than organizational form that so often make the difference between successful action and continuous struggle.

RACIAL POLARIZATION IN NEWARK, NEW JERSEY

In the early days of the "war on poverty," the community action program in Newark, New Jersey, was a leader in the development of resident participation. With the establishment of neighborhood organizations called "area boards," the Newark program seemed to have one of the firmest bases for grass-roots control.

The ideological foundation of the Newark approach, however, was not home-grown but instead originated across the Hudson River in New York City's Harlem. It was imported into New Jersey by Cyril Tyson, the first executive director of Newark's antipoverty program who had been serving as project director of HARYOU.

HARYOU was established in July, 1962, to plan a youth development program with funds from the President's Committee on Juvenile Delinquency, supplemented by a grant from the City of New York. Under the leadership of Kenneth Clark, who served as chairman of the board and chief project consultant, HARYOU in 1964 published Youth in the Ghetto, a 620-page report on its findings and recommendations, and requested federal financial support for a major demonstration program. This report stated:

> The core of the HARYOU program and the basis upon which any claim for innovation must be judged is in the persistent emphasis and insistence upon social action rather than dependence upon mere social services.
>
> Social action, in its operational sense, means and demands the stimulation of concern among individuals who share a common predicament, who

are victims of long-standing community problems and injustices, who can be induced not only to identify these problems but to seek to determine the methods by which they can be resolved, and who are able to develop and sustain the initiative for the type of collective action which, in fact, does resolve or ameliorate these problems.[3]

Three vehicles were proposed to carry out this social action emphasis: local neighborhood boards, a community action institute to train staff and neighborhood leaders, and a youth-operated program called Harlem Youth Unlimited. The neighborhood boards, the main concern here, were proposed on the assumption that "effective social action in a community so populous and complex as Harlem requires decentralization."[4] Five local boards would be organized to carry out the following mandates: "(1) to develop social action, educational and social welfare programs, (2) to conduct systematic community research, and (3) to inform local residents about available community resources."[5] The neighborhood boards would be assisted by professional consultants supplied by HARYOU and by an experienced community agency, and the board themselves would have lay staffs in the form of part- and full-time aides. Most of the major service programs would be operated by other agencies.

Clark and his colleagues were denied the chance to implement their ideas. Instead, when the action funds became available, HARYOU was taken over by allies of Congressman Adam Clayton Powell, who at the time was the powerful chairman of the House Committee on Education and Labor, which had jurisdiction over the juvenile delinquency program and the new Economic Opportunity Act, an even larger source of funds.

---

[3]Harlem Youth Opportunities Unlimited, Inc., <u>Youth in the Ghetto</u> (New York, 1964), p. 388.

[4]<u>Ibid.</u>, p. 391.

[5]<u>Ibid.</u>, p. 392.

HARYOU was merged with ACT, another juvenile delinquency project already controlled by Powell. Tyson went to Newark to head its community action program.

Newark was organized to benefit from the Economic Opportunity Act even before congressional action was completed. The mayor's staff looked over the bill and decided that the city itself should operate manpower-related programs, such as the Neighborhood Youth Corps and the Adult Work-Experience Program, and that a new nonprofit organization should be created to conduct the community action program. In August, 1964, Mayor Hugh J. Addonizio called together a group of public officials and civic leaders, who formed the United Community Corporation (UCC) and obtained a state charter. The city, the Board of Education, and the United Community Fund each put up $15,000 to get the program under way. Tyson was hired as a consultant, and an application for OEO funds was prepared. When UCC received a $184,000 program development grant from OEO in January, 1965, Tyson was appointed full-time executive director.

In the months that followed, UCC's basic strategy began to unfold. In terms of organizational arrangements, this strategy had five manifestations: corporation membership, area boards, task forces, board of trustees, and new service agencies.

UCC is a membership corporation open to anyone age 15 or older living or working in Newark. All members automatically belong to the area board for the sections of the city where they live or work.

The city was divided into nine areas, including the poor and not-so-poor sections. An area board was planned for each; three were organized the first year, and eventually eight came into being. The role of the area boards, following the HARYOU model, was expressed in the manual of procedure:

> The Area Boards are the vehicles for . . . social change with the responsibility of identifying those in need of service with the aid of community action researchers; recommending and selecting programs; referring individuals and families to appropriate programs; and its

members participating, as individuals, in various capacities as administrators, supervisors, sub-professionals and workers-in-training in the various service programs.[6]

Each board would be assisted by staff hired by UCC upon the recommendation of the area board.

To review program proposals, whether developed by area boards, established agencies, or its own staff, UCC created five task forces--on employment, education, housing, community action, and special projects. During the first year, their membership ranged from 30 to 100, including representatives from area boards, public and private agencies, and the public at large.

From the beginning, policy control was vested in the board of trustees. At first the board consisted of 53 persons: 5 city officials and 48 persons chosen by the corporation members. Board membership was increased to 82 in 1966 to give direct representation to the area boards and then to 114 in 1967. But in 1968, the Green Amendment to the Economic Opportunity Act forced a reduction in size to 45, with 15 public officials, 16 representatives of the poor chosen by the eight area boards, and 14 representatives of private groups and interests (with 6 other seats reserved for future expansion). Through all these changes, the board of trustees had a black majority.

The fifth part of the organizational strategy was designed to prevent the established agencies from capturing complete control of the program. This was accomplished by quickly setting up new agencies that would be controlled by blacks and representatives of the poor. When UCC got its first OEO action grant in the summer of 1965, two such new agencies, the Pre-School Council and the Legal Service Project, began operations, and funds were given to the already existing, black-controlled Blazer Community Employment Training Program. In addition, OEO money was

---

[6]United Community Corporation, *The Community in Action: The Area Board*, Newark, N.J., 1965, p. 2. (Mimeographed.)

channeled to the city's Senior Citizens Commission on the condition that it have a policy advisory committee involving representatives of the area boards. This OEO grant also permitted UCC to organize three more area boards, bringing the total that year to six.

In sum, resident involvement was the major theme of the United Community Corporation from the beginning, and it seemed to be well expressed in organizational structure. OEO had great praise for the Newark program, and it was cited by advocates of citizen action as one of the advanced community action agencies. In many respects, the highlight of Newark's citizen action approach came in September, 1966, when 1,000 residents went to Washington to support legislation to continue OEO. The area boards (then numbering 7) and the 15 delegate agencies combined their forces to mobilize this turnout of citizen support and to raise funds to rent 22 buses.

Though Congress did extend OEO, the appropriated funds were less than the amount necessary to keep all the community action agencies going at their then current program level. This meant that cities, such as Newark, which had organized quickly and had received more than their share in the early days, had their allocations reduced. Newark's area boards were particularly affected, because by then they had developed proposals for a variety of new programs, and new funds needed to get them started were not available from OEO. The area boards turned on UCC's total budget and proposed that such programs as those of the Pre-School Council and the Senior Citizens Commission be cut back so that the area boards could have a greater share. This did not happen.

Until that time, the area boards had been concentrating on neighborhood organization, with the prospect of eventually running neighborhood programs. With no funds available, about all that was left was social protest as a means of sustaining organizational interest. This was already a major approach of Area Boards 2 and 3, and in the first half of 1967 other boards moved in that direction.

Area Board 3 was particularly noted for its activism. In this section in 1961, the Clinton Hill Neighborhood Council, under black leadership, had fought a proposed urban renewal project. In 1964, a group (mostly white) from Students for a Democratic

Society moved into the neighborhood and formed the Newark Community Union Project, using demonstrations against city agencies and litigation against landlords as major organizing tools. When Area Board 3 was formed, the militant blacks and whites from these two organizations became the dominant forces. Most of their protest activities were directed at municipal agencies, landlords, and local businesses alleged to be exploiting consumers. But in the struggle over the UCC budget, this and other area boards directed some of their energies against the central staff and board of UCC itself.

This internal dissension was mild, however, compared to the steadily worsening relationship between UCC and City Hall. It first came to the fore in the summer of 1965 when UCC asked the city to put up matching funds for the second OEO grant. This gave some councilmen who were hostile to the program an opportunity to conduct an investigation and to issue a report condemning the work of UCC. Then in the fall of 1966, a black leader who was vice-president of the UCC board of trustees took a leave of absence from that position and ran for mayor. Although he was defeated, he forced Mayor Addonizio into a runoff.

This election campaign was but one of many signs of the racial polarization developing in Newark. Although Addonizio had built a liberal voting record in seven terms in Congress, had been first elected in 1962 with the combined support of Italians and blacks (the two dominant racial-ethnic groups in Newark), and had made several appointments of blacks to high city positions, he had not kept up with either the population changes in Newark or the growing demands of the blacks. From 1960 to 1966, Newark's population had shifted from 65 per cent white to 52 per cent black and 10 per cent Spanish-speaking, but the top municipal jobs and boards gave little indication of that change.

To add to the stress, the city administration, trying to get a medical school located in Newark, promised developers 185 acres of land, to be obtained by removing residents and demolishing homes in the heart of the black ghetto. Although a survey conducted by UCC indicated that the majority of neighborhood residents wanted the medical school in Newark and slightly over half favored it even if forced to move, the medical school land deal was a natural issue for anti-administration blacks, especially in view of the poor results of past relocation efforts. During May and June, 1967, the City Planning Board held stormy hearings on whether to declare the area "blighted" and thus make it eligible for federal renewal assistance. In spite of strong objections, the Planning Board approved the project.

At the same time, another dispute was raging over the appointment of a new secretary of the Board of Education. The mayor proposed a councilman without a college education; the NAACP suggested the city budget director, a black with a master's degree in accounting. After a noisy hearing lasting more than ten hours, the Board of Education ducked the issue by persuading the incumbent to remain for another year.

During the disputes over the medical school site and the school board appointment, many rallies and demonstrations were held, and feelings ran high. To many it was apparent that Newark was about to explode. It did on July 13 in five days of civil disorder that took 23 lives--21 black and 2 white.

After it was over, two city councilmen and a police detective told a congressional committee that "the community action programs in the city of Newark have definitely played an important part in setting off the riots."[7] They cited people from Area Board 3 in particular. However, Governor Hughes' Select Commission on Civil Disorders, after a six-month study, concluded that in the events immediately before the outbreak of disorder, UCC activities did not worsen the situation, and during the riot its "personnel did participate in individual efforts to prevent violence, to bring food and emergency supplies to persons in the riot area and to offer medical assistance and legal aid to those needing it."[8]

---

[7]Hearings before the House Committee on Education and Labor on the Economic Opportunity Act Amendments of 1967, 90th Cong., 1st Sess., Pt. 4, p. 3537.

[8]Governor's Select Commission on Civil Disorder, State of New Jersey, Report for Action, February, 1968, p. 95.

However, in the broad sense that the riot was a product of the polarization of blacks and whites in Newark, UCC was a factor inasmuch as its general thrust was on the side of the blacks. Blocked from other sources of municipal power, Newark's blacks had little voice other than UCC. UCC did not create the disputes, but a few of its neighborhood leaders and staff seem to have been heavily involved in the struggle against the medical school site and the mayor's nominee for the school position. In this situation, UCC did not serve as a bridge between blacks and whites--but neither did the churches, business organizations, social welfare councils, or any other community leadership.

UCC survived the investigations that followed the disorder, but after that summer the area boards were never the same. The agency was vulnerable to criticism of its inadequate procedures on internal management, and OEO, under pressure from Congress, pressed hard for reforms, including much tighter central control over the area boards. Tyson had left in the fall of 1966 to take a job as deputy administrator in New York City's new Human Resources Administration. His successor lasted only about eight months; an acting director filled in until September, 1967, when Sylvester Odum took over, coming from a job at OEO headquarters. Since then, he and other new staff seem to have achieved the management improvements that were needed.

Part of the reform was to switch the emphasis of the area boards. The staff division handling this activity changed its name from "community action" to "community development," and a modest service program has replaced the previous emphasis upon neighborhood organization and social action. By early 1969, the area boards were concentrating on such activities as recreation (karate, boxing, basketball, music, and art), sewing classes, tutorial programs, welfare rights, certification for surplus food, and multiphasic health examinations. They were assigned slightly less than 20 per cent of the UCC budget.

On two different days in March, 1969, I visited the headquarters of five area boards and found very few residents there, although I was told that after school and in the evenings children and youth show up for the scheduled activities. In contrast, I have been in dozens of multiservice centers around the country that were full of people during the day. The difference is that in Newark the action is elsewhere--at the field offices and neighborhood centers of the delegate agencies, which run pre-school, manpower, senior citizen, and other major programs. Even most of the lawyers from Neighborhood Legal Services, once located at the area board offices, have moved to a central location.

There are exceptions. The once controversial Area Board 3 has organized a separate delegate agency, the Bessie Smith Community Center, which gets its own funds from UCC and which is supported by a white suburban group called Friends of Clinton Hill. Area Boards 1 and 3 have plans under way to start cooperative supermarkets. Area Board 5 has organized a cooperative day care program. But with only the eight-man staff provided by UCC and with no operating funds except small amounts for rent and supplies, the area boards have little capacity for innovation. Attendance is lagging at most of the area board membership and trustee meetings, and one board has had no meetings for several months. Even UCC itself had only about 300 people attend its last membership meeting even though it has 12,000 members on the rolls.

In May, 1968, UCC indicated that it was willing to delegate staff and programs to any area board that demonstrated the capacity to run its own program. As of March, 1969, three boards were contemplating incorporation, but none had been approved by UCC to become delegate agencies.

In the meantime, City Hall has organized a Model Cities Program in a section that encompasses parts of the territory of three area boards. In the summer of 1968, 6,000 people voted in an election held to select members for the Model Neighborhood Council. The 13 districts from which the 52 members were chosen had separate boundaries from those of the area boards, and although some area board officers competed in the election, the Model Cities citizen apparatus is essentially controlled by a different group of citizens than the Community Action Program. In terms of legitimacy based upon extent of citizen participation in board election, the Model Cities Program in Newark has moved ahead of UCC and its area boards.

However, it would not be fair to judge the United Community Corporation solely on the basis of the three boards, for they are no longer the main thrust of the total program. Instead, the main emphasis is now upon such programs as pre-school education, legal services, senior citizens, and others conducted by delegate agencies and upon the Concentrated Employment Program, jointly operated by UCC and the municipal government. Reports indicate that most of the programs are operating satisfactorily.

The civil disorder of July, 1967, severely jolted Newark, and since then efforts have been made to reduce the extreme polarization of black and white that previously existed. The question of the medical school has been resolved through a mediation process which allocated less land to the school and called for the construction of more relocation housing. Odum has developed an effective working relationship with City Hall, and the UCC staff is working closely with the Model Cities agency. The police department and some of the area boards are conducting joint police-community relations activities. When the city was threatened with civil disorder in April, 1968, following the assassination of Dr. Martin Luther King, UCC and the area boards played a major role in keeping things cool. UCC is now much more of a bridge between the black and white communities than it previously was.

COLUMBUS, OHIO: EAST CENTRAL CITIZENS ORGANIZATION

Shortly after joining the Sviridoff study group in early 1966, I called on David Hunter, executive director of the Stern Family Fund, to discuss some of the preliminary ideas the group had for reorganizing New York's antipoverty program, including my proposal to establish community corporations. In the course of our conversation, he mentioned that the Stern Fund had given a small grant to a Columbus, Ohio, group that was forming a neighborhood corporation. Milton Kotler of the Institute for Policy Studies in Washington was an adviser to the Columbus group. I went to see Kotler two weeks later.

For about two years, Kotler had been developing the idea of forming what he then called "community foundations," which would develop into a new level of local government. In his first memo on the topic, he wrote: "The neighborhood government, through the Community Foundation, will be small enough for political life and important enough to make its participation satisfying and relevant--particularly since its decision will intimately affect the everyday living conditions and activities of the citizens."[9]

Early in 1965, Kotler presented his concepts at the Urban Training Center for Christian Mission in Chicago. Pastor Leopold Bernard of the First English Lutheran Church of Columbus was in the audience; Kotler's proposal immediately appealed to him.

Bernard's church was located in the inner city. In the prosperous years after World War II, most of its white middle-class members moved to the suburbs. Blacks and low-income whites took their places in the neighborhood, but not in the church. Unlike many other similarly situated churches, this congregation decided to stay put and to develop a program that would serve the changing neighborhood. Attention was first given to youth recreation, and then in 1961 a full-scale settlement house program was launched. By 1964, the annual operating budget was $24,000, and there were many volunteers, both from the neighborhood and from area universities. But by then it was becoming apparent that the church acting alone could not continue this level of support, much less expand to respond to other unmet needs of the neighborhood.

In March, 1965, the church's neighborhood center applied to the Columbus United Community Council for support but was turned down. At about this time, Kotler came in as a consultant to the center, and his ideas for a neighborhood foundation began to be influential. By midsummer, the church council agreed to turn over control of the neighborhood center to an elected neighborhood board. An interim executive council was formed, consisting of the previous members of the operating committee of the neighborhood center (five church members, five social service professionals, and five neighborhood residents) plus five additional residents selected by the four active neighborhood clubs in the area served. To help with

---

[9]Milton Kotler, <u>Community Organization as Political Government</u>, 1965, p. 8. (Mimeographed.)

organizing expenses, the Stern Family Fund and the Columbus Area Council of Churches each put up $3,000. In September, the group incorporated as the East Central Citizens Organization and has been known as ECCO ever since. Its area encompasses 6,500 people, of whom 70 per cent are black and 30 per cent white, mostly migrants from Appalachia.

To get a full-scale program going, ECCO applied to the Office of Economic Opportunity for a demonstration grant to run a "neighborhood foundation project." Emphasis in the application was upon achieving a "self-governing settlement" controlled by the residents of the total neighborhood community. The hypothesis was that "service programs arising on this self-determining basis would be different in character and value than programs derived from professional control." Although having a self-governing settlement house was a modest objective in comparison to achieving neighborhood government, some of the founders had this broader goal as a long-range target. For instance, the application started with one of Kotler's favorite quotes from Thomas Jefferson:

> Each ward would thus be a small republic within itself, and every man in the State would thus become an acting member of the common government, transacting in person a great portion of its rights and duties, subordinate indeed, yet important, and entirely within his competence. The wit of man cannot devise a more solid basis for a free, durable, and well administered republic.[10]

OEO approved the application in January, 1966, and ECCO called the first meeting of its general assembly for March. Membership in the assembly is open to anyone 16 and over living in the area served, and by the time of the meeting about 1,400 had signed up, representing nearly half of those eligible. Four hundred and fifty attended the first assembly, elected

---

[10] The Neighborhood Foundation Project: Columbus, Ohio (Application submitted by the East Central Citizens Organization to the U.S. Office of Economic Opportunity, 1965.)

13 representatives to the executive council, and chose the council officers. Each of the four neighborhood clubs also selected two council members. The new executive council then selected as executive director Randolph Holland, a social worker who had been serving as program director for the neighborhood center when it was under church control.

The OEO demonstration grant provided funds for central administration and some corporate aides (nonprofessionals) to conduct neighborhood organization, but not for the operation of service programs, not even for the neighborhood center that ECCO was taking over. For these funds, ECCO went first to the Columbus Metropolitan Area Community Action Organization (CMACAO), reasoning that it could run some programs on behalf of the over-all community action program. This was to no avail, and 1966 passed without this central component being funded.

However, ECCO was successful in getting a demonstration grant from the Department of Health, Education and Welfare's (HEW) Office of Juvenile Delinquency for the purpose of opening a youth civic center. This center was governed by a board selected by the neighborhood youth; the board in turn chose the staff, with ECCO serving as the fiscal agent.

The failure to obtain funds for the neighborhood center was frustrating, and part of the responsibility was assigned to Holland, who was alleged to be ineffective in negotiating with federal agencies and political forces in Columbus. Things came to a head in November, 1966, and Holland resigned under pressure. His replacement was Mrs. LaVerne Love, a former neighborhood aide, who was given an interim appointment. Kotler, who was still serving as a consultant, had always been opposed to Holland, and he now favored a candidate other than Mrs. Love. After the board refused to follow his recommendation, his consultative services were sharply reduced, a process an ECCO board member compared to a growing youth rejecting his parent.

By then, it was near the end of the first year of the OEO demonstration, and re-funding had to be arranged. Mrs. Love apparently improved relations with CMACAO so that funds for ECCO's neighborhood center were included in a package of seven neighborhood centers funded by OEO for Columbus in 1967.

Part of the difficulty that had to be overcome was the attitude of OEO's Chicago regional office, which apparently did not like headquarters funding a demonstration project in its territory.

The second ECCO election was held in January, 1967, with 150 in attendance. By then, the bylaws had been changed, so that the general assembly elected 14 members to the executive council and approved 16 selected by the neighborhood clubs. In this election, neighborhood youths campaigned actively and won eight of the at-large seats and two of the club selections. A report later filed with OEO indicated that the change in board composition occurred because "it was generally felt that club representatives are more accessible and responsive to the will of their constituents than councilmen elected at large."[11] But the assembly retained ultimate authority.

With the neighborhood center funded, ECCO's program grew rapidly in 1967. The center's services included the following: education--pre-school, adult, office procedures, tutoring; counseling--financial, legal, planned parenthood, psychological; employment--interviewing and job referral; recreation; emergency welfare; housing--referral and financial counseling; and health services--referral to city programs. The youth civic center provided activities in education, employment, recreation, and social action, and both black and white youths participated in contrast to the neighborhood center which served mostly blacks. Some of ECCO's aides, on their own, opened a small cooperative store. As another by-product of ECCO, an active education committee emerged in the local elementary school district and in September carried out a boycott of the school on the issue of quality education. In addition, the ECCO area was selected by the city for a project to raze condemned and unsafe houses.

ECCO started 1968 with its service program stabilized, but there were clouds on the horizon. Funding for the two-year OEO demonstration and the neighborhood center was to expire in April, and the

---

[11]History Part III of ECCO--November 1966 to June 1967, 1967, p. 3. (Mimeographed.)

youth center demonstration grant would run out in July. Relationships between ECCO and CMACAO were still touch and go, and it was by no means certain that CMACAO would re-fund the neighborhood center much less pick up the tab for ECCO's administration, which was coming from the OEO demonstration grant. Meanwhile, Columbus had received a Model Cities planning grant, but since the program was quite slow in getting under way, it offered no immediate program funds. At the same time, ECCO had no good prospects for obtaining contracts with the city to conduct various municipal services in its neighborhood, which was the next step in the program postulated by Kotler. In anticipation of its financial difficulties, ECCO had talks with the Ford Foundation about possible assistance, apparently with the encouragement of some of the foundation staff. An application was also submitted to OEO for an extension of the demonstration for another two years. In the midst of this uncertainty, Mrs. Love resigned and was replaced by James Cooper, who had previously worked at the neighborhood center and the youth civic center.

Fortunately, surplus funds in the OEO demonstration and neighborhood center accounts made it possible for these grants to be extended until mid-summer of 1968 while ECCO's application for an extension was reviewed by OEO. However, in April the Ford Foundation turned down ECCO's request for assistance. Funds for the youth civic center expired during the summer. Meanwhile, it became apparent that OEO would not re-fund a demonstration project dealing with more of the same, so the application was reshaped to emphasize a new direction for ECCO: the achievement of economic self-sufficiency. On this basis, OEO made a new demonstration grant to ECCO in August, 1968. By then, CMACAO had also continued funding the neighborhood center for another year through the community action funds it controls.

The program to achieve economic self-sufficiency got under way in September. The ECCO leaders quickly decided that to engage in manufacturing was infeasible and that instead they should concentrate upon services related to the fundamental needs of food, clothing, and shelter. Based upon that decision, they started exploring the purchase of a neighborhood grocery store. To assist and advise in this new phase, ECCO set up a marketing and investment committee, consisting of an executive from a research

THREE APPROACHES TO COMMUNITY CORPORATIONS 71

and development corporation, an investment counselor from a local bank, a certified public accountant, and ECCO's lawyer, executive director, and deputy director. An economic advisory committee was also organized within the executive council. To run whatever businesses might be formed or purchased, steps were taken to organize ECCO Enterprises Corporation, a profit-making stock corporation. By the end of 1968, ECCO was considering the purchase of two grocery stores, a food carry-out, and a florist shop. For capital resources, it had $25,000 in seed money from the OEO grant. It also decided to hire a fund-raising organization to assist in obtaining additional financial contributions.

After three years, how successful is ECCO? One answer was given by Pastor Bernard, still serving the First English Lutheran Church: "If you measured it on the yardstick as a social service agency, ECCO is a flop. Its success is in political awareness. ECCO has endeavored to proved that poor people can take hold of their own destiny."[12] The word "flop" is too strong, but I do know that a pair of consultants sent about that time by the Ford Foundation were unimpressed by ECCO's service program.

My own judgment, based upon a visit to Columbus in November, 1968, is that the service programs are of average quality in comparison with others I have observed. The organization is on the rebound from the period when future funding was in question. The programs at the neighborhood center have the look of similar ones in other communities: Head Start, rudimentary vocational training, sewing activities, senior citizens program. The youth civic center was still operating part-time with volunteer leadership because the funds had run out. The program appears to be on a par with the typical settlement house run by professional social workers and controlled by an absentee board of upper-middle class citizens.

Clearly, these East Central Columbus residents have shown that they have the capacity to run their own programs and to handle funds. Their performance has not been faultless, though, for staff of the neighborhood center have been laid off because the center director misread the balance sheet and spent at too fast a rate. This situation arose in part

---

[12]*Columbus Dispatch*, April 19, 1968.

because each component of the program--administration, youth civic center, and neighborhood center--was derived from different grants and the funds handled separately. ECCO is now in the process of centralizing financial control.

Of course, ECCO never offered itself as a demonstration in service programs but rather in resident participation and community control. Pastor Bernard is right in indicating that there is now more political awareness. The school boycott and the transfer of experience gained in ECCO to participation in local politics by some of the residents is evidence of this. However, ECCO has never gained the strength and know-how to negotiate effectively with the "powers that be," such as those who control CMACAO, the United Community Council, and City Hall, to promote its own self-interests--not to speak of the broader interests of neighborhood residents. Thus, once again ECCO has had great difficulty in getting funds through CMACAO to run the neighborhood center; the central community action agency deleted ECCO from its 1969 budget, forcing it to appeal to OEO for direct funding. So far, the City of Columbus has not entered into any contracts with ECCO, although this was an expectation of the founders.

ECCO's success in resident participation has been more internal, in operating as a self-governing settlement house. Over the months, the executive council has emerged as the principal point of resident control rather than the general assembly, which meets only twice a year. In an analogy with local government, ECCO is governed by a "city council" and not by a "town meeting," although it was the latter that Kotler had in mind. When I visited the council meeting, I found the members well informed and articulate. Except for two youths, all members in attendance were adults, the majority over 40 years old. There was considerable reliance upon the staff, but the staff was not nearly as dominant as in some of the other boards I have observed.

Perhaps it might be fair to conclude that ECCO is more of a model for turning settlement houses over to resident control than for organizing neighborhood government. Even if this broader goal of the founders is not being achieved, ECCO has had a greater social role in the United States than its local accomplishments might suggest. It has served as an inspiration, a point of departure, for other groups. It has had dozens of visitors who return to their own communities not merely to copy it but to try their own approach to community control. Representatives of ECCO appeared before Congress, and Senator Robert Kennedy visited the neighborhood, each case adding to the national discussion. The neighborhood was used as a site for training persons for the five pilot neighborhood service centers run by community corporations (see Chapter 7). In sum, the mere existence of an organization like ECCO has been valuable.

Whether ECCO can achieve self-sufficiency as envisioned in its newest OEO demonstration grant remains to be seen. I am skeptical of its ability to gain complete self-sufficiency from enterprises it runs or controls. But to the extent that it can obtain additional sources of funds, the greater independence and flexibility it will have. In the long run, more and more government funds will be flowing to neighborhood boards through community action agencies, Model Cities agencies, and their successors, and it will be proper and desirable for ECCO to be at the receiving end. Thus, it is necessary for ECCO to strengthen its relationships with the local agencies that control the pipe-line to federal funds. In part, this will require ECCO to become a more forceful spokesman for the entire neighborhood it serves, and not merely a sponsor of a couple of service facilities. So far, ECCO has survived in the face of adversity mainly because it could obtain federal demonstration funds directly from Washington. When these special funds run out, ECCO will face the test of standing on its own in the competition for locally controlled resources. How it meets this test will be an important measure of its success.

COMMENTARY

These three cities--Washington, Newark, and Columbus--are quite different in their approach to the Community Action Program and in the roles given to neighborhood organizations. UPO in Washington uses community corporations in four of the ten neighborhoods it serves. UCC in Newark has a city-wide network of area boards, but as a result of committing most funds to other agencies and backing off a strong citizen action approach, it has not developed the boards into major community-controlled institutions. In Columbus, ECCO has operated a resident-controlled neighborhood house with OEO demonstration funds and has struggled hard to get continuing support from the local community action agency, which otherwise has no neighborhood-controlled programs. In spite of these differences, a key factor in all three cities is commitment--and lack of commitment.

On the whole, UPO has had a commitment to neighborhood control and has allowed citizens in four neighborhoods to take over what it was previously running directly. However, in another neighborhood where a resident-controlled pilot neighborhood center is being organized (see Chapter 7), UPO has vacillated on how far and how fast to extend neighborhood control over other UPO-operated centers, and this uncertainty has been a handicap to the neighborhood center corporation. Newark, once strongly committed to area boards has backed off this approach. The community action agency in Columbus has fought against control by residents of the ECCO area and has thus made life much more difficult for that community corporation.

Another thing that stands out from the experiences in Washington and Newark is that it is hard to sustain citizen organizing in the face of opposition from public officials. The issue-oriented, city-wide committees in Washington were de-emphasized when they became too controversial, and the social protest and organizing activities of the Newark area boards were curtailed. With citizen organizing played down and with no significant programs to operate because most of the funds were otherwise committed, the area boards in Newark have not been able to maintain the support of large numbers of residents. In Washington, though, the community corporations are conducting service programs as well as organizing citizens, and delivery of services protects the organizing process.

There are social theorists who do not favor community corporations getting involved in program operations. Residents of poor neighborhoods, though, have many specific needs and look to the corporations for assistance. The agency that can deliver on services has a much stronger base for mobilizing neighborhood support for action on broader issues. What is necessary is a reasonable balance between services and social action.

CHAPTER 4   COMMUNITY ACTION IN APPALACHIA

As the previous chapters have indicated, my work experience has been almost entirely in urban settings. When this current study got under way, I resolved to see more of the rural program firsthand.

I began my quest for a better understanding of rural problems by going to Appalachia. Because time was limited, I decided to visit some counties where the Community Action Program was organized so that poor rural residents had some degree of control over program operations beyond selecting persons for the governing board. Thus, the counties chosen do not represent a scientific cross section of all Appalachia; rather, they were selected to provide illumination of issues related to community control of program operations. The description of these county programs emphasizes the process of community involvement and does not attempt to provide a comprehensive exposition of the program content.

In the heart of the Appalachia coal area, successive booms and busts not only have vastly changed the physical character of the mountains and streams but also have left thousands of broken, worn-out people in place of the rugged and fiercely independent mountaineers who occupied the land a century ago. The coal empire has always been absentee-owned, and the territory was treated virtually like a colony by industrial and financial interests in the Eastern and Great Lakes regions. The coal companies own vast tracts of land and virtually unrestricted mineral rights; until recently, company housing and company stores with their own scrip were commonplace. Moreover, the mining interests have exercised pervasive influence on local government, but paid almost nothing in local taxes as they extracted the natural wealth of the land.

In the process, the coal industry brought a long boom period, which burst in 1927 as a forerunner of the great national depression. World War II brought a revival only to be followed by prolonged decline during the 1950's. In recent years, coal production has increased, but automation has substantially reduced the number of jobs, and newer methods of strip and augur mining are despoiling the countryside in an unprecedented manner. Thousands and thousands of people have moved away, generally the young and better educated, leaving large numbers of retired, crippled, and unemployed people for whom welfare has become a way of life.

In June, 1968, I visited eight counties in this grievously depressed area. Four were in the southern part of West Virginia: McDowell, Raleigh, Mingo, and Mercer. Each of these has its own community action agency. In Kentucky, the four counties I visited, Leslie, Knott, Letcher, and Perry, have combined for the purposes of operating a community action program.

These are all mountainous counties. Roads generally snake along the valleys, climbing the mountains only to get to another valley. Compared to the other six, Raleigh and Mercer had wider valleys and the hills seem less steep. The West Virginia Turnpike transverses Raleigh County and has its southern terminus in Mercer County, with the capital, Charleston, at the opposite northern end. Hazard, Kentucky, the county seat of Perry, is connected to Lexington and the more open blue grass country by a new state highway (built under the Appalachia Regional Development Act), a toll parkway, and an interstate highway. The other five counties have more difficult highway connections with the outside world.

Within all the counties, topography and widespread dispersal of population make it a major problem for people to get around and for programs to operate effectively. The resulting isolation reduces accessibility of jobs for residents and of markets for manufactured goods and in intangible ways contributes to a certain backwardness stemming from lack of a regular interchange of ideas and experience with other localities.

ISSUE COMMITTEES IN
McDOWELL COUNTY, WEST VIRGINIA

The first of these eight counties to organize a community action program was McDowell. In 1964, a small group of citizens in the county seat of Welch got together and initiated efforts to deal with the county's social problems. If they had lived in a city, it is quite possible that they would have worked through a council of social agencies, a united fund, or some other organization of that sort, but such institutional structures are largely absent from most rural areas. Instead, they turned to the Council of Southern Mountains, a 50-year-old organization dedicated to helping the mountain people help themselves, serving parts of nine states with headquarters in Berea, Kentucky. Not only did the McDowell County leaders receive technical assistance, but they were also provided an organizational base through the establishment of the McDowell County Chapter, West Virginia Branch of the Council of Southern Mountains, in reality a unique unit created for their purpose.

This occurred while the Economic Opportunity Act was making its way through Congress. With the establishment of the Office of Economic Opportunity, the McDowell County Chapter had a new potential source of financial support, and OEO had an opportunity to fund a rural program at a time when rural areas were much less prepared than cities to receive community action funds. This marriage of interests led to McDowell County's receiving a program development grant in the first series awarded by OEO, and in 1965 OEO provided funds for a sizable action program, which was heralded as a rural model for the national Community Action Program.

The McDowell program was built around eight multipurpose service centers, which were scattered around the county in abandoned schoolhouses and former company stores. In some respects, they were copies of urban settlement houses and even were called "neighborhood centers," although their locations were not really "neighborhoods" as that term is used in cities. Staff was hired by the county-wide agency and assigned to these centers. The initial program basically included Head Start, social service, adult education, and recreation, with virtually no attempt to engage in social action activities. Resident participation was through community action groups organized in various mining camps and hollows throughout the county.

Within a year, it was found that this approach was not working as well as had been hoped. Poor persons were not coming in large numbers to the centers, which were operating programs designed by the staff at the county seat, with little or no say from the residents served. Also, establishing small community action groups merely for the sake of having an organization in each community proved insufficient to sustain the interest of the residents. Instead, these residents were more oriented toward special issues rather than small geographic areas as such. Different residents of a particular community would have varied concerns, and such concerns were shared by some of the residents of other small communities.

Based upon this experience, the program has been modified and is still evolving. Early in 1967, neighborhood council boards were organized to oversee the operations of the multiservice centers. A board consists of two representatives from each of the 10 to 12 community action groups within the service district of the center. Each board has an employment committee to select all center personnel but the center coordinator has to be approved by the central office. There are program committees to advise on the operations of Head Start and community improvement activities.

In early summer, 1968, issue committees were organized on a county-wide basis to deal with the following topics: roads, welfare, cooperatives, disabled miners and widows, election reforms and voting education, senior citizens, community action group projects and self-help, technical referrals, health and sanitation, and youth. These issues cut across the geographic boundaries of community action groups and multiservice centers. There is a committee for each issue, with membership consisting of a contact person from each of the eight districts, and through the multiservice centers there are further contacts to the community action groups that have a concern for the particular issue. The issue committees are staffed by coordinators who are assigned part-time from the multiservice centers. Although the issue committees were just beginning to operate when I visited the county, I sensed that their approach would likely reflect the style of the McDowell County Chapter, which emphasizes "talking with people across the table," rather than "creating an uproar."[1]

This moderate stance was a major factor in keeping the county court (the county governing board) from taking control of the community action program under the Green Amendment, which enables the local government to become the community action agency or to designate that agency. In McDowell County, the commissioners took no action, and this permitted OEO to continue funding the existing agency.

In the evolution of the McDowell County program, the next likely step will be to give the neighborhood council boards a greater say in the allocation of funds assigned to their respective centers. They will have more flexibility in adapting the program to the needs in their districts rather than having virtually identical programs in each center. Funds will still be handled by the central office, but it will act mainly as a fiscal agent with policy control delegated to the neighborhood council board. The boards will eventually incorporate. However, at the end of 1968, this form of decentralization had not yet begun.

COMMUNITY DEVELOPMENT VOLUNTEERS IN RALEIGH COUNTY, WEST VIRGINIA

In Raleigh County, the community action program has taken a somewhat different direction. In the beginning, the program was organized by local education and city leaders and received a program development grant of $25,000 from OEO in July, 1965. The program was developing slowly until the summer of 1966, when a contingent of summer associates of the Appalachian Volunteers entered the county.

---

[1] Interview with Harold Cooper, Executive Director, McDowell County Chapter, West Virginia Branch of the Council of Southern Mountains, June 26, 1968.

The Appalachian Volunteers (AV) is an organization originally created in Berea, Kentucky, by the Council of Southern Mountains as a means of drawing new talent into an area that has long been experiencing a brain drain. Operating on its own since 1966, the Appalachian Volunteers recruits and assigns personnel, mostly young college graduates, to varied community development activities. In some instances, the AV's team with other volunteers recruited directly by OEO through VISTA (Volunteers in Service to America). In 1966, AV summer associates joined the year-round AV's and VISTA's, and together they created quite a stir in West Virginia.

Along with recreational activities for children, the volunteers in Raleigh County spread throughout the county getting acquainted and informing poor rural residents of programs that could benefit them. As one part of this effort, the volunteers promoted attendance at the July meeting of the Raleigh County Community Action Association. By happenstance, at this meeting the incumbent president resigned, and as membership was based upon attendance at one meeting, these new participants were eligible to vote for the new president at the August meeting. They elected Chester Workman, an outspoken coal miner who was to become known as the "community action preacher." By October, all but one of the old officers had been replaced and a new executive director appointed. He was Gibbs Kinderman, a 23-year-old Harvard graduate who had come to the county as an AV field representative. With the required approval of the membership at monthly meetings, other former AV's were added to the staff as well as many poor people from throughout the county.

Once in command, the leaders of the poor on the board and the former AV's on the staff proceeded to develop an unusually large program, which by the summer of 1968 was drawing to the county about $2.5 million a year in federal funds. Programs include Head Start, adult education, health education, a medical clinic, bus transportation, Neighborhood Youth Corps, and cooperatives.

Around the county, 27 community action groups have been organized in particular geographic areas. The county is divided into eight districts, with a weak district organization based upon the general

membership within the district. For each of the major
programs, there is a county-wide committee whose
membership is drawn largely from district program
committees on the same topic. The county program
committees play major policy roles and participate
in the recruitment and selection of program personnel.
For certain programs, such as Head Start and health
education, district program committees have a say in
hiring the personnel that work in their districts.
In Head Start, both teachers and aides are drawn from
the ranks of the poor.

The size of the operating budget and the details
of program administration have absorbed most of the
energies of the committee members, board of directors,
and staff. As a result, Raleigh County has not made
very much noise on issues, and there has been relatively little conflict with county officials--although
such an outcome might have been expected after the
AV-stimulated takeover. The education committee is
most involved in citizen action, promoting parental
involvement in the educational process and attempting
to work with the county board of education on the
use of funds under the Elementary and Secondary Education Act. Significantly, the education committee
has the least funds to administer whereas the health
committee, which handles the largest budget, and the
Head Start committee are not particularly issue-
oriented.

Until July 1, 1958, when the Green Amendment to
the Economic Opportunity Act required that policy control reside in a board of directors, the 4,000 members of the Raleigh County Community Action
Association were in control and ratified all decisions of the board at monthly meetings attended by
300 to 400 people. After July 1, not only did decision-making power shift to the board of directors
but also the addition of public officials and agency
representatives to the board reduced the representatives of the poor to a minority. At one stage, the
county court even indicated its intent to take the
program over, apparently in order to control the
funds and jobs and not to change the program content
particularly, but later it withdrew and designated
the Association to continue.

MINGO COUNTY, WEST VIRGINIA: POLITICS AND THE COMMUNITY ACTION AGENCY

Poor residents of Raleigh County resisted the threatened takeover by the county, but their protests were mild in comparison to the battle that raged in Mingo County. According to a broad consensus of informed observers, the political machine in that county is the most corrupt in the state, with voting irregularities commonplace and kickbacks by contractors and public employees to political slush funds a widely established pattern. There the community action agency is more directly engaged in political action than in any place I know, approaching the extreme limit of legally permissible activities under the Economic Opportunity Act.

The program started quietly enough when the Chamber of Commerce of Williamson, the county seat, petitioned the county court to create a community action program, apparently to attract additional federal funds to this impoverished area. The six businessmen appointed to the original board of the Economic Opportunity Council proceeded to submit an application for program development funds to OEO in Washington and to hire an executive director. Their choice was Huey Perry, a junior high school teacher who was a member of an old Mingo County family and thus considered "safe" by the political machine. But Perry was misjudged, for he turned out to be the strongest opponent ever faced by the Democratic organization, which has long dominated the political scene in Mingo County.

The basic focus of the Economic Opportunity Council has been to develop among poor people democratic community organizations that are tools for effecting political and institutional change. The actions that flow from this focus inevitably have led to conflict with the political forces controlling the county's institutional structure, and the resulting struggle for power is a major theme of the events marking the development of the community action program.

Perry started quietly by organizing community action groups in rural hollows and old mining camps, working with the occasional assistance of board members and after a while with the help of a community aide. Within a year, there were 17 such groups. During that period, the governing board was expanded to provide representation both for these new community action groups and for established organizations, such as the Kiwanis, the NAACP, the Izaak Walton League, and several public agencies. However, the representatives of the poor came to have a majority as Perry, his staff, and some AV's organized more community action groups until their number reached 30. As the poor on the board began to express themselves and take control of decision-making, some of the original businessmen dropped out. Ultimately, the first president, Gerald L. Chafin, a mortician from the small town of Delbarton, was ousted through a series of complicated parliamentary maneuvers. With his removal, Perry and the representatives of the poor were in full control.

While the struggle for control was going on, programs were beginning: Neighborhood Youth Corps, Medicare Alert, home improvement activities, and Head Start. These activities were carried out within the broad framework of the basic objective of institutional change. Head Start was controlled by representatives of the poor; nonprofessionals were hired from the subcommunities as both teachers and teacher aides, and the Head Start centers were commonly used as the meeting place of the community action groups. These groups were issue-oriented, although inevitably they were drawn into special projects, such as roads and recreation, to benefit their immediate community.

Perhaps even more important, the community action groups formed the basis for county-wide issue committees. An education committee has focused on the need for a school lunch program and on the use of federal elementary and secondary education funds received by the county board of education. More controversial has been a fair elections committee, which has concentrated on election irregularities, such as votes cast in the names of deceased persons and former residents of the county. So widespread are such irregularities that the committee challenged 6,000 names on the voting register in the spring of 1968--this in a county of 40,000 where 15,000 people were recorded as voting in the 1964 Presidential election.

Whereas the education committee and fair elections committee operate within the structure of the Economic Opportunity Council, an independent Political Action League was organized by many of the same persons; it endorsed anti-machine candidates in the spring primary election and lost. Although the League has its own governing structure, friend and foe alike see it and the community action agency as virtually synonymous.

Nonetheless, political action is not the sole pursuit of the Economic Opportunity Council. The home improvement project, for example, hires unemployed carpenters to supervise unskilled workmen who are assigned from work-relief programs and puts these crews to work improving, and in some instances completely rebuilding, the homes of the poor. For materials, they rely mainly upon salvage and the small amount of new materials the homeowners themselves can buy. Occasionally a workman, himself on welfare, will buy nails and other supplies. The decision of whose house to repair is made by a district home improvement committee (there are four districts), which is formed from representatives of the community action groups.

The 16 Head Start centers also have policy advisory committees which choose personnel and select the children to participate. Two community action groups operate community work programs under the Nelson Amendment to the Economic Opportunity Act, and they select the workers and the projects. Thus, efforts of institutional change are founded on local bodies in which poor people have a real voice in decision-making.

It is no wonder that this structure was seen by the political organization as a major threat, even before the Political Action League backed candidates in the primary. Consequently, the county initiated steps to take over the community action program under the provisions of the Green Amendment. Apart from the contest for control, the Economic Opportunity Council was somewhat vulnerable because administrative practices have been shoddy, with inadequate accounting procedures and lack of formal personnel policies. Thus, the opponents could use the claim of mismanagement as a mask for a takeover that has deeper roots. However, in early 1969, the newly inaugurated governor blocked the county takeover, and the Mingo County Economic Opportunity Council continued in operation.

COMMUNITY ACTION IN
MERCER COUNTY, WEST VIRGINIA

What has been occurring in Mingo County is weakly echoed in Mercer County, where a similar power struggle has been waged, but with mcuh less militancy and considerably fewer funds and jobs at stake. Originally, the program there was set up by officials of the local government with the support of business leaders, and these members of the local power structure controlled the board. After a fairly unproductive planning period, the first executive director resigned, and in his place the board hired James Overdorf, an ordained minister who was serving a Presbyterian church in a northern West Virginia county and who was a lay member of the local community action board.

Overdorf arrived in Mercer County in November, 1966, just after Congress had passed an amendment requiring that at least one-third of the board of each community action agency consist of representatives of the poor. For Mercer County, this meant a change from the two poor members out of 27 then serving. Starting with the required one-third, other poor persons were gradually added as unrepresented groups of poor petitioned for board seats, utilizing a rarely used provision of the 1966 amendments. Through this process, poor persons and their representatives came to have majority control of the board, and this in turn led some of the agency representatives who had previously been in command to become less active. The bylaws were changed so that a general membership was created, and the members were given control of policy, previously the exclusive domain of the board of directors. The vast bulk of members were poor people.

By the time this transformation had occurred, OEO was operating on a tight budget and was unable to fund a major program in Mercer County. Partly for this reason and partly by preference, the program has concentrated on community organization and local issues that affect the lives of the poor. Through the efforts of six community aides on the staff and ten summer volunteers, 16 community action groups have been organized. One of the groups developed a water system for its hollow, another forced the removal of an incompetent elementary school principal,

and several have sought to improve local roads. A
sum of $300 per year is available to each group if it
provides equal matching funds or the equivalent in
volunteer services. Some have used this money to
fix up a meeting place; others have undertaken small
community improvement projects.

County-wide issue committees have been formed to
unite the efforts of the community action groups.
The education committee has been especially active,
pushing for greater parental involvement in Head
Start, which the county schools operate, and trying
to influence the use of federal education funds.
This committee, at the urging of various community
action groups, fought a school bond issue that seemed
to favor urban areas, neglect rural areas, and discriminate against Negroes. After the bond issue was
defeated, the superintendent of schools, who like
many of his counterparts in Appalachia is an important county political figure, protested vigorously,
supported by the owner of both county newspapers,
the local television station, and a radio station.

About the same time, the community action group
in one of the neighborhoods in Bluefield, the largest
city in the county, was involved in a dispute with
the city manager over a firehouse location. Soon
after, the community action agency left its free
quarters in City Hall (voluntarily, the city manager
says; evicted, Overdorf says), and the board of education took back the office furniture that had been
loaned to them.

At the time of my visit in June, 1968, the poor
persons involved in the program were seeking to complement their pursuit of issues with the operation
of concrete programs. Among other things, they were
trying to shift control of Head Start from the board
of education to committees of parents. In the fall,
they succeeded in gaining such control over Head
Start. By then, the Mercer County program had a new
executive direcotr, Joe Hatfield, and finally some
OEO program funds; by the end of 1968, they had the
following programs in operation: Head Start, Neighborhood Youth Corps, legal services, cultural enrichment for youth, training of household workers,
organization of cooperatives (such as quilt-making,
a bus line, domestic service), activities for the
elderly, and community organization.

In the summer of 1968, the county court expressed its intent to take control of the program under the Green Amendment. It held a public hearing in August but delayed making a decision for several months; finally, in November, it decided not to take control and instead to designate the existing agency. As required by law, public officials were appointed to one-third of the positions on the 24-member board, but representatives of the poor were given 12 seats. Policy-making powers were transferred from the general membership to the board.

MULTICOUNTY AGENCIES IN EASTERN KENTUCKY

Each of the counties in southern West Virginia has its own community action agency. Initially, this was the same pattern in eastern Kentucky, but after a while, with a strong push from OEO, multicounty agencies were formed. For example, the counties of Leslie, Knott, Letcher, and Perry each had its own agency and received a program development grant, but in July, 1966, they merged into the LKLP Community Action Council.

This four-county agency operates a wide range of of programs, including Head Start, rural child care, Neighborhood Youth Corps, on-the-job training, community work projects (Nelson Amendment), basic education, health services, a sewing center, a demonstration housing program, guidance and referral, and community information depots. The latter are the particular interest of this section.

When Letcher County had its own program, it hired poor persons as guidance and referral aides to go around the county uncovering personal problems, referring persons to social agencies, driving them there if necessary, distributing clothing, helping people obtain food stamps, and doing a variety of other tasks that responded to individual needs. At the same time, community development aides were stimulating the formation of community action groups in mining camps and hollows. The work of these two types of aides was conducted through six outreach offices.

After the four-county merger, the Letcher County outreach program was continued, and similar efforts were begun on a more modest basis in the other three counties. After about a year, this activity in Leslie, Knott, and Perry Counties was redirected and expanded through the initiation of community information depots (CID). Within these three counties, 45 communities—mostly rural hollows and small settlements—were selected by a committee consisting of representatives of the poor on the four-county area council. Each community would be the locus of a community action depot, which would be staffed by an "operator." Information about the depots and the jobs was distributed to every household in these communities, interested persons submitted applications for the positions, and the four-county committee selected the persons to be hired.

Once hired, the operators began to canvass their communities, organize committees, and help the residents to incorporate. Unlike the West Virginia counties where incorporation of community action groups is a rarity, most of the CID groups in Leslie, Knott, and Perry counties have incorporated. This results from the easy incorporation procedures in Kentucky and from the presence of two lawyers on the staff of the LKLP Community Action Council. The director of the CID program believes that incorporation also helps to affirm the responsibility the residents have and requires them to make decisions when they might want to avoid policy issues for fear of offending their neighbors.

Each CID corporation has an allocation of $500 for heat, supplies, and other needs, provided that it matches this amount in cash or services. Most of them have acquired the use of a building, such as an abandoned one-room school or an old store. Assistance in fixing up the building is often given by one of the work programs, such as Neighborhood Youth Corps, Work Experience and Training, or the Nelson Amendment. Two of the groups will have centers provided under the neighborhood facilities program operated by HUD. Project activities include sewing clubs, garbage hauling, park construction, beautification, day care, medical transportation, and recreational activities.

Every community with an information depot selects one of its low-income residents to serve on a county-wide citizens advisory committee. This committee in turn elects three of its members for the four-county board of directors, and the 12 so elected constitute the CID committee. Whereas initially the CID committee chose the operators, this function is now being handled by the three representatives from the particular county.

At this stage, the CID corporations do not hire staff, handle funds, or operate local portions of the established programs, such as Head Start and Neighborhood Youth Corps. Thus, their main policy role is in determining what community projects should be undertaken and how their $500 allocation should be spent.

However, there is one community corporation in the LKLP area with more authority--the Millstone Sewing Center in Letcher County. It was organized by Mrs. Mabel Kiser, a dynamic long-time resident of the Millstone community, once a mining camp. She got leaders from three other small communities to join with her, and with donated legal services they incorporated. The board of education turned over an abandoned school building, and some youths and adults from work projects rehabilitated it. A neighbor permitted the men to salvage tin from a dilapidated building for under-floor insulation; at Mrs. Kiser's request, U.S. Gypsum donated wallboard; and the Mennonite Service Committee provided two sewing machines. After a year of voluntary operation, the Millstone Center became a delegate agency of the area council and received enough OEO funds to put Mrs. Kiser on the payroll, hire two supervisors and ten half-time seamstresses, and buy additional sewing machines and supplies. The product of their work is distributed free to poor people throughout the county.

The corporation is governed by 12 persons, three named by each of the participating communities. They are fully in charge of program policy and hiring of personnel, but bookkeeping is handled by the area council. It may be that the administrative staff takes a disproportionate amount of the corporation's budget, and some observers believe that the director and supervisors could handle a number of centers in different locations around the county.

The LKLP community action program from the beginning has been strongly service-oriented in contrast to the issue focus of Mingo and Mercer counties in West Virginia. However, as community action groups have been organized, residents of poor rural communities have gained experience in working together. In at least two instances in Letcher County, this new-found organizational conciousness has been manifested as a side effect in matters not directly a part of the LKLP program. In one case, parents became greatly concerned about the deplorable physical conditions of the schools in Whitesburg, the county seat, and after a strenuous campaign that included a protest demonstration the county and state education authorities responded by making immediate improvements and embarking upon a long-range school building program. In the other case, residents organized to protest the planning and construction of the Kingdom Come dam by the U.S. Corps of Army Engineers, a project residents felt was inimical to their interests; the vigor of their opposition at a public hearing was sufficient to block the project from proceeding further.

Because citizen action on these issues was a byproduct rather than a direct result of the community action program, the LKLP Community Action Council was not seen as the instigator. Nor has the Council stimulated other significant action on public issues. Largely for this reason, the four counties are content to keep the Council in existence and not to place it under county control. The main change that occurred as a result of the Green Amendment was in the composition of the board of directors; representatives of the poor now have only one-third of the membership compared to the 50 per cent they previously had.

COMMENTARY

One can observe both differences and similarities in the community action programs in these eight Appalachian counties. The differences emerge in the style of operation and the order in which different developments have occurred.

These community action agencies use techniques that fall into three broad categories. One is "community development," which consists of efforts to assist community residents to identify their local problems and organize to carry out solutions, often through self-help activities. The community problems focused on are not always related to the elimination of poverty, although they might deal with conditions that result from a lack of income, such as poor clothing. Sometimes the problem stems from the neglect of public agencies, such as inadequate roads and water systems in the hollows.

A second category is "services and programs," particularly those which ameliorate the conditions of poverty, such as social services, child care, food stamps, housing improvement, buying cooperatives, health services, and recreation. Less frequently, these services provide exits from poverty, such as manpower training when effectively linked to job opportunities (which is not always the case) and, over the long run, Head Start and elementary and secondary education.

A third category is "issues and action," with an orientation toward institutional change. Sometimes such action is directed toward influencing, and if possible controlling, programs with an anti-poverty focus, such as local programs under the Elementary and Secondary Act and the Work Experience and Training Program. In other cases, the action relates to broader issues, such as government financing (bond issues and taxes), election reform, and ultimately the election of public officials.

In McDowell County and the LKLP area in Kentucky, the initial thrust was directed toward services, mainly those which ameliorate the conditions of poverty, although the LKLP areas also have had sizable manpower trianing efforts. As these services were being put into operation, a small-scale community development effort was begun, leading to a number of local projects. Only recently have these two agencies taken the first tentative steps toward becoming involved in action on county-wide issues.

The Raleigh County program as it exists today is a product of community development efforts of volunteers who came from outside the county. When their efforts led to representatives of the poor taking control, the emphasis shifted to a large-scale service program, built upon a foundation of continuing community development work. Heavily involved in program operations, the staff, board, and general membership have scarcely had the time or energy to become engaged in broader issues.

Both Mingo County and Mercer County (after Overdorf became executive director) also started from a base of community development, but with a difference. The establishment of community action groups and of the other parts of the county structure was intended to provide an organizational base for a much wider campaign of institutional change. However, in both counties the community participants have not been content with only the long-range struggle and have organized a variety of services to bring about more immediate improvements in their lives.

Thus, over a two- to three-year period, all five programs have moved toward a middle ground in which community development, services and programs, and issues and action are combined. To be sure, the mix is different from one county to the next, but all blend techniques drawn from the same three categories.

There are also other similarities. All have organized community action groups (called community information depot committees in the LKLP area) in small settlements of 200 to 300 people, in hollows with houses scattered along a creek, and to a lesser extent in low-income neighborhoods in towns. These groups are democratic institutions, generally operating through a "town meeting" approach with all residents having a voice and a vote at public gatherings. In some communities, steering committees have been organized with members elected by the residents. The resulting gain in the broadening of the democratic process is significant though intangible. Although statistical measures on program results are not available, the value of these grass-roots organizations is unmistakably clear.

Most of the residents of the communities in which these groups have been organized are poor. Like most other people, the poor crave concrete results rather than vague theoretical goals. Consequently, the community action groups have tackled local problems, such as road improvement, water supply, recreation for youngsters, libraries, sewing clubs, and related activities, and have usually obtained an old building for a community center. Some of the staff executives would prefer that energies not be sapped by these activities so that the residents can concentrate upon more basic institutional change, but without these close-at-home activities it is unlikely that residents would sustain their interest in the community action group. Without continued citizen support, the groups could not be available as the organizational basis of broader efforts.

For in all of the counties, the community action groups are building blocks for other parts of the community action structure. In four of the five programs, the community action groups elect representatives to district committees or boards, such as the neighborhood council boards that govern the multi-service centers in McDowell County, the district health committees in Raleigh County, the district housing improvement committees in Mingo County, and the county-wide citizens advisory committees in the four-county LKLP area.

In a hierarchy of representation, the district committees in McDowell and Raleigh counties select some of their members for the county board, and the county-wide citizens advisory committees in the LKLP area choose representatives to the area council. In Mingo County, the community action groups designate representatives to a county-wide association, which in turn selects the board of directors, a portion of whom are members of community action groups.

The community action groups and district committees also form the building blocks for county-wide program committees, such as the ten issue committees in McDowell County, the program policy committees (education, health, transportation, Head Start) in Raleigh County, education and fair elections committees in Mingo County, and roads and education committees in Mercer County. In Mingo County, members of the community action groups also form the representative structure for the independent Political Action League.

Altogether, the programs reviewed have six different kinds of units with some degree of decision-making authority: community action groups, general district committees, district program committees, county program committees, board of directors, and membership. The extent of policy control given each type of unit varies considerably.

The community action groups have a say over the local projects they undertake and how the $300 to $500 grant available to them should be used; none of them, except the Millstone Sewing Center, has authority to hire or fire personnel, although they often can give guidance to staff assigned to work with them. The district-level neighborhood council boards in McDowell County guide the work of the multiservice centers, select all the personnel, and may eventually be given power to alter budgets and programs. District program committees, such as those for Head Start in Mingo County and those for health in Raleigh County, also have a say in who is hired, and the district housing improvement committees in Mingo County decide whose house will be improved. County-wide program committees tend to have significant policy roles in their particular fields, and the ones in Raleigh County are active in the selection of personnel. Until the Green Amendment decreed otherwise, the general membership had ultimate policy control in Mercer and Raleigh counties, but now in all instances the board of directors is the ultimate policy-making body, and except in the cases noted above, controls the hiring of staff.

As to the expenditure of funds, central administration is virtually universal. Bank accounts, disbursements, and bookkeeping are all handled by the central office. However, the area council office is mainly a fiscal agent for the Millstone Sewing Center in Letcher County, and the county office in McDowell County intends to fill this fiscal role when greater authority is delegated to the multiservice centers. But none of these organizations functions as a full delegate agency that handles its own funds. Among other reasons, if every one of the small groups had its own bookkeeper, a large portion of the limited funds would be eaten up by administrative expenses and thus unavailable for programs.

With no funds of their own, very few of these groups and committees have incorporated--with the major exception of the community information depots in the LKLP area. Other exceptions occur when a community action group or district committee is in line for special federal funds, such as for the construction of a neighborhood center; then the nature of the grant requires incorporation.

Are community corporations desirable for rural areas, such as these Appalachian coal counties? Are they feasible? At the grass-roots level where the community action groups are organized, I would say they are not. These groups serve too few people to justify the administrative costs of complete delegation of program and financial control. More feasible from an administrative point of view would be community corporations at the district level, formed by dividing a county into districts, each of which combined 10 to 15 small communities.

However, only McDowell County is pursuing a course that could lead directly to district-level community corporations. In both Raleigh and Mingo counties, the general district units are weak compared to district program committees that operate as subunits of county-wide program committees. (This is another instance of the classic problem of specialized functions versus generalized integrative administration.) Mercer County has no district organization In the four-county LKLP area, there is an outline of a district structure in the remnants of the previously independent county committees, with a new increment in the county-wide citizens advisory committees which oversee the community information depots, but the operational functions of these units are quite limited.

It seems to me that the formation of district-level community corporations that would encompass the activities of the existing district program committees along with over-all responsibility for determining district needs, developing and implementing programs, hiring staff, and handling the necessary funds would be worth exploring. Although the community action groups might serve as building blocks for the district corporate structure, they should remain free and flexible for the type of local action community residents choose to undertake, and they might combine in issue-oriented efforts on a county-wide level somewhat apart from the district corporation. In such an arrangement, district corporations would tend to be service- and program-oriented. Community action groups working separately would engage in community development activities; working together, they would become involved in issues and social action. The county (or multicounty) community action agency would provide the structure for issue committees and special program units, would deal with county-wide delegate agencies (such as the board of education), would provide technical assistance and training to the district corporations and community action groups, would deal with federal and state agencies, and would orchestrate the total approach. Such a division of responsibility would combine the necessary elements of a broad-scale community action program.

An alternative approach would be to form multi-county community action agencies, governed by the required tripartite board, and then to organize in each participating county a community corporation largely controlled by the persons served. There is a strong trend, encouraged by federal agencies, to organize multicounty agencies for the purpose of economic development. To complement this thrust, the multicounty community action agency could have coterminous boundaries but delegate major operating responsibilities to incorporated county units.

One final observation. What seems to be the most significant action in the counties visited has almost always been the result, in part at least, of the intervention by a person, group, or agency outside the traditional governing group of the county. Two of the founders of the McDowell County program were ministers, thus professional itinerants; one--Jeff Monroe--became head of the West Virginia Economic Opportunity Office, and the other--Ed Thomas--became the first executive director of the program and later moved out of the county. The Council of Southern Mountains gave the McDowell County program not only technical assistance but also its name. The Appalachian Volunteers were instrumental in reinvigorating stodgy programs in Raleigh and Mercer counties and in assisting representatives of the poor to gain control. Several AV's joined the staff in Raleigh County, and in Mercer County the activist director, James Overdorf, was a former minister who moved to the county to take the position. The first executive director of the LKLP Community Action Council, Edwin Safford, came from the staff of the Council of Southern Mountains. Only in Mingo County, which has the most controversial program, was the director, Huey Perry, a county native. And, of course, over-all was the Office of Economic Opportunity, which was able to dispense funds largely free from the influence of county politicians and greatly assisted in the statehouse by Jeff Monroe.

Yet these outsiders could not have succeeded by themselves. Where they have been effective, they have worked in partnership with the residents of the poor communities for whom the program is intended. The program ingenuity of outsiders has become allied with the persuasive power of mobilized numbers of the poor, and as they gain experience, the representatives of the poor themselves become program initiators. This is not to say that all established agencies have been uncooperative, for some of them have participated in significant ways. But for the program to succeed, the power of the poor has had to be released by the intervention of a force most often drawn from outside the county.

Almost in a Hegelian manner, the social stagnation and political backwardness derived from the long "colonial" history of the coal fields can apparently be counteracted only by the vigorous, sometimes irritating, intervention of an outside force. Hopefully, the resulting synthesis will leave the county residents in a better position to carry out long-lasting solutions to their problems. Already some of the outsiders have moved on and their replacements have been local people, perhaps not as imaginative but with qualities that ease apprehensions and make more friends for the program. If enough change has occurred so that the old ways cannot be reimposed, the lessening of conflict might lead to greater mobilization of all segments of the community to combat poverty, which is the real enemy of poor and rich alike.

Most of the community action agencies in Appalachia have remained in existence under the Green Amendment and have not been taken over by the counties. However, more public officials have been added to the boards of directors, and those which previously gave power to a general membership have had to transfer control to the board. As these changes occur, the greatest risk is that the community organization process will be terminated prematurely and that the fragile community action groups will not survive. Without this grass-roots foundation, efforts toward change will be greatly weakened and perhaps become virtually impossible.

CHAPTER 5 — THREE RURAL AREAS

Rural America is richly varied, with great differences in natural resources, agricultural products, terrain, and climate. Historically, the settlers came from different places, and today rural residents still have diverse backgrounds. The social system varies in different parts of the country, particularly as to who the poor are and how minority groups are treated. This being so, I decided to expand my rural sample by visiting Tulare County, California; Guadalupe, Arizona; and the Mississippi Delta.

THE TULARE COUNTY (CALIF.) COMMUNITY ACTION AGENCY

Tulare County is located in California's fertile San Joaquin Valley, between Bakersfield and Fresno. The county is vast in area, equal in size to the state of Connecticut, and half mountainous, encompassing the entire Sequoia National Forest. Most of its 190,000 people live west of the mountains in the valley. The population is widely dispersed; there are only five communities over 5,000, the largest being Visalia (20,000) and Tulare (14,000). Tulare County's crops (oranges, peaches, plums, apricots, grapes, olives, walnuts, cotton, and alfalfa) and beef production place it among the top U.S. counties in the value of agricultural products. In spite of this wealth, about one-third of the people are poor. The largest group of poor are Mexican-Americans, plus a small black population and the Indians of the Tule River Reservation.

By and large, the established leaders in Tulare County are conservative, but for years a small number of concerned citizens have supported local social programs sponsored by the Americans Friends Service Committee and the Migrant Ministry. In September and October of 1964, just after the passage of the Economic Opportunity Act, these interested citizens held two meetings to talk about a community action program for the county. From this discussion emerged the Tulare County Community Action Agency, Inc. (CAA), a private nonprofit agency with a 15-man board of directors, largely hand-picked, one-third poor, one-third public officials, and one-third from private agencies. In December, the County Board of Supervisors designated the new organization as the antipoverty agency for the county and requested all county offices to cooperate with it. The board appointed Everett Krackov, a local grower who had been a board member of the Friends project, as executive director. The first OEO grant came in February, 1965.

One of the first programs to get under way was Operations Grassroots. A core of nonprofessional community workers was hired and put to work organizing community action groups throughout the county. They concentrated mostly in the unincorporated communities, of which there are more than 50. These are small settlements and migrant camps dating back to the 1930's when large-scale irrigation first brought the land into production. After three years, 19 community action groups were organized. Fourteen were predominantly Mexican-American in membership, three black, one Anglo, and one on the Indian Reservation.

The community action groups form the backbone of the county program. With membership ranging from 50 to 150, members meet to discuss the needs of their communities and to formulate action programs. They have developed proposals that led to federally funded programs, such as day care, adult education, and a community center in Visalia; these programs in turn relate back to the residents through the community action groups. They also raise funds and run activities on their own without outside support, such as citizenship education, sewing classes, auto repair instruction, and recreation. Although they get involved in services, they have a strong action orientation and direct their energies toward getting local government to respond to their needs. For example, when I visited the county in October, 1968, a number of the groups were working together to improve the services at the county hospital.

Once a community has an organized group, it is allowed to hire and fire the community worker assigned to it. Until recently, these workers have been on the payroll of the CAA. They are organized into a staff that divides the county into five districts that correspond to those in which the county supervisors are elected. There are no regular district citizen organizations as such, but on an ad hoc basis some community action groups in the northern part of the county have banded together to work for park development. It may be that similar district alliances will emerge in the future.

In early 1969, delegates from the community action groups formed a county-wide organization called Rural Action Groups, Inc. This new nonprofit corporation entered into a contract with the CAA to conduct Operations Grassroots (with a budget of $150,000) and Project Demeter (economic development, with a budget of $237,000). This approach was chosen in order to reduce the direct operations of the CAA but to keep the project staffs intact and not let them be divided among many small groups, which would have happened if each community action group was given its own funds. In the process, the Grassroots staff have gained greater freedom of action than before, for they are now responsible to a board controlled by poor people rather than the tripartite board of the community action agency. Although the corporate form of this resident-controlled organization is county-wide, it is built on the foundation of local community action groups.

In the beginning, the CAA operated the day care centers, but after a couple of years most of them were turned over to the county schools, except two that are handled by community action groups. This program combines day-long care of children and preschool education, similar to Head Start in other communities. In Tulare County, the only Head Start as such has been a fairly small summer program. In the day care program, most of the staff consists of nonprofessionals drawn from the communities served.

The CAA's adult education program, called Proteus, sometimes conducts classes directly and sometimes turns this responsibility over to community action groups. In the latter case, Proteus field staff meet with the group to explain the kind of adult education programs available. The group decides upon

THREE RURAL AREAS							101

the program it wants and selects a teacher and a teacher aide; the latter has to have at least a high school education. Proteus trains these personnel, makes available the necessary material, and provides over-all supervision.

In addition, the county schools offer adult education courses, using regularly certified teachers, and recently have begun to use teacher aides, who are recruited through the community action groups. In reciprocity, Proteus has an advisory committee of school personnel.

The Tulare County CAA has organized credit unions in each of the five supervisory districts, and it provides consumer education. Under consideration are various types of small business developments. The CAA operated a self-help housing program for a year, but it is now run by a seven-county organization. Legal services are also delegated to an independent agency. Although there has been a pattern of program delegation, including activities conducted initially by the CAA, Krackov believes that it is necessary for the agency to continue to innovate and to operate new programs for a period before delegating them to other sponsors. He believes that merely functioning as a funding and technical assistance agency is not sufficient to give the CAA the standing it needs in the county.

When the Tulare County Community Action Agency was organized, it had 15 members, of whom one-third were representatives of the poor. Two years later, it doubled this representation by permitting the community action groups in each of the five districts to select two members instead of one. In the meantime, one of the private agency delegates had dropped off, and the representatives of the poor had a numerical majority, 10 to 9. In 1968, the Green Amendment of the Economic Opportunity Act required restoration of one-third membership of governmental officials, who were then given 10 places. One seat on the enlarged, 30-man board was given to the Tule River Indian Reservation, and the other 9 were given to private agencies.

These shifts in board composition do not seem to have made any particular difference in the operation of the agency. Krackov (who resigned in the spring of 1968) was a strong and effective executive director, respected by both the Anglos, who control the economic life of Tulare County, and the Mexican-Americans, the largest minority group. The first board chairman was a county supervisor. The staff of Operations Grassroots is solidly based in the communities served. Many of the community action groups have endorsed the grape boycott campaign led by Cesar Chavez and the United Farm Workers Organizing Committee. All these factors produce what is generally considered the best and most forward-looking rural community action program in California.

Tulare County shows how a community action agency can reach the poor while maintaining the support of the broader community. In the process, the CAA serves as a bridge between various elements of this rural county that tend to be isolated from one another. Gradually the activities of the community action groups have been enlarged, and they are becoming part of the basic agency structure in the county, illustrating the role of the Community Action Program in institution building.

TEN YEARS' EXPERIENCE IN GUADALUPE, ARIZONA

Guadalupe, Arizona, a town of 6,000 residents, is located 15 miles southeast of downtown Phoenix. Three-fourths of the people are Mexican-Americans, and the rest are Yaqui Indians (except one black, two Chinese, and ten Anglo families). Of those employed, 70 to 80 per cent are agricultural workers, and most of them do not have jobs the year round. Over half the families are poor by federal poverty standards. Although the majority of the houses are owner-occupied, the 1960 census reported that three-fourths of them were substandard, and many lacked water, sanitary facilities, and electricity.

Faced with these conditions, the residents are working together through the Guadalupe Organization, Inc. (GO), which is their instrument for self-help, community improvement, and personal betterment. The Guadalupe Organization was founded in 1964, but its roots can be traced back to 1960 when Father Fidelis, a local parish priest, stimulated the formation of the Christian Family Movement and the Young Christian Workers. Among other accomplishments, these two groups provided a means through which Mexican-Americans and

Yaqui Indians could work together, in spite of their different languages and cultural heritages.

One of the greatest concerns of the Guadalupe residents was the lack of adequate health services. There were no doctors in the community, and the county health department ran a clinic only one day a month. To respond to this need, they formed the Guadalupe Health Council in August, 1962, and within three months they had raised $800 to lease a mobile health unit. By the following spring, eight doctors and seven nurses, mostly part-time volunteers, were providing health care and treatment. To get a permanent facility, they obtained land owned by the Presbyterian Church and by 1964 had constructed a clinic.

As the Guadalupe residents worked together, they came to realize that some of their problems could be solved by a better response from the local government, particularly Maricopa County. However, they had little or no influence because relatively few were registered voters. This was due in part to apathy, but it was also because Guadalupe was included in a large voting district and did not have its own local precinct. Under the initiative of the Health Council, a Guadalupe voting precinct was approved in June, 1963, a voter registration drive was undertaken, and within a year the number of registered voters increased from 150 to 800, of whom nearly 85 per cent voted in the 1964 election. This new-found power at the polls helped lay the groundwork for later gains.

The Presbyterian Church continued its support by giving a grant to the Industrial Areas Foundation of Chicago, headed by Saul Alinsky, so that it could send an organizer to Guadalupe, as the Foundation has done for many urban and rural communities over the last two decades. Later, the Catholic Diocese of Tucson also contributed funds for this purpose. The organizer, Fred Ross, spent a year in Guadalupe, and with his technical assistance and advice, the residents formed the Guadalupe Organization in April, 1964. In many respects, it was a transformation of the Health Council, whose chairman, Lauro Garcia, Jr., became executive director of GO.

Membership in GO is open to all residents, and about 500 pay the $1.50 annual membership fee. Each year in July, the members elect an eight-man board of directors; candidates are nominated by petition and from the floor during the annual meeting. So far, candidates have run as individuals and not as part of slates. Other membership meetings are held at least monthly and more often if necessary. In October of each general elections year, candidates for public office are invited to a meeting, and in 1968 most of the candidates for governor and Congress came to Guadalupe.

During the first year of its existence, the Guadalupe Organization depended upon membership dues for its source of funds. Then in June, 1965, it received an OEO grant of $57,000 to pay for administration, a service center, a credit union, and a health aid program. Later, it got $175,000 from OEO for an adult education program. In addition, GO recruits children and teacher aides for the Head Start program operated by the county schools, and it is assigned youths who are participating in the county's Neighborhood Youth Corps program to work in the GO office, distribute its newsletter, and take part in community improvement activities.

GO has its headquarters in the service center. The center has a very practical orientation, rendering such services as reading, drafting, and typing letters; making phone calls; obtaining money orders; getting birth and baptismal certificates; distributing surplus commodities; referring people to social service agencies; obtaining driver's licenses; getting property deeds; and putting persons in contact with legal aid or attorneys. GO has three community welfare aides full-time, and the county welfare department sends caseworkers to the center every Wednesday. GO's employment officer canvasses employers for jobs, keeps in touch with the State Employment Service, and helps unemployed residents find work.

The health aides get residents to the seven health clinic sessions held each month in Guadalupe: family (2), maternity (2), well-child (2), and pediatric (1). Day care is provided in a building constructed by students in a summer project sponsored by the World Council of Churches and the Presbyterian Church. This building is also used for the adult education program, which teaches basic literacy, citizenship, child care, home economics, science, social studies, electric wiring, upholstery, carpentry, and welding. In two years, 53 persons obtained high school equivalency certificates. The OEO grant also pays for the manager and clerk for the credit union, which is an important asset to this poverty-stricken community.

The Guadalupe Organization received its first grant directly from OEO. When Maricopa County formed a community action agency, OEO required GO to go through that body for funds. The county community action agency accepted this requirement but has not attempted to exercise strict control over GO's program and personnel; however, it does require financial reports, which are developed by a certified public accountant hired by GO.

The Maricopa County Community Action Program has a 27-man board. The one-third representation of the poor is provided by area councils, which are organized in various poor rural communities. However, the Guadalupe Organization is not considered to be one of these but rather is viewed as a "single-purpose agency," to use OEO jargon, and is provided one seat on the county CAA board.

Even though OEO funds have given the Guadalupe Organization a much broader program than it could have had otherwise, GO has produced many other results for the community, such as water mains to serve all the homes; stop signs at all major intersections; ten miles of paved streets, with a commitment for two additional miles of paving each year; a deputy sheriff assigned to provide police protection; a post office and home mail delivery; a community baseball diamond, watered daily. It is now working for street lights and for new housing.

Throughout the years, Father Fidelis has continued to support and assist the residents of Guadalupe, and as we have seen, other forms of technical assistance have been available. But the leaders of the community, when given the opportunity, have shown that they have the capacity to do things for themselves. Guadalupe seems to have achieved a good combination of indigenous leadership, expert technical assistance, and government funding of self-help programs.

When OEO funds became available to Guadalupe, the organizing efforts had been completed, the culmination of several years' development. Most of the rural communities surveyed have had to start organizing from scratch when they received community action funds, and they seem to be taking at least two years and sometimes three or four to develop the capacity to run varied programs. This leads to the conclusion that if we really believe in the development of self-help among the rural poor, we must be patient and back our patience with sufficient technical assistance that helps to harness the native talents of local leaders.

RURAL MISSISSIPPI: THE ROLE OF OUTSIDE INITIATIVE

Mississippi is the poorest of the 50 states. It has the lowest per capita income, the highest rate of infant mortality, and the largest percentage of persons rejected for the draft due to educational deficiencies. It makes the lowest monthly welfare payments, and it spends the least per capita for hospital care. It has the highest percentage of black population, and it is the oppression and neglect of this population which explains the state's low rankings on these social indicators.

Conditions are worst in the Mississippi Delta area, a section of the state lying between the Mississippi and Yazoo rivers from the Tennessee line to Vicksburg and encompassing all or part of 18 counties. In this flat, rich land, cotton has reigned for more than a century. Until about a decade ago, production depended upon a large supply of manual labor, but in recent years machines and herbicides have drastically altered production methods and displaced thousands upon thousands of black farm workers. As this happened, large numbers of young adults moved north, leaving behind a population dominated by children (the median age is 14) and older adults, mostly unskilled and scarcely educated. With vast numbers out of work, hunger has been widespread.

In response, OEO and the cabinet-level Economic Opportunity Council decided that Mississippi should receive considerable attention under the "war on poverty." This was not easy, for the Mississippi power structure was not inclined to develop new opportunities for blacks, and the idea of maximum feasible participation of those served was an anathema to those who controlled the state. Indeed, one of the challenges was to figure out ways to fund programs the governor could not veto, which he was permitted to do under certain parts of the Economic Opportunity Act.

One of the first of these new programs was the Mississippi Child Development Group, usually known as CDGM, which was organized in the spring of 1965 to operate Head Start programs in various counties. Its founders included persons from the Delta Ministry (an affiliate of the National Council of Churches) and others active in the civil rights movement. It was funded through Mary Holmes Junior College; the governor could not veto a grant to an institution of higher education. With its first grant for $1.4 million, CDGM opened 84 Head Start centers and served about 6,000 poor children during the summer of 1965; when the funds ran out, 50 centers were kept open by volunteers. The next summer, the grant was increased to $5.6 million for 121 centers to serve 12,000 children in 28 counties. Most of the centers' staffs were local residents, drawn primarily from the ranks of the poor; parents and other residents were involved in local advisory boards. The staffs included quite a few who had previously been active in the Student Non-Violent Coordinating Committee (SNCC) and the Freedom Democratic Party (FDP), which in 1964 had challenged the right of the regular Democrats to represent Mississippi at the Democratic National Convention. And therein was the source of the troubles that descended on CDGM.

When Sargent Shriver, director of OEO, came before the Senate Appropriations Committee in late summer 1965, he was confronted by Senator John Stennis, who was prepared with charges against CDGM related to fiscal mismanagement and political activity. To some extent, CDGM was vulnerable, for it ran a loose shop the first year, and some of the staff were not discreet in activities conducted on their own time, apparently sometimes using CDGM-rented cars to attend voter registration rallies and for other civic ventures that went beyond the purpose of the grant (though not beyond community action, broadly conceived). But the real issue was whether a group of black leaders and white civil rights activists would be permitted to operate with federal funds in Mississippi. At first, Shriver stood his ground and approved a second grant to CDGM in February, 1966, but by the following fall he gave in. Working undercover with White House encouragement, OEO arranged for the organization of a new group, called Mississippi Action for Progress, Inc. (MAP), led by moderate whites and blacks, to take over much of the CDGM Head Start program; the rest would be absorbed by community action agencies, which by then had been organized in a number of counties. MAP was announced, and CDGM was told it would not be re-funded because of "serious deficiencies and irregularities"[1] in program and audit. Shortly before the federal decision was announced, Walter Reuther, acting as president of the Citizens' Crusade Against Poverty, appointed a board of inquiry composed of nationally known persons; two weeks after CDGM was denied re-funding, this board reported that the charges were exaggerated and recommended the continuation of CDGM. This was followed by a national campaign which, by December, forced a reversal at OEO, and in January, 1967, CDGM received $4.9 million to operate in 14 counties.

When I visited Mississippi in April, 1967, with the Senate Subcommittee on Employment, Manpower and Poverty, feelings were still running high and charges and countercharges were still being made. Returning in February, 1969, I found that things had settled down considerably. A third multicounty Head Start agency, Friends of the Children of Mississippi (FCM), which had been organized to keep alive some of the CDGM centers on a voluntary basis, had also received OEO funds. CDGM, MAP, and FCM were now working together on matters of mutual concern, such as developing a staff training institute, and previous antagonism among them had greatly diminished.

By 1969, CDGM was operating 72 centers in 14 counties (none of which has a community action agency), serving 5,300 children, and maintaining a staff of about 1,300, of whom one-fifth are part-time. Originally, the CDGM board was composed largely of professionals and middle-class leaders, although from the beginning many grass-roots people were involved in program operations. Now representatives of the poor constitute a majority of the board. Each center has a community committee selected by the residents of the area served, and each committee sends a

---

[1]Office of Economic Opportunity, CDGM Situation Report, September 27, 1966.

representative to an area council, which also includes some professionals. Each of the 12 area councils chooses a representative to the central board, and these 12 select eight others to round out the CDGM board.

Administration is still handled by Mary Holmes Junior College, which handles the entire payroll and has tighter financial control than in the beginning. But each area council has a bank account that can be used for certain purchases; for nine councils, headquarters must countersign, but for three the signature of the area director and chairman suffice. Each center also has a bank account, and the director is authorized to purchase food and minor supplies. The centers hire their own staffs.

The program continues to be almost exclusively Head Start, that is, a combination of pre-school education, health services, two meals a day, social services, and parental involvement. Here and there, a Head Start community committee gets involved in other concerns of the poor, such as the need for a better water supply, but these are rare exceptions. Each year CDGM has had a crisis of re-funding and a lapse between grants, and the organization is worn down by the struggle for existence. Although its programs are solid and productive, its creative edge seems to have been dulled.

In contrast, the Friends of the Children of Mississippi is beginning to use its Head Start centers and local committees as points of departure for community development activities, such as organizing credit unions and cooperatives and starting housing programs. To do this, FCM has a community development specialist for each of the four counties in which it operates.

In three of the counties, the centers were originally started by CDGM, and the fourth was functioning on a voluntary basis in anticipation of CDGM funding. At first, MAP was to have jurisdiction over these four counties, but FCM claimed them. For 18 months they were operated with volunteers and funds from the Field Foundation (which also supported CDGM during fund crises). In May, 1968, FCM became a delegate agency of MAP and in the following November arranged for its own funding through Tougaloo College in another veto-proof grant.

FCM is organized from the grass roots up. Each center has a committee elected by ballot of the poor people in the area served, and at least half the committee must consist of parents of participating children. Each center sends its chairman and one other to a county council. The central board is composed of the county chairman, a parent member from each county council, and two delegates at large from each county, chosen by the county council, making a total of 16. The county council and the central board have professional advisory committees, and each year FCM has a two-day convention consisting of delegates from each center.

FCM has a centralized payroll, pays all rent, but allows the county councils and local centers to have their own bank accounts for food and certain supplies. The local committees also select teacher trainees, cooks, and janitors and recommend teachers and center administrators, subject to the approval of the central staff. FCM wants to move toward greater decentralization, but it wants to achieve orderly procedures first. As noted earlier, it is working with CDGM and MAP to develop a staff training institute.

One of the counties where Head Start is under the jurisdiction of the community action agency is Bolivar County. Located on the Mississippi River halfway between Vicksburg and Memphis, about two-thirds of its 55,000 people are black. CDGM ran a Head Start program during the summer of 1965, and this alerted the county leaders to the possibility of operating a community action program and also to the "danger" of having it done by an outside group. Thus, with staff assistance from the Chamber of Commerce of Cleveland, the county seat, a leadership group consisting of two county commissioners, several white planters, and the Negro mayor of Mound Bayou prepared and submitted an application for community action funds. OEO awarded a planning grant in September, 1965, and the Labor Department gave the newly founded Bolivar County Community Action Program, Inc., funds for a Neighborhood Youth Corps in December.

Concurrently, some of the black residents who were associated with CDGM organized the Association of Communities of Bolivar County (ACBC). ACBC applied for Head Start funds for the summer of 1966, and so did the Bolivar County CAP. After prolonged negotiations, OEO approved a single Head Start grant with the requirement that half the program be operated by CAP directly and the other half by ACBC as a delegate agency.

Gradually the Bolivar County CAP added other programs, such as Operation Mainstream (a work program, later dropped), emergency food and medical assistance, and a multiservice center. Its board has the required tripartite membership of public officials, representatives from private organizations, and representatives of the poor. The existence of such a biracial board here and elsewhere in the South is an important contribution of the Community Action Program but the board is fairly well contained by the local "establishment," and the executive director has his office in the county courthouse. ACBC leaders fear that the county CAP wants to take over their Head Start center, but the executive director of the county CAP says that this is not so, even though "from a business standpoint, the job could be done under one organizational structure."[2]

ACBC, though, is strong enough to hold on to its Head Start program. In recent months, it has acquired some land for the purpose of building low- and moderate-cost housing and erecting a shopping center. This would provide better housing for blacks while giving the organization a stronger economic base.

In several other Mississippi counties, former CDGM Head Start groups have continued in existence and obtained funds as delegate agencies of the county community action agency. They were able to bargain for their share of funds because they already had operating experience and an organizational base. As far as I know, there are no examples in Mississippi of the community action agency taking the initiative to organize a delegate agency controlled by the poor and to make funds available to it.

Another of the independent antipoverty organizations controlled by Mississippi blacks is the Delta Opportunities Corporation (DOC), formed in September, 1965, with the assistance of the Delta

---

[2] Interview with R. T. Gernert, February 12, 1969.

Ministry. However, two years elapsed before it
launched its first major program, Freedom Village,
which was a response to the desperate housing needs
of farm workers who lost their jobs and were displaced from the shacks they occupied on plantations.
To dramatize their plight as well as to seek an
instant remedy, a group of members, along with leaders of the Delta Ministry, moved into empty barracks
on the Greenville Air Base in 1966; they were quickly evicted. Others carried the protest to Washington
and camped in tents in Lafayette Park across the
street from the White House.

After the Greenville Air Base sit-in, some of
the homeless families lived in a "tent city" in
Issaquena County; others stayed at the Delta Ministry's conference center, a small abandoned college
near Edwards, Mississippi. These families then
moved to temporary housing erected by DOC on 400
acres of land in Washington County. After these
buildings were destroyed by a storm in November,
1966, they lived in a barn and other buildings while
DOC negotiated for funds to provide a more permanent
solution. For that purpose, the Delta Opportunities
Corporation acquired another tract of land in Washington County and announced plans to construct Freedom Village. This was where things stood when I
visited Mississippi in the spring of 1967. I was
frankly skeptical, but when I saw the village under
construction almost two years later, I changed my
opinion.

Located about 12 miles southeast of Greenville,
Freedom Village is being built on 80 acres of land.
When I was there, 14 cement block houses were at
various stages of construction, and eventually 50
will be built on one-acre lots, with gardens in the
rear. A small shopping center will occupy a central
space. Already built is a community center (a ware-
house-like structure), which is being used for
offices and classes. Also erected is an experimental
frame house, which is being converted into a health
center. However, it is not the village itself that
is so impressive but rather the way in which a
number of program elements are tied together in its
construction.

At the community building in Freedom Village,
DOC has a ceramics class, which is intended as the
first step toward home production, small businesses,

and the cooperative sale and purchase of supplies. Other small business development efforts include assistance to a handicapped man who is setting up a TV repair shop, training in construction for 20 displaced farm workers from Sunflower County who intend to form a construction company, and help for two graduates of plumbing training who want to open a laundromat. A separately chartered farmers' co-op is seeking a $1 million government loan. In each of these cases, DOC helps the individuals and groups to take advantage of various governmental programs.

DOC, through a program called Grassroot Organization, conducts adult education classes one night a week in each of five counties. Participants with no incomes are paid a $3.50 stipend, which enables them to purchase food stamps. Some of these enrollees as well as the trainees at Freedom Village are obtaining general equivalency diplomas, and three of these have been hired as part-time teachers. A tuition support program is helping needy youths get to college.

In the beginning, the DOC board consisted of black civil rights leaders, but at OEO's insistence the board added some whites who were interested in the program. In February, 1969, the structure was changed to provide better representation for the poor. In each of nine counties where DOC works, an advisory board of 15 to 25 members was selected at county-wide meetings. Each county advisory board will then appoint three of its members to the central board for three-year overlapping terms. Once this transitional period is complete, DOC will be more broadly based, but it will continue to operate as a centralized organization.

Funding comes from various outside sources: Ford Foundation for the self-help housing program; OEO's Migrant Division for adult education, vocational training, and tuition loans; Economic Development Administration for job placement; Farmers Home Administration for housing loans; Church Women United for a nurse and medical supplies; the Delta Ministry; the World Council of Churches; and various individuals. None of these grants can be vetoed by the governor, not even the one from OEO, which comes under a part of the Economic Opportunity Act not subject to veto. This gives DOC considerable freedom of action, and they are using this opportunity well.

Another veto-proof project in the Mississippi Delta is a comprehensive health center at Mound Bayou in the northern part of Bolivar County, operated by Tufts Medical School of Boston. Tufts received a grant from OEO in 1965 to develop two health centers, one at Columbia Point, an isolated public housing project in Boston, and a second one somewhere in the South. The search for the southern location started with about 20 very poor counties and narrowed to a choice between the Mississippi Delta or Georgia hill country; finally in the summer of 1966, Bolivar County was chosen. By then, the Tufts team had had experience at Columbia Point in organizing citizen participation around an ad hoc committee of apparent leaders, only to find the group demanding more control but being neither representative of nor accountable to the community.

In Bolivar County, citizen involvement was built more slowly but on a much stronger foundation. The staff spent a lot of time going to villages and scattered houses where the poor live, talking, listening, observing, figuring out which persons and groups had the most interest and might provide the strongest organizational base. They found that the most viable indigenous organizations were churches. The civil rights groups tended not to reach many of the scattered rural poor in that county, and there seemed to be considerable economic pressure on those who participated in such activities. The Tufts staff concluded that a new organizational base was needed and set out to form health associations that recognized natural community groupings. For each one, the organizer used the main concern of the community--mosquitoes, poor water supply, inadequate food, and so on--as the focus for organizing. This took about a year, and by October, 1967, ten health associations had been established. The following July they joined together to form a Health Council, consisting of the chairman and one other member of each association. By the spring of 1969, the health associations had signed up 4,000 members in a service area that has 6,000 black adults.

As this was going on, the Tufts professional staff was developing plans for health services and a building at Mound Bayou, a small all-black community located about ten miles north of Cleveland, the county seat. The service area of the health center covers about 500 square miles in northern

Bolivar County; only about one-tenth of those to be served live in Mound Bayou. Nonetheless, the traditional middle-class leaders of Mound Bayou felt that they should have control of the health center. The more militant blacks, such as those active in the Delta Ministry, felt that control should be in their hands. But the Tufts staff resisted, believing that the poor would never be able to play a role if these more sophisticated blacks took over from the beginning. The health center that emerged represents current professional concepts: examining rooms, maternity and well-child facilities, emergency room, pharmacy, social service office, children's playroom, and a 24-hour maternity unit to be used when the nearby hospital is full. Many of the subprofessional personnel are from the communities served.

Meanwhile, around the county the Tufts staff was becoming acquainted with the enormous problems of environmental health and the vast void in appropriate services: polluted water, no water at all, no sewers, dilapidated housing, broken-down outhouses, mosquitoes, rats. Soon a major environmental health program was under way.

Everywhere people were suffering from malnutrition. They lived on some of the most productive soil in a nation with the greatest agricultural output in the world, but they were hungry. The government programs of commodity distribution and food stamps were not reaching many of the poor, and the people were not equipped to raise, store, and distribute food for themselves. To deal with this basic need, the North Bolivar County Farm Cooperative was formed through the efforts of the Tufts staff and the health associations. Land was acquired, seeds planted, vegetables grown, and food distributed and frozen for future use. The effort was aided by an OEO grant under the Emergency Food Program. The next step to be undertaken is the construction of a cannery to produce food for local use, to broaden the market, to provide jobs, and to gain income for the cooperators. This will involve dealing with several federal agencies, and citizen representatives from the Farm Cooperative and the health associations will participate in this process.

When the Health Council came into existence in July, 1968, the Tufts group had a formal means for consulting with representatives of those served.

As time passed, the agenda became more and more the concern of the residents and less that of the professional staff. When the 1969 budget was being drawn up, the Health Council placed priority on legal services (a lawyer and three lay advocates), youth guidance and health careers, better transportation, and improvements in emergency relief and social service. In fact, they offered to take over the transportation system and provision of emergency relief. These concerns and the Farm Cooperative are a long way from the medical school curriculum, but they reflect the real needs of the people. They might have been approached through a Head Start center, an adult education program, or some other phase of the Community Action Program, but it was the health center which provided the stimulus for organization, and the Tufts team was willing and able to adapt the program to respond to these needs.

So far, the Health Council has expressed no interest in becoming the true governing board of the health center, thereby controlling all policies and hiring. This kind of power is too much an abstraction, the residents' needs are more immediate and concrete. Perhaps it will come, but it has not happened yet.

The Tufts Delta Health Center, the Delta Opportunities Corporation, and the several Head Start agencies reviewed in this chapter are all engaged in the development of grass-roots leaders and organizers. This is done as an integral part of program operations. One other organization in the Delta, Mississippi Action for Community Education, Inc. (MACE), is training organizers somewhat apart from direct programs. MACE was organized in January, 1968, with a Ford Foundation grant, and during its first year its seven-man staff provided community development training for 22 members of organizations in seven Delta counties. Forty persons were to be trained in 1969, and the number of counties served was to increase to 13.

About 25 per cent of the training program takes place at MACE's headquarters in Greenville, and the rest is done on the job in the counties. The fundamental mission of the field work is to help blacks in each of the participating counties to develop a united front to deal with matters of major concern: election of blacks to public offices, greater participation on local agency boards, control of resources coming into the county from government programs, economic development, and other things that advance the political, social and economic life of the black community.

As an example of what can be done, leaders of MACE cite Holmes County, where the Freedom Democratic Party (which is really more a black coalition than a political party) has the county well organized; can mobilize mass rallies on 24-hour notice; has helped get blacks elected to the school board, the election commission, the Mississippi House of Representatives, and the Agriculture Stabilization and Conservation Committee, which passes on federal benefits to landowners; and has effective control of a Head Start agency operating as a delegate of the county community action agency. MACE would like to see similar membership-based organizations in all the Delta counties, not to operate programs but to provide a base for united action.

MACE can offer participating county organizations these incentives: training for local staff, technical assistance related to federal programs, and economic development assistance. For the latter, MACE is preparing a 12-county economic development plan (to be extended later to six more counties), and it has Ford funds to be used as seed money for various enterprises.

MACE was organized with the assistance of the Citizens' Crusade Against Poverty and is now being funded through the Center for Community Change, a new national Ford-financed organization which in December, 1968, absorbed the Citizens' Crusade and several other groups. The MACE board consists of two representatives from each county organization. However, it seems to be an operation in which staff plays a dominant role both in program operation and policy determination.

During my visit in February, 1969, I found that most of the persons in the other Mississippi organizations discussed here were uninformed about what MACE is doing. Moreover, several of them had an interest in economic development programs, but each was working more or less separately from the others and quite apart from the Research and Development Center at Greenville, which has both state and Ford funds for this purpose. By and large, they have common concerns and might benefit from mutual support.

The organizations visited in Mississippi have various combinations of outside assistance and local leadership, but all have both elements. The National Council of Churches organized the Delta Ministry, sent in white clergymen to head the staff, but hired local blacks. This staff had a hand in starting CDGM, and it organized the Delta Opportunities Corporation, which is locally controlled; by now, the principal staff members of the Delta Ministry are Mississippi blacks. CDGM had other nonresidents in key roles in its first years; each executive director has come from out of state. The current one is the first black to fill the post, and control is shifting more and more to representatives of local centers. ACBC and several other county Head Start groups were organized when CDGM was in trouble with OEO, and they are locally controlled. The Tufts Delta Health Center is wholly a product of outsiders; of those agencies reviewed here, it is the slowest in moving toward local control although it has a great breadth of resident participation through the health associations and the Farm Cooperative. As its local organizational efforts progress, the persons served are reshaping the nature of the program. MACE was organized by the Citizens' Crusade Against Poverty, but it is broadening its local base.

However, I should point out that my interest in community control has led me to concentrate on Mississippi organizations where this factor of outside intervention is particularly evident. There are other community action programs run by county leaders without particular outside assistance except for federal funds. Moreover, the state government is conducting programs of economic development, manpower training, food stamps, and other activities that benefit the poor.

But those programs with the most participation by the poor tend to have had outside initiation or at least outside assistance in the beginning. All are achieving a broader base of local involvement, and the role of the poor is gradually being enlarged. However, except for the Associated Communities of Bolivar County (and a few Head Start programs in some counties not discussed), none of the organizations has independent county entities in which the poor community controls policy, budget, expenditures, and hiring of all staff. Although such grass-roots community corporations are a rarity in Mississippi, there are now several multicounty organizations controlled by blacks. All of these operate either with foundation grants or veto-proof federal funds. This outside money has been an exceedingly useful force and an absolutely necessary ingredient to help broaden the base of civic participation in rural Mississippi.

COMMENTARY

Several times in my analysis of rural programs in West Virginia, Kentucky, California, Arizona, and Mississippi, I have noted the importance of funds, technical assistance, and program initiation coming from the outside but at the same time the crucial need for local leaders whose leadership capacity can be enhanced. One other generalization should be emphasized: the importance of an adequate time span to develop local organizations in poor rural communities.

In all of the counties reviewed in this chapter and the previous one, there were virtually no civic organizations with significant participation by the poor when the rural Community Action Program began in 1965. The main exception was the Guadalupe Organization, which was formed in April, 1964, but which has antecedents traceable to 1960. It takes time and patience to build rural community action groups that deal with the concrete needs of poor citizens. To use these small groups as building blocks for district, county, and sometimes multi-county organizations takes even longer, particularly if council delegates and board members are to be both representative of and accountable to the persons served. Judging from the experience of a number of agencies committed to this approach, this process takes from two to four years.

Yet, most of these programs have been funded by the Community Action Program on a year-at-a-time basis. For part of this period, decisions on refunding have been delayed as Congress failed to appropriate funds before the fiscal year began; in the case of CDGM, funding was discontinuous because of political opposition. If there is to be meaningful rural community development, federal support must be put on a more permanent basis, and congressmen, federal executives, journalists, and the general public who pass judgment on the program must realize that this effort cannot succeed overnight.

CHAPTER 6 INDIAN RESERVATIONS

When the Economic Opportunity Act was under consideration by Congress in the spring and summer of 1964, Sargent Shriver's task force was hard at work designing ways to implement its provisions. One of the principal planners of the Community Action Proram was Richard Boone, who had been with the President's Committee on Juvenile Delinquency and most recently had been working on a special White House project to design a domestic version of the Peace Corps. To help develop an approach to Indian reservations, Boone brought in Robert A. Roessel, Jr., from the Indian Education Program at Arizona State University and Forrest Gerrad of the Indian Public Health Service. They consulted with Indian leaders and kept in touch with the Bureau of Indian Affairs (BIA).

As a group, Indian reservations are among the most poverty-stricken areas in the United States. Eighty per cent of the Indians living on reservations are poor. Unemployment averages 40 per cent, and on a number of reservations almost everyone is out of work during the winter months. Natural resources are vastly insufficient when compared to the population they must support. Industrial development is meager and is made more difficult by the isolated location of many of the reservations.

Faced with this situation, it was apparent that the Economic Opportunity Act did not have all the answers to Indian poverty, but it could help. It was Roessel's idea that OEO should pursue two main courses in its Indian program: first, deal directly with tribal leaders and make grants to tribal councils; and second, provide a source of independent sympathetic technical assistance. This would be a significant new approach for the Federal Government in dealing with Indian reservations. To understand this difference, we must understand our history.

The coming of white explorers, traders, and settlers to North America set in motion many changes in the lives and customs of the Indian tribes. For example, the introduction of horses changed the life style of Plains Indians. As the European powers contended for territorial control, they pulled various tribes into their colonial struggles through ever-changing alliances. As settlement moved westward, Indians were repeatedly displaced, aggravating tribal competition.

After the colonies gained independence, the first attempt of the United States to define an Indian policy was in the Northwest Ordinance of 1787:

> The utmost good faith shall always be observed towards the Indians; their land and property shall never be taken from them without their consent; and in the property, rights, and liberty, they never shall be invaded or disturbed, unless in just and lawful wars authorized by Congress; but laws founded in justice and humanity shall from time to time be made, for preventing wrongs being done to them, and for preserving peace and friendship with them.[1]

The essentials of this policy were confirmed two years later by the first Congress under the new Constitution. But both the spirit and the word of this declaration were broken many times in the years that followed.

The Constitution gave the national government the power to make treaties with Indian tribes, to regulate commerce with them, and to control the public land they occupied. Nontheless, all reservations are considered to be parts of states, politically and legally. These federal powers were

---

[1] Quoted in <u>The Indian, America's Unfinished Business</u>, compiled by William A. Brophy and Sophie D. Aberle (Norman, Okla.: University of Oklahoma Press, 1966), p. 17.

INDIAN RESERVATIONS

implemented by early Congresses in various statutes, most notably in a comprehensive act of 1834, which also established the Bureau of Indian Affairs in the War Department. The BIA was transferred to the Interior Department in 1849, where it has remained. Over the years, treaties were signed, turning over large areas of Indian land to federal ownership in exchange for cash, goods, the establishment of reservations, and the promise of certain services.

When the West was being settled after the Civil War, the General Allotment Act of 1887 attempted to make homesteaders out of Indians by allotting them individual tracts of tribal land. However, Indians were not accustomed to private ownership or farming, and no provision was made for their training or for granting livestock and implements. The net result was the reduction of tribal holdings from 138 million acres in 1887 to 48 million in 1934 when the practice was halted. This loss of land was a major contributor to contemporary Indian poverty.

The Indian Reorganization Act of 1934 brought about a generally more enlightened approach. It recognized the value of Indian communal life, confirmed Indian self-government, provided for federally chartered tribal business corporations, and established a system of federal loans. For the next seven years, there was considerable economic advance on the reservations, but during World War II federal appropriations were reduced and skilled manpower drained away. After the war, the Bureau of Indian Affairs was under leadership less sympathetic to the principles of the 1934 Act.

Then in 1953, Congress passed House Concurrent Resolution 108, which had as its intent the freeing of Indians from federal control and supervision and the ending of their wardship. In the next few years, the reservation status of several tribes was terminated and federal services were withdrawn, but with such inadequate preparation and safeguards that the results were disastrous. After five years, the push for termination abated. Since 1961, the emphasis has been upon improvement of services and facilities and upon development of greater capacity for local determination and self-government.

Nonetheless, the official federal policy still rests on a trust relationship. No matter how much authority seems to be given to tribal governments, the Bureau of Indian Affairs has ultimate power to approve or disapprove tribal decisions on the use of land and other resources. Indeed, in one case a tribe managed a forest with very little supervision, lost money, and successfully sued the BIA for allowing mismanagement. For the most part, services are run by the BIA and the Public Health Service, and the level of funds is determined by Congress.

In many respects, the tribal governments are themselves part of this system of continued dependency, and they are not eager to press for complete independence for economic and psychological reasons. In many cases, the form of tribal government is more the design of the BIA for its administrative convenience rather than an expression of the Indians' traditional style of running tribal affairs. Thus, no matter how enlightened the federal administrators are or how much good will they display, the system itself perpetuates dependency.

TRIBAL ADMINISTRATION OF OEO FUNDS

In contrast to the historical federal approach, OEO decided to relate to Indian reservations not as a trustee but as a grant-in-aid agency dealing with a local grant recipient. This meant that the tribal council could determine the activities, design the program, apply for a grant, receive the funds, and hire the staff. This is no more or no less than any city, county, state, or nonprofit organization also does with a federal grant, but for the Indian reservations it marked an entirely new procedure.

In 1968, OEO granted $14.3 million to 63 grantees, encompassing 115 tribes. In the same year, the Bureau of Indian Affairs and the Indian Health Service spent $347 million for services to Indians.

Since 1965, OEO has also made funds available to a consortium consisting of Arizona State University, the University of South Dakota, and the University of Utah for the purpose of providing training and technical assistance to the tribal councils and the operating staffs of Indian community action programs. In 1968, the University of Montana, the University of New Mexico, and Bemidji

State College in Minnesota were added to this consortium.

Because it is a departure from previous federal policy, the provision of community action grants to tribal councils can be seen as a variation on the theme of community control. I had heard Indian leaders praise this new approach at a public hearing conducted by a Senate subcommittee in Albuquerque, New Mexico, in the spring of 1967. To see at firsthand what was going on, I returned to the Southwest in August, 1968, and visited three Indian community action programs: Zuni, Northern Pueblo, and Navajo.

The Zuni Indians

Of the three groups, the first to be contacted by Europeans were the Zunis; in 1539, Fray Marcos de Niza claimed he had discovered the fabled Seven Cities of Cibola with their gold and other great riches. Two years later, Coronado led an expedition there and as he explored what are now New Mexico and Arizona he found 70 other pueblos, or villages, of adobe buildings. By then, the Pueblo Indians had occupied that general territory for at least 600 years and had developed a flourishing civilization. This did not keep the Spaniards from conquering them, however, and the Roman Catholic Church from sending its missionaries. In 1680, the Pueblos overturned Spanish rule only to be reconquered 12 years later. About this time, the Zunis began building their present principal town on the site of Halona, one of the Seven Cities. When Mexico gained its independence in 1821, Indians were declared citizens on an equal basis with non-Indians, but otherwise life changed little. Following the Treaty of Guadalupe Hidalgo in 1848, the land became the territory of the United States. For decades thereafter, the holdings of the Pueblos were challenged by white settlers, but a court decision in 1924 confirmed most of the Indian land claims.

"The Zuni," Ruth Benedict wrote, "are ceremonious people, a people who value sobriety and inoffensiveness above all other virtues. Their interest is centered upon their rich and complex ceremonial life."[2] They are also well known for their fine

---

[2] Ruth Benedict, Patterns of Culture (New York: New American Library, June, 1948), p. 54.

silver and turquoise jewelry, a craft that has come into its own only during the last 35 years.

With 5,300 people on the reservation, the Zunis are the largest group of Pueblo Indians. Most of the population is concentrated in the town that surrounds the ancient pueblo, about 40 miles south of Gallup, New Mexico. The reservation encompasses a little over 600 square miles, which is about the size of a typical county in the midwestern states. The land is not very productive, the people are poor, and unemployment is high. Tribal income from leases, lumber, fees, and fines is only about $50,000 a year. The Gallup-McKinley County school system runs two elementary schools and a high school, and two parochial elementary schools also operate in Zuni. The high school produces 50 to 60 graduates a year, and in recent years quite a few of them have gone on to college. However, job opportunities on the reservation are insufficient to absorb these better-educated youth.

The civil government of the Zunis is in the hands of a governor and a council of seven members elected by the people for two-year terms. Of the present incumbents, five speak English. Following the general pattern established by OEO's Indian program, the council serves as the governing body for the Community Action Program. This program consists of seven major components: Head Start, Neighborhood Youth Corps, housing improvement, legal aid, arts and crafts cooperative, economic development, and administration.

Head Start is an important program, and one of the most successful, because many Indian children, raised in homes where traditional culture is preserved, are unprepared for school. Head Start permits them to overcome their shyness, to develop socially, and to make a start in learning and speaking English, which is essential for their future education. The Zunis built their own Head Start center. Much of the work was done by participants of the Neighborhood Youth Corps, who learned some construction skills in the process.

In 1967 and again in 1968, the Zunis were awarded an "incentive" grant by OEO on the basis of their performance in running programs, and they used the money for housing improvements. The houses to be improved were selected by the community action staff, based upon published criteria related to family needs and housing conditions. OEO funds were used to hire workers from among the unemployed, and 32 persons were selected by the tribal council and put to work in 1968. The BIA provided materials, and so did some of the owners. Additions were built for bathrooms, plumbing and hot water heaters were installed, walls and ceilings were repaired, and screen doors were put on. Unfortunately, the program lasted only five months the first year and three months the second because of limited funds.

To oversee the legal services program, a special seven-man advisory board was created, consisting of four Zunis and three Anglos (two traders and a BIA employee). The legal services staff consists of a lawyer, a lay counselor (who also serves as interpreter), and an investigator. The cases involve matters related to social security and welfare, domestic affairs, consumer problems, and a few misdemeanors. The legal staff performs some legal education functions and is concerned with law reform but does not have much time to pursue this interest. However, a recently enacted Indian Civil Rights Act requires the tribes to write out their tribal codes and to revamp their judicial systems, and the legal services staff is assisting the tribal council in this task. Unlike some other Indian legal programs, relationships with the Bureau of Indian Affairs are friendly.

The Zuni Craftsmen Cooperative Association, Inc., was organized in 1966 with the support of OEO funds in order to train craftsmen and other personnel and to act as a base for wholesale and retail operations. Its purpose is to market Zuni jewelry for the best possible return to those who produce it, to advance the interests of Zuni craftsmen, and to promote the highest standards of design and workmanship. More than 100 silversmiths are members of the cooperative, or about one-third of the full-time Zuni silversmiths. The nine-man staff consists of a manager, bookkeeper, assistant bookkeeper-secretary, two salesmen, two instructors, and two who buff jewelry. The cooperative buys the highest quality jewelry produced by its members and then resells it, using the salesmen to develop new markets around the country. The cooperative also buys silver and turquoise and sells it to its members at a slight profit. The instructors train less experienced persons to make better jewelry. Gradually the OEO subsidy is being reduced so that the association can become economically self-sufficient.

As important as this traditional craft is to the economic life of the Zunis, tribal leaders realize that other efforts at economic development are needed. In recent years two electronic plants have opened, one with 160 employees, the other with 9; both have intentions to expand. The larger plant was built and equipped by the tribe with loans obtained from the Bureau of Indian Affairs, and the other one secured private financing. An industrial park is being developed with assistance from the Economic Development Administration and the Water Pollution Control Administration and with other loans obtained by the tribe. In 1968, OEO funded staff to promote further developments, and among the enterprises being considered are a supermarket, a motel, an automobile franchise, jewelry manufacturing, and a restaurant. As it is, as much as 90 per cent of the funds earned by Zunis leaves the reservation because of the lack of competitive businesses located in Zuni.

The Community Action Program was the first public service activity operated by the tribal council. More recently, the BIA has contracted with the council to take over police services. When the council wanted a higher level of service than contract funds would provide, they put in some of the tribal funds. BIA is now considering contracting other services, such as roads and building maintenance.

Governor Robert Lewis believes that OEO made a bold and dramatic move by granting funds directly to the tribal council for the Community Action Program. It showed the Indians that they have untapped administrative ability, and it has developed feelings of greater self-confidence. He is looking forward to having the tribe run other programs, especially as more and more of the young people receive college educations and move into positions of tribal leadership.

The Northern Pueblo Community Action Program

In the Rio Grande Valley north of Santa Fe there are eight Pueblos, some of which have occupied their sites for more than 600 years. When the Spanish Government claimed possession of this territory in the sixteenth century, it made grants to the individual Pueblos for the purpose of defining and protecting the boundaries of Pueblo lands. The general practice was to fix boundaries at one league in each of the cardinal directions from the mission church, making the grant four square leagues, or 17,712 acres. (This amounts to a little over five miles square, which is slightly smaller than the six-mile-square townships that surveyors laid out in the Midwest.) Today six of the Northern Pueblos are in this size range, and two take in some adjacent mountain land and are two and one-half times as large. The eight are among the smallest Indian reservations in the United States.

In the Treaty of Guadalupe Hidalgo, residents of the territory ceded by Mexico to the United States were given the option of retaining their Mexican citizenship, but none of the Pueblo Indians did and they thus became citizens of the United States. In 1854, however, Congress excluded them from voting for territorial officials, except local overseers of ditches, and they did not gain the franchise until 1924, when all Indians in the United States were given the right to vote.

The Bureau of Indian Affairs established the Pueblo Agency in 1872. Until recently, it dealt with 18 Pueblos from headquarters in Albuquerque, but now the branch office in Santa Fe has become a separate agency for the Northern Pueblos.

The eight Northern Pueblos and their reservation population, which totaled 4,673 in 1968, are as follows: Nambe (257), Picuris (165), Pojoaque (60), San Ildefonso (319), San Juan (1,255), Santa Clara (916), Taos (1,470), and Tesuque (231). Six of them speak a common language (Tewa), while two (Taos and Picuris) belong to a different linguistic group (Tiwa). They are well known for their pottery, which is a major economic product. Farming is important, but many work off the reservation in such places as Santa Fe and Los Alamos.

Each Pueblo has its own tribal government with an elected governor and council and is independent for internal affairs. However, being close together and having common interests, the eight have been loosely associated for a number of years through the Northern Pueblos Governors Council.

OEO started its Indian program in the summer of 1965 by giving grants to 16 Indian tribes on a pilot basis. Two of these were Northern Pueblos: Santa Clara and Tesuque. Later that year, the eight governors joined to develop a program for all eight Pueblos, and they submitted a joint application which was approved in April, 1966. Although the component activities are carried out within the individual Pueblos, they operate under a common policy. The governors tend to be conservative and to proceed cautiously, reserving judgment until they can consult with other tribal leaders, but in at least one instance they moved rapidly to apply for special funds for senior citizens when OEO demanded fast action.

The programs include Head Start, Neighborhood Youth Corps, adult education, home enrichment, arts and crafts, senior citizen activities, economic development, and the "incentive" program. Except for the latter, these are basically the same as such programs elsewhere.

The Northern Pueblos are using their incentive funds, awarded by OEO for good performance, to improve community facilities and homes. When I visited the Pueblos, men were erecting a new cement block community building at the Santa Clara Pueblo, and at San Juan they were constructing new houses with materials supplied by the Bureau of Indian Affairs. Elsewhere, they have built and enlarged Head Start buildings, repaired private homes, and developed a canyon recreation facility. Each Pueblo's personnel selection committee chooses its own workers, who are then placed on the payroll of the over-all community action agency. Like a related program on the Zuni reservation, this one has been funded for short periods whereas year-round work is needed, and it has suffered from insufficient funds to buy building supplies.

During 1968, the Northern Pueblos joined with other community action agencies to form the North Central New Mexico CEP Association to run a Concentrated Employment Program with funds supplied by the U.S. Department of Labor. This is bringing about much greater cooperation among Indians, Mexican-Americans, and Anglos than previously existed.

INDIAN RESERVATIONS   131

    For the Northern Pueblos, the experience of
running the Community Action Program has been
favorable, but so far they have not entered into
contracts with the BIA to operate other services.
Indeed, they seem to be apprehensive of this idea
because they fear it might be the first step toward
termination of all federal support, a result that
would be economically disastrous from their point
of view.

    Relations between the staff of the Northern
Pueblo Community Action Program and the Bureau of
Indian Affairs seem to be good. It was reported to
me that at first the BIA's Pueblo Agency was skeptical about OEO's approach of direct funding, but that
now it sees value in it. Following a directive from
Washington, the Pueblo Agency has set up local school
boards with advisory powers to relate to the BIA
schools. Otherwise, there is little movement toward
community control.

    One of the governors expressed the view that
there was not much difference between OEO and the
BIA. Neither would let the Pueblos have the autonomy
they want in spending federal funds. He would prefer
to get the money directly and not have any siphoned
off for administrative expenses of the community
action agency--exactly the same statement made by
community corporation officials in New York City (see
Chapter 2).

                    The Office of Navajo
                    Economic Opportunity

    The Navajos are the largest Indian tribe in the
United States, with a population of 109,000 in 1967.
Their reservation encompasses nearly 24,000 square
miles in northeastern Arizona and adjacent parts of
New Mexico and Utah, a territory about the size of
West Virginia and one and one-half times as large
as Connecticut, Massachusetts, and Rhode Island
combined.

    When the land they now occupy first became
part of the United States, the Navajos were not a
tribe in the sense of being a political entity.
Rather they were a group of people sharing a common
culture and language but with no over-all political
organization. There were local bands led by headmen, whose powers depended mainly upon persuasion,

not force, and coalitions of headmen were few and of short duration.

The U.S. Government, in trying to suppress the Navajos, had difficulty in making treaties with a tribe that had no central leadership. When the American military sent the Navajos into exile at Fort Sumner in 1863, it tried to bring about the formation of a tribal government, but to no avail. When the Navajos returned to their homeland in 1868, the traditional form of social organization, characterized by the extended family and small bands, was re-established. The BIA's Navajo agent sometimes arranged for councils of headmen, but these had neither permanence nor continuity of membership. To facilitate control and communication, the BIA in 1901 divided the sprawling Navajo reservation into separate agencies, finally totaling six (including the Hopi), each with its own superintendent. In 1927, one of the superintendents began to develop local community organizations, called chapters, as a vehicle for encouraging the improvement of livestock and agricultural techniques, the advancement of education, and other BIA objectives. Chapter houses were built as meeting places, and by now there are about 100 chapters located throughout the reservation.

In 1921, oil was discovered in Navajo country, and the need for a body to approve oil leases provided the stimulus for establishing a tribal council. The council was formed by 1923 and consisted of 12 delegates and 12 alternates, apportioned among the six agency districts on the basis of population. The chairman was chosen from outside the council; the vice-chairman was one of the delegates. The commissioner of the Navajo Tribe (a BIA official) called all meetings, and the council could meet only in his presence. For its first ten years, the council met once a year, usually for two days. However, the true leadership of the Navajos remained at the local level in the hands of headmen.

By the 1930's the Navajos had experienced considerable population growth, and their livestock far exceeded the grazing capacity of their lands. Their economic future depended upon stock reduction and range control, and the BIA worked toward that objective through the tribal council. However, the controls were not favored by many Navajos, and this led to charges that the council did not truly represent the people. After several turbulent years, a constitutional assembly was called in 1937, with members chosen from among local headmen, but instead of framing a new constitution, it constituted itself into a new de facto tribal council. A year later, with the approval of the Secretary of the Interior, it developed "Rules for the Navajo Tribal Council," which to this day provide the basis for Navajo government. Under these rules, 74 delegates are elected by secret vote (at first colored ribbons, now pictorial paper ballots) from local election districts, and the council chairman and vice-chairman are elected at large. Since 1940, the chairman has had a regular salary. For 20 years, the council members received per diem pay, but now they meet more often--about 100 days a year--and are paid an annual salary. When the rules were adopted in 1938, the requirement that council meetings be held only in the presence of a BIA official was eliminated.

The Navajo tribal council oversees the expenditure of more than $13 million in tribal funds, derived from oil leases, timber operations, and other enterprises. With these funds, the tribe pays for the operations of the tribal council, the chairman and his staff, resources development (forestry, water supply, range conservation), public services supplementing federal programs (education, health, welfare, youth services, police), and public works (roads, water systems, construction of chapter houses).

Because they were experienced and well organized, the Navajos were in a position to take advantage of the Economic Opportunity Act. Within four weeks of the Act's passage in August, 1964, the Navajo tribal council authorized the tribe's participation in the Community Action Program. In December, the council sent to Washington a plan to participate under five different titles of the Act, and the first federal grant was approved the following April. In that month, the tribe also established the Office of Navajo Economic Opportunity (ONEO) to run the program. ONEO is governed by a ten-man board consisting of the chairman of the tribal council, a representative of each of the five agency districts, and a representative from the BIA's Navajo Agency, the Public Health Service, the BIA school administration, and a county superintendent of schools. (The Hopis, who occupy the sixth agency district, have their own program.) Council Chairman Raymond Nakai persuaded Peter McDonald, a Navajo with a degree in electrical engineering, to return to the tribe from Los Angeles and to serve as executive director.

By late 1968, ONEO had ten programs in operation: local community development, home improvement training, tribal housing and training, Navajo culture center, Head Start, Neighborhood Youth Corps, migrant and agriculture placement, alcoholism treatment, legal aid, and VISTA. The program is directed from ONEO's headquarters at Fort Defiance, Arizona, but most of the component programs have branch operations quartered at the five agency centers.

The purpose of the local community development program is to develop a feeling of hopefulness by motivating the chapter communities to unite and then to identify and solve problems by initiating and carrying out their own programs. This is no easy task after more than a century of oppression and paternalistic management, which led to widespread dependency and defeatism.

As a basis for local community development, most of the chapters have formed community action committees and have appointed chapter development workers. These workers visit homes, enroll young children in Head Start, refer adults to services, and work with the community action committees. The committees have dealt with such problems as water supply, roads, bridges, electric power, facilities for preschool programs, and other matters of concern to the chapters. In many respects, they are similar to the community action groups found in Appalachia (see Chapter 4), except that distances between houses are much greater in Navajo country.

The Housing Improvement Training Program (HITP) is designed to improve housing conditions while training unskilled unemployed adults. Trainees are nominated by the community action committees and approved at chapter meetings, and at any one time a chapter may have ten trainees participating. Under the supervision of journeymen carpenters, the trainees spend two hours in classroom instruction related to their day's work and five hours on the job repairing old homes or building new ones. In addition, every day they receive an hour of adult basic education from teachers who are mostly Navajos. A trainee stays in the program for 90 days and then is helped to find employment. Of the 5,500 enrolled the first two years, about 20 per cent found work off the reservation and others found employment in Navajo country, but more than half remained unemployed because of the lack of sufficiently developed skills as well as the lack of employment opportunities.

The families that benefit from the HITP are chosen by the chapters on the basis of need. Each family is allocated $145 for materials, and this amount may be increased if endorsed by the community action committee and chapter officers. Some owners supply their own logs. Those on tribal welfare may be given as much as $600 for materials.

During the past year, some of the HITP trainees have been placed in a new mutual-help housing program called Tribal Housing and Training (THAT). This program allows low-income families to purchase a home by contributing 600 hours of labor as a down payment. A construction crew consists of a superintendent, a foreman (usually with carpentry experience), a plumber, an electrician, and a number of HITP graduates, who do all of the carpentry and serve as helpers to the plumber and electrician. Materials are supplied by tribal funds, the BIA pays the superintendent and the cost of streets, the Public Health Service provides sewers, and the Department of Housing and Urban Development makes available mortgage funds. The program started with the construction of 20 homes; if it proves successful, it will be expanded.

The Navajo Culture Center is collecting legends, history, mythology, and other information pertaining to the Navajo. Older adults are interviewed, and their recollections recorded on tape. The Center's staff is writing a book on Navajo history, which will be used in local schools. This will be the first book on the history of an Indian group written by Indians themselves, and this is another means of restoring self-pride and building hope.

The alcoholism treatment program is dealing with a major problem in Navajo life. The migrant labor program assists Navajos to find agricultural employment off the reservation and to protect these workers from exploitation and mistreatment. Head Start,

Neighborhood Youth Corps, and VISTA are local adaptations of national programs.

Legal aid is handled by a separate corporation called DIBEBEIINA NAHIILNA BE AGADITHE, Inc. (DNA). The name comes from the Navajo language and means "attorneys who contribute to the economic revitalization of the people." The board includes Navajos and non-Navajos who are practicing lawyers and law professors. DNA provides legal services through six different offices: a typical office has two lawyers, two counselors, two interpreters-investigators, and three secretaries. The lawyers assist people with state and federal law problems, and the counselors help with tribal law and tribal courts. DNA's organizational independence enables it to deal with Navajo authorities on behalf of its clients.

Chairman Nakai, a strong supporter of the Community Action Program, told the Senate Subcommittee at its 1967 Albuquerque hearing that the Bureau of Indian Affairs and the Public Health Service exercise strong controls over the functions and funds they handle on the Navajo reservation, and they are more engulfed in red tape than OEO. He said, "The community action programs which allow program innovation geared to local needs as determined by the people have been very successful on the Navajo Reservation."[3]

COMMENTARY

These brief descriptions of three programs in the Southwest provide but a sample of the Indian Community Action Program. They reflect only a small part of the rich and varied heritage of the American Indians. Nonetheless, with many local variations, the same theme emerges on dozens of other reservations: Indian tribes clearly have the capacity to run their own programs. To be sure, OEO has been concerned with such matters as nepotism in hiring, which arises in part from the Indians' traditional concept of clan loyalty but which is unacceptable under conventional standards of public administration.

---

[3]Hearings before the Senate Subcommittee on Employment, Manpower and Poverty, Examination of War on Poverty, 90th Cong., 1st Sess., Pt. 3, p. 1132.

On the whole, however, local administration by tribal councils has been about the same as that by non-Indian local agencies: some very good, some very bad, and most, average.

The Community Action Program is, of course, not the cure-all. Before poverty can be eliminated from Indian reservations, much greater effort must be made to achieve better economic development and to raise the educational and job-skill levels of the Indians. So far, the Community Action Program has been relatively weak in these areas.

CAP's major accomplishments have been threefold. First, it has instituted new services, such as Head Start, home improvements, and adult education, which have benefited the participants. Second, it has had a psychological effect upon tribal leaders, who have gained greater confidence in their capacity to do things for themselves. Third, it has reversed the long-time approach of federal paternalism. Out of inspiration, threat of competition, and demonstrated results, the Bureau of Indian Affairs has been challenged to try new approaches. This surely must be of great assistance to Commissioner Robert L. Bennett, who took office in 1966 as the first Indian to head the BIA and who undoubtedly needs outside pressures to help change this stiff old bureaucracy.

The BIA is now entering into contracts with a number of tribes to run their own services, and this practice is certain to expand. Another step is for the tribes to receive direct federal grants from other federal agencies, and the Economic Development Administration, for one, has started to do this. In moving toward greater community control on Indian reservations, grants and contracts provide the middle ground between abrupt termination of reservation status, which the tribes fear, and the government's paternalistic services, which they despise.

CHAPTER 7 NEIGHBORHOOD CENTERS PILOT PROGRAM

Civil disorder in urban ghettos began in 1964, occurring that year in New York City and Rochester in the State of New York; in Jersey City, Elizabeth, and Paterson, New Jersey; and in Chicago and Philadelphia. In August, 1965, serious disorder raged in the south central area of Los Angeles for nearly a week. In 1966, the pattern spread throughout the nation, with 43 occurrences.

As civil disorder became more prevalent, there were increasing demands for national response. In midsummer 1966, President Johnson instructed the White House staff to search for ideas on the most appropriate course of action. A major product of this search was a speech given by the President in Syracuse, New York, on August 19. Among a great variety of program proposals, he stated that he had requested the Secretary of the Department of Housing and Urban Development "to set as his goal the establishment--in every ghetto in America--of a neighborhood center to serve the people who live in that area."[1] These were to be one-stop service centers, ministering to a wide variety of needs.

This idea was not new. Eighty years earlier, the first settlement house had opened in New York City, and by 1964 about 800 settlements and neighborhood centers were in operation throughout the United States. With the passage of the Economic Opportunity

---

[1] Lyndon B. Johnson, "Remarks at Columbus Circle, Syracuse, New York, August 19, 1966," <u>Public Papers of the Presidents of the United States: Lyndon B. Johnson</u>, Bk. II (Washington, D.C.: Government Printing Office, 1967), p. 846.

NEIGHBORHOOD CENTERS PILOT PROGRAM 139

Act of 1964, hundreds of other centers went into operation, and as this program evolved more and more emphasis was placed upon neighborhood control in contrast to a board with a nonresident majority which governed most traditional settlements. In the Housing Act of 1965, federal aid was made available to cities for the construction of neighborhood centers.

A second part of the President's proposal was to achieve coordination of federal agencies in support of neighborhood centers. This was not wholly new either, for during the 1960's several other attempts had been made along these lines--by the President's Committee on Juvenile Delinquency, chaired by Attorney General Robert Kennedy when his brother was President; by the Concerted Services Project sponsored by HEW and the Public Housing Administration and focusing on housing projects in five cities; and by OEO, using broad coordinative authority given by the Economic Opportunity Act. However, the President's Committee lost its impetus under the Johnson Administration, the Concerted Services Project was a complete failure in coordination, and by 1966 OEO was losing presidential favor.

President Johnson turned to the Department of Housing and Urban Development, the newest federal department, not yet a year old. The President had recently given HUD authority to serve as "convener" of federal agencies in order to deal with interdepartmental matters related to urban problems. Using this convener authority, HUD brought together representatives of the Department of Labor, the Department of Health, Education, and Welfare, the Office of Economic Opportunity, and the Bureau of the Budget to form the Washington Interagency Review Committee (WIRC). The Bureau of the Budget had been studying the idea of one-stop neighborhood centers that would integrate service delivery systems, and it made a report on this topic available to WIRC. HUD made a quick study and found that the cost of placing such a center in every ghetto would be about $500 million. The White House and the Bureau of the Budget realized that such resources were not available, and therefore only a pilot program could be initiated. Thereupon, HUD, with some consultation with the other agencies, selected 14 cities, most of which already had applied to it for funds to build neighborhood centers. In November, the mayors of these cities were notified of their selection, and regional office personnel were organized into Federal Review Teams (FRT), with the HUD regional administrators as chairmen.

In January, 1967, the federal machinery seemed to be sufficiently ready to invite representatives of the cities to Washington. They found their instructions a little fuzzy and the assurance of federal funding somewhat uncertain, but they learned enough to start local planning. Federal support seemed assured in March when the President, in his Message on Urban and Rural Poverty, confidently predicted that $120 million would be spent on neighborhood multiservice and multicounty centers in the coming fiscal year. But this statement must have been referring to all types of neighborhood centers, and not necessarily the pilot program, since the only firm commitments for the special project had been $750,000 in demonstration funds from OEO, $500,000 for job-oriented services from the Labor Department (which later evaporated), and perhaps as much as $12 million from HUD for the construction costs of neighborhood facilities. HEW was still studying ways to find funds for this program. The program was also lagging because of disagreement on purpose and procedures, so the matter was placed on the Cabinet's agenda in April and the program was given a boost by the President.

By that time, at least the guidelines for planning grants were ready and were sent out to the cities. Applications were hastily prepared, and in June, 1967, OEO awarded planning funds to the 14 cities, mostly to community action agencies.

During this first year, WIRC had an ongoing debate about who should be in charge of the neighborhood centers. Because OEO was the only agency willing and able to put up funds immediately, it had considerable leverage. First it offered to make demonstration funds available for seven centers to be operated by neighborhood corporations, and later it agreed to finance core services in all centers provided funds were channeled through community action agencies. It appeared that neighborhood corporations were most likely in Chattanooga, Jacksonville, Louisville, New York City, Philadelphia,

St. Louis, and Washington, D.C. However, as planning progressed, local officials in Chattanooga and Jacksonville were found to be resistant to the corporation idea, thus leaving only five cities in which to try this approach.

Finally in January, 1968, nearly a year and a half after the President's Syracuse speech, the federal agencies were able to announce the approval of operating funds for 11 pilot centers, including Louisville, Philadelphia, St. Louis, and Washington, where neighborhood corporations would be organized. Two others, including the fifth corporation city--New York--were announced in March.

As other case histories described in this report indicate, practical experience in the operation of neighborhood corporations is quite limited. Recognizing this, OEO decided that the corporation approach could be facilitated by providing free technical assistance to those cities using this approach. Consequently, OEO entered into a contract with the Organization for Social and Technical Innovation (OSTI), a nonprofit agency in Cambridge, Massachusetts, organized by a group of social scientists and public administrators with experience in community programs. OSTI actually has had three roles: providing technical assistance to the community corporations, serving as a communications link from OEO to the corporations, and reporting back to OEO the problems and achievements in the five cities.

Before OSTI entered the picture, the federal agencies in Washington had already formulated their own concept of a neighborhood center, and some of them had committed funds, mostly for predetermined uses. But responsibility for implementation was in the hands of the localities, each with its own style of operation and organizational arrangement. This meant that as the program progressed, differences would occur among the participating cities. But there would also be similarities, resulting from the uniformity of federal rules and policies. These similarities and differences can be illustrated by the four cities I have visited that have developed pilot neighborhood centers operated by community corporations: St. Louis, New York City, Washington, and Philadelphia.

THE ST. LOUIS YEATMAN DISTRICT COMMUNITY CORPORATION

In St. Louis, the mayor designated the Human Development Corporation (HDC), the community action agency, to be the prime sponsor for the pilot neighborhood center. HDC assigned the program to the Yeatman district, which has about 65,000 residents of whom 95 per cent are black and which is the largest of the 14 districts in which HDC sponsors programs.

When the Community Action Program first began in St. Louis, the Human Development Corporation contracted with the Urban League to operate a neighborhood services program in the Yeatman district. However, relations between HDC and the Urban League were seldom smooth, and by the spring of 1967, HDC had withdrawn the Yeatman program from Urban League sponsorship. By then, the residents wanted a greater voice in program operations, and in response HDC organized a district advisory committee. This 60-member body was elected by the residents and was composed of 15 persons from each of four subsections. At this stage, the committee was unincorporated.

St. Louis was in line for a planning grant under the Neighborhood Centers Pilot Program, and HDC wanted to operate through a community corporation in the Yeatman district. However, the federal agencies were not satisfied with the process of selecting members for the district advisory committee. Therefore, another election was held in August, at which all district residents 21 and over were eligible to vote. Again, 60 persons were chosen, 15 from each of the four subsections. The election was hotly contested, particularly by a slate advanced by a neighborhood association called Jeff-Vander-Lou, Inc., which succeeded in winning about a dozen seats. The new directors then incorporated as the Yeatman District Community Corporation. They appointed as executive director, Alphonse Lynch, who had been assigned to Yeatman when HDC took control away from the Urban League. The Yeatman residents were already overseeing the HDC-funded services in their neighborhoods, and after the corporation was formed, control of funds was subcontracted to it by HDC, including the planning funds for the pilot neighborhood center.

In January, 1968, when HUD announced the funding of operating programs for the first 11 cities, it appeared that the Yeatman District Community Corporation would receive $2,253,000: $161,000 from OEO for core services; $10,000 from OEO for planning a parent and child center; $780,000 from the Department of Labor for participation in the Concentrated Employment Program; $500,000 from HEW for projects in education, health, social services, and programs for the elderly; and $800,000 from HUD for the construction of a neighborhood center building. This prospect turned out to be an illusion.

Half of the OEO funds for core services were those already transferred by HDC to the Yeatman corporation, so only half were actually new funds for the demonstration. The $10,000 planning funds for a parent and child center were new, but OEO had already largely predetermined what such a center would be like and what kind of operating programs could be funded. Closer reading of the announcement revealed that the Labor Department promised "resources" not funds, and these were in the form of personnel from the State Employment Service assigned to the Yeatman center and job training programs to which Yeatman residents could be referred. The HEW funds were "reserved," not granted; this meant that applications would have to be made through the regular channels of state agencies and HEW regional offices. However, the State Division of Welfare did station some personnel in the Yeatman center, and the State Department of Education transferred funds to the University of Missouri to conduct an adult basic education program in the Yeatman district.

The development of a health center has required prolonged negotiations involving the Yeatman corporation, the city, the state, and HEW, and not until 1969 were funds for the health program granted by HEW. The $800,000 reserved by HUD for the construction of a new neighborhood center dwindled to $300,000 as the city, which has local control of such funds, assigned $1 million of St. Louis' $1.3 million over-all reservation to two other neighborhoods. This situation has been further complicated by disagreement between the Yeatman corporation and the city on the site of the center and on the selection of an architect. Moreover, with the failure of a bond issue in November, 1968, the city was having difficulty finding its share of the costs, a prerequisite for a federal grant. All of which proves that a federal press release masks many complex problems in the concerted financing of a neighborhood center.

Not all aspects of coordination in the Yeatman district were negative. The Yeatman corporation has become the neighborhood participant in the Concentrated Employment Program, so that it can tie together this program, sponsored by the U.S. Labor Department, with other neighborhood programs financed by OEO. The St. Louis Model City Agency selected five districts, including Yeatman, for its operation and contracted with neighborhood organizations to develop their own plans. The Yeatman District Community Corporation received a small contract ($4,200) to develop Model Cities human resources programs, but a similar amount was given to Jeff-Vander-Lou, Inc., to develop a physical development plan for Yeatman, thus reopening an old dispute. With this exception, the Yeatman corporation is in a position to pull together these three major federal programs, which in some other cities have been divided among competing groups at the neighborhood level.

In the fall of 1968, the Yeatman corporation sought funds to expand its operations. Highest priority was given to a training program for board members and staff. Funds were also needed for economic development, additional manpower programs, and housing rehabilitation. The latter, though, would compete with Jeff-Vander-Lou's principal program emphasis, indicating that this internal rivalry continues.

The first bylaws of the Yeatman corporation called for a re-election of one-third of the board of directors in November, 1968. However, this was changed, and there was an election of the entire board in January, 1969, coinciding with the election of other neighborhood corporations in St. Louis. In this election, 29 of the 60 incumbents were re-elected to the board.

By the end of 1968, the Yeatman District Community Corporation had over 12,000 members. However, affairs were run entirely by the board, which had 13 committees consisting only of directors, none of whom were from the general membership. The bylaws were changed to allow persons 18 and older to be members of the corporation (previously 21 was the limit), and the minimum age of directors was lowered from 24 to 21.

Compared to other community corporations visited, the officials in Yeatman tend to be older and less militant. The programs are solid but not particularly innovative. The primary emphasis has been upon services, not protest and social action. However, in the winter of 1968-69, rent strikes were initiated to pressure landlords to bring their apartments up to minimum housing standards, a departure from the previous less militant approach.

NEW YORK CITY: THE HUNTS POINT MULTI-SERVICE CENTER CORPORATION

In New York City, the Hunts Point section of the Bronx was selected for the pilot neighborhood center. This represented a coming together of two new super-agencies in Mayor Lindsay's administration. As reported in Chapter 2, the Human Resources Administration was formed in August, 1966, by combining agencies running programs in welfare, youth services, manpower, and community action. About the same time, the Housing and Development Administration (HDA) was created by joining the agencies that operate public housing, urban renewal, building inspection, and other housing improvement activities. The study groups that developed plans for these two super-agencies were headed by Mitchell Sviridoff and Edward Logue, who had worked closely together in New Haven during the 1950's. Their close association set the stage for an initial effort to develop joint programming in the social and physical aspects of urban improvement.

New York City had reserved federal funds for building several neighborhood centers. Responsibility for their construction fell to HDA, but it was apparent that most of the services provided in them would come under the jurisdiction of HRA. Thus, the agencies developed a common strategy for site selection and program development. It was obvious to all concerned that the southern part of the Bronx was greatly deficient both in facilities and services and deserved priority. Also, one of HDA's constituent agencies was planning an urban renewal project there, and the persons displaced would require special services which HRA could help provide. Perhaps, then, a neighborhood center could be located in or near the renewal area.

Early in 1967, WIRC invited New York City to participate in the Pilot Neighborhood Center Program. After considerable internal discussion, HRA and HDA agreed in May, 1967, that the pilot neighborhood center should serve two health areas in Hunts Point. (Health areas in New York City are sections demarcated for statistical purposes and do not necessarily denote natural neighborhoods.) These two health areas were among nine to be served by the Hunts Point Community Corporation, which was being formed at the time (see Chapter 2). The interim chairman of the corporation-organizing committee appointed a special committee to develop plans for the pilot center, and Ramon Velez of the corporation staff was assigned to work with that committee. The committee set up 16 planning subcommittees in various service fields, brought in other residents to serve on these subcommittees, and during the next several months developed a host of proposals. Almost from the beginning, they talked about becoming a separate corporation, and after a while OEO, which was providing funds, concluded that this should be required. At first, the Community Development Agency downtown and the Hunts Point Community Corporation resisted, but by the first of the year they gave in. In February, 1968, the 17 members of the multiservice center committee filed papers of incorporation and developed a set of bylaws for the Hunts Point Multi-Service Center Corporation. Velez, the staff planner, then became executive director of the new corporation.

The bylaws called for a board of directors of 25 members: 16 elected by area residents, 2 from each of eight sub-areas; 5 chosen from standing committees; and 4 at large, the first year to be representatives previously elected by residents of the multiservice center health areas to the Hunts Point Community Corporation and thereafter to be chosen by the other members of the multiservice center board.

In October, 1968, the first election was held for the multiservice center board with 1,750 residents participating. Of the 16 elected, 13 were Puerto Rican and 3 black; when the other 9 members were added, Puerto Ricans held about 80 per cent of the board seats. As with the parent Hunts Point Community Corporation, ethnic division is a major factor in the internal workings of the Hunts Point Multi-Service Center.

A unifying factor, though, is a desire to gain even greater independence from the Hunts Point Community Corporation and indeed from the whole anti-poverty administration of New York City. The Multi-Service Center would prefer to deal directly with the federal agencies, and it sees the Federal Review Team as its best protection against the municipal bureaucracy. However, its current status is that of a delegate agency, with regular program funds channeled from City Hall through the community corporation to the center. In the case of manpower programs, the center receives a proportionate share of Hunts Point's allocation, but for general program operations out of versatile community action funds it obtains relatively less. Leaders of the community corporation believe that the two health areas served by the center are getting extra federal funds under the pilot program and that scarce program funds should be used elsewhere. The center leaders counter that Hunts Point's over-all allocation is based upon the percentage of poor in the total community and that the community corporation should not be allowed to withhold the fair share of the center's two health areas. The board of the Hunts Point Multi-Service Center has petitioned for equal status with the Hunts Point Community Corporation, but it is doubtful that the city-wide Council Against Poverty will accede to this re-request.

As these organizational procedures have been going on, the Multi-Service Center has been developing a variety of programs. One of the first programs in operation provided day care services starting in June, 1968. General intake and referral staff were hired during the summer. A manpower program began in the fall when the State Employment Center stationed counselors in the center. By the end of the year, plans were being developed for programs related to youth services, senior citizens' homemaking, housing development, a parent-child center, physical and mental health, and board and staff training.

The Hunts Point Multi-Service Center set up operations in a small corner office, and similar storefront facilities were opened as new program components were added. In November, 1968, these scattered operations were consolidated into a single building--a former nurses' dormitory. Meanwhile, a site has been selected for the new neighborhood center, and the city agencies are processing the papers necessary to obtain HUD construction funds. Eventually the programs will be shifted to this new facility.

Like most of the other corporation cities in the Neighborhood Centers Pilot Program, the Hunts Point Multi-Service Center is encompassed in a Model Cities area, which takes in not only the entire area served by the larger Hunts Point Community Corporation but also the territory of two other community corporations, South Bronx and Morrisania. The Multi-Service Center has been in a good bargaining position with the Model Cities Program, for its executive director served as chairman of the interim Model Cities committee, and some of its board and staff have been selected to serve on the permanent South Bronx Model Cities Policy Board.

THE PEOPLE'S INVOLVEMENT CORPORATION OF WASHINGTON, D.C.

In Washington, the first federal-local contact on the proposed pilot neighborhood centers was between HUD officials and the office of the Engineer Commissioners who was then one of three commissioners who governed the District of Columbia. The Commissioners' staff had recently published a report on a Community Renewal Program, which proposed 45 community progress centers to be scattered throughout the city. Since these were to have functions similar to those proposed by WIRC, it seemed logical to deal with the District staff that had been working on this matter. In January, 1967, a meeting of local officials was held in the District Building (D.C.'s "city hall") to develop plans for participation in the federal pilot program. OEO, through its membership on WIRC, learned of this meeting and encouraged the executive director of its local counterpart, the United Planning Organization, to attend, which he did.

For the next several months, there was a lot of "pulling and hauling," but by April it was decided that UPO would submit an application for planning funds. This happened partly because OEO, not HUD, was willing to put up the planning money, and OEO insisted that these funds go to the community action agency. The grant was announced in June.

NEIGHBORHOOD CENTERS PILOT PROGRAM

As mentioned in Chapter 3, UPO sponsors neighborhood development centers (NDC) in ten sections of the nation's capital. At that time, three of these were run by community corporations and a fourth was in transition to that status; two were operated by settlement houses; one by the Urban League; and two (NDC 1 and NDC 2) by UPO directly. The territory served by the last three covers a large area northwest of the Capitol. UPO's application stated that the pilot neighborhood center would be located somewhere in this area, that a planning team would be formed consisting of staff from the three existing centers, and that the neighborhood advisory committees of these centers would provide citizen participation. Conceivably only one of these centers would be chosen, but until a decision was made all would participate.

As soon as the choice of area was known, Thomas Appleby, executive director of the Redevelopment Land Agency (RLA), became concerned that this new planning grant might duplicate the social planning role of the Model Inner City Community Organization (MICCO). MICCO is an organization funded by the RLA to undertake citizen-controlled planning in the Shaw urban renewal area, which takes in some but not all of the same territory. (See Chapter 8 for more on MICCO.) He raised this concern with UPO, and at the same time Rev. Walter Fauntroy, president of MICCO, took it up with OEO directly. As a result, in its June grant to UPO, OEO wrote in conditions requiring that this relationship be more clearly defined. UPO provided a response in August that satisfied OEO but not MICCO.

In August, UPO also appointed one of its staff as project director, and by mid-month he was ready to recommend that the Urban League area be chosen. This was outside MICCO's territory, and it included part of another urban renewal area which had available land for the construction of a new neighborhood center. A month later, he changed his choice to the NDC 1 area. Early in October, representatives from the three neighborhood advisory committees got together to form an interim board with five members from each group. A month later, the name "People's Involvement Corporation" (PIC) was chosen. It was largely decided by then that PIC should operate in all three areas. Altogether there are about 110,000 residents, almost all black, making this the largest population served by a pilot neighborhood center.

These organizing details took most of the energies of the planners, and little was accomplished in the way of developing a concrete program. Nonetheless, OEO gave UPO a grant for core services for PIC and also planning funds for a parent and child center in January, 1968, along with ten other cities participating in the Neighborhood Centers Pilot Program. An interpretive article in the Washington Star indicated that eventually the three existing neighborhood development centers would be absorbed by PIC.[2]

Relations between UPO and MICCO were still uneasy, and once again OEO attached a grant condition that this situation would have to be clarified. By then, the District of Columbia had a new mayor, Walter Washington; UPO had a new executive director, Wiley Branton; and the newly established City Council had Walter Fauntroy, head of MICCO, as its vice-chairman. These three men worked out an understanding that would have MICCO concentrate on physical planning (which was its primary emphasis so far) and PIC on social service planning. The interim PIC board concurred. However, a formal agreement was held up until PIC incorporated and hired a permanent executive director.

PIC's incorporation took place in April, 1968, and the interim board hired Richard Brown, who had been working at OEO headquarters, as executive director. UPO's contract with PIC gave the parent organization the right to veto the board's choice of executive director, but this right was not exercised. With the hiring of its own man, PIC was substantially free of heavy dependence on the UPO staff, which had been handling all funds, recording and editing board minutes, and performing other ministerial tasks.

When Brown came on the job in mid-May, he found that the interim board had scheduled an election for June 15 but had done relatively little to mobilize neighborhood participation. This election had first been planned for the end of April but had been postponed because civil disorders on April 6 and 7 following the assassination of Dr. Martin Luther King had left the PIC area in a state of disarray.

Immediately, Brown hired a staff of 24, the majority of which were neighborhood workers, to build

---

[2]The Evening Star, January 21, 1968.

NEIGHBORHOOD CENTERS PILOT PROGRAM

support for the election. By election day, they had signed up 11,000 members for PIC and had 93 candidates (each with at least 20 signers on a nominating petition) for the 25 board positions. About 3,000 actually voted. In each of 11 districts, one poor person and one nonpoor person were chosen, and three youths were elected at large. Those elected divide approximately in thirds by age: under 25, 25 to 40, and over 40. The board elected as its chairman an 18-year-old youth. Membership is open to persons age 13 and older who live or work in the area, which may explain why this community corporation board has the youngest average age of any of the boards in my acquaintance.

With its regular board elected, PIC finally moved into the development of programs during the summer of 1968. After several months of planning, it came up with an economic development package with five major enterprises: Beneficial Construction, Inc., a stock company to purchase, rehabilitate, sell, and lease housing and to provide construction bonds and seed money for other housing improvement efforts; The Musicians Shop, Inc., for retail sales, instrument repair, and musical instruction; Power and Action for Youth, Inc., to allow unskilled unemployed youth to develop manufacturing enterprises; Jet Food Stores, to operate as a franchise; and an offset printing company. Each of these would provide jobs, training opportunities, and economic return for PIC and stockholders. PIC proposed to use OEO "block grant" funds as seed money for this program, but as of mid-February, 1969, the proposal had not been approved by UPO or OEO.

Simultaneously, PIC formed three coordinating councils to serve as a means of communication among agencies and organizations active in the neighborhood and to develop linkages between related programs. Membership consists of both organizational representatives and interested individuals. Each council is concerned with the service area of one of the neighborhood development centers previously organized by UPO. The centers also have separate neighborhood advisory committees.

In July, 1968, PIC told UPO that it wanted to take over the operation of these three centers, but UPO so far has not agreed to this request. In October, Wiley Branton, UPO's executive director, wrote PIC expressing concern that it was not developing a coordinated delivery system and not conducting needed community services. PIC replied that it had barely gotten under way and that it needed control of funds and staff from the existing centers if it was to achieve a better service network. In this and other ways, relations between sponsor and the neighborhood corporation have been strained.

PIC, however, did get into center operations in October when it took charge of an urban progress center opened by the District government in that part of PIC's area where the Urban League runs the UPO-funded neighborhood development program. The District converted an old convent into a temporary center pending the construction of a new building, lined up some of its agencies to provide services, but lacked someone to be in charge. PIC volunteered, with the concurrence of the Urban League which lacked the staff to undertake this role. Eighty-eight organizations were invited to send representatives to a meeting on the new center, and the 18 who showed up became the interim board, which was appointed by the mayor. This center, though, is more a common shelter for staff from various agencies than a truly coordinated service delivery program.

In the meantime, PIC has developed plans for the construction of three new centers, using the $1.3 million which HUD earmarked for the PIC area. These plans are slowly moving through the complicated review procedures of the federal city.

PIC and MICCO have yet to sort out their respective roles. They do not seem to be in open contention, but they are not involved in joint activities either. PIC, however, appears to be working things out with the Model Cities Program, which encompasses the PIC area and an equal-sized adjacent area. PIC board members tried to get elected to the Model Cities Citizen Board, but only one succeeded. At the staff level, relationships are smooth, and the two organizations are developing a written memorandum of understanding. But unless PIC can develop a similar mutual understanding with its own sponsor, UPO, it will have a long uphill struggle to achieve success.

NORTH PHILADELPHIA'S
HARTRANFT COMMUNITY CORPORATION

Philadelphia was the only one of the five cities with pilot neighborhood centers run by neighborhood corporations in which funding and other arrangements were not worked out through the community action agency. The reason for this has historical roots.

As related in Chapter 1, in the latter part of 1961 staff from the Ford Foundation met with leaders in a couple dozen cities, offering the hope of a major grant for comprehensive programs in the inner city. In Philadelphia, the response was spearheaded by a group of social scientists from Temple University, who allied themselves with persons associated with the civic reform movement who had held municipal power during the 1950's. They organized the Philadelphia Council for Community Advancement and got a Ford grant. However, from the beginning they were engaged in a constant struggle with the old-line regular Democrats who had taken control of City Hall in the spring of 1962 when Richardson Dilworth resigned as mayor to run for governor of Pennsylvania and was succeeded by James Tate. This power struggle was one of several factors that prevented this new group from accomplishing very much.

When the Economic Opportunity Act was passed by Congress, Mayor Tate made it clear that City Hall intended to control the new community action program. Nonetheless, when the Philadelphia Anti-Poverty Action Committee (PAAC) was established in February, 1965, it appeared to be broadly based. Of its 30-man board, 12 persons were selected by 12 community action councils located in poverty areas and elected by residents of poverty areas; 12 were appointed by leading private agencies, most of whom had been active supporters of the reform movement; 5 were appointed by the mayor; and 1 was chosen by the County Court. As the program unfolded, however, it became apparent that the dominant influence was Samuel L. Evans, a close political ally of Mayor Tate, who as vice-chairman of the board and chairman of the community action subcommittee was the most powerful black in PAAC. It was also clear that ten years of reform administration had not removed an earlier style of political operation, and very soon OEO had to crack down on the community action councils for extensive use of nepotism in the selection of personnel. As the years progressed, PAAC was by far the least effective of the large-city community action agencies.

For this reason, the Washington Interagency Review Committee decided to bypass PAAC and to develop a pilot neighborhood center in Philadelphia through the school board. By then, Dilworth, having lost his bid for governor, was president of the school board, and a new superintendent and other new central staff were making the school system more innovative. One such endeavor was a plan to replace the obsolete Hartranft School in North Philadelphia with a new community school. Already the Deputy Superintendent for Planning, Graham Finney, was working with neighborhood residents of the Hartranft area, and they were talking about the community school serving as a neighborhood services center. It was natural that this could form a point of departure for a pilot neighborhood center run by a community corporation. The service area would take in about 30,000 residents, of whom 50 per cent were black, 15 per cent Puerto Rican, and 35 per cent white.

Before joining the school board staff, Finney had served as executive director of the Philadelphia Council for Community Advancement, which still operated on Ford funds. Finney got this council to initiate organizational efforts in the Hartranft area, which it did with a staff paid by a grant from the Field Foundation. However, after things got going it was necessary to attempt a reconciliation with PAAC, and the PAAC community action council serving that area was permitted to appoint an interim board to develop a community corporation. This group consisted of both residents and nonresident professionals working in the area; in August, 1967, they formed the Hartranft Community Corporation.

The bylaws made membership open to all persons 16 and older who lived or worked in the area. The board of directors would consist of 24 members: 20 elected annually by the members, of which two must be age 16 to 20, eight must be poor, and, of the remaining ten, at least two must reside in the neighborhood; the other four directors would be appointed, one each by the mayor, the governor, the president of the school board, and the chairman of the local community action council, the neighborhood affiliate of PAAC.

The first election was held in January, 1968, with about 400 people participating. Members and staff of the community action council actively campaigned and won 12 of the 20 elected positions plus a seat filled by appointment. However, of these about half were somewhat independent and not completely committed to PAAC, so that the Hartranft board has not been PAAC controlled.

In the summer of 1967, the school board received a planning grant from OEO, entered into a subcontract with the interim board of the Hartranft Community Corporation, and made these funds available to it. One of the contract conditions was that the school board and the Hartranft board of directors would jointly select the executive director of the corporation. In reality, the Hartranft board made the selection, and the school board concurred in the corporation's choice--James Roberts, who was then director of a settlement in another part of North Philadelphia.

To undertake program development, the corporation set up seven committees--on education, financial development, social services, recreation, housing, job opportunities, and health. These committees were assisted by staff, and the first four had available the help of "advocates," i.e., professional consultants who were hired to give one-day-a-week service. The preference of the board was to hire all black advocates, but they also insisted upon competence. After considering those available, they chose two blacks and two whites. In addition, they received technical assistance from OSTI.

As with the other pilot neighborhood centers, Hartranft received some federal funds and promises of more. The OEO demonstration grant was used mostly for a basic administrative and planning staff, and an OEO grant for core services made possible the opening of four satellite centers to conduct intake and referral to other organizations, but no direct services. OEO's planning grant for a parent-child center led to a clash; Hartranft, with the support of one set of federal officials, wanted the program to be an integral part of the neighborhood center with a neighborhood resident as director, but OEO/Head Start, which was putting up the funds, demanded separatism and an outside professional director; its wishes prevailed. The manpower "resources" committed by the Labor Department proved to be ephemeral, since Philadelphia's Concentrated Employment Program was bogged down in mismanagement and also questioned placing responsibility in a corporation like Hartranft.

One part of the federal package was a $974,000 reservation by HUD for the construction of a neighborhood center, which would be part of the community school complex. To be in a better bargaining position with the city, which controls the funds and constructs the building, the Hartranft corporation hired its own architectural advocate, who worked with a special board committee to draw up a plan for the building, including space for the corporation's headquarters, central intake, maternal and child health services, and other program components.

In the meantime, OEO Health Services funded a comprehensive family health center through a corporation established by Temple University. This new center opened a few blocks away and serves half of the Hartranft area. Although the health center's board provides representation for neighborhood residents, it is a separate entity, and effective ties have not yet been established beween these two federally funded centers.

In the latter part of 1968, the Hartranft Community Corporation set up a youth program with OEO funds. It is run by a subsidiary board consisting of three representatives from each of six identifiable youth groups in the neighborhood plus some members of the corporation board.

Internally, the Hartranft corporation has suffered growing pains. During its first year, the board dealt with administrative matters more than most boards do, partly because of inexperience in distinguishing between policy and management, and partly because decisions on hiring determined who would receive economic gain from the project and to the board this was a policy matter. Another reason seems to have been lack of complete confidence in Roberts, the executive director. In November, 1968, after 14 months' service, Roberts resigned. For a while, the vice-chairman of the board served as acting director, and then a staff member filled that role. As of February, 1969, a permanent executive director had not been chosen.

In the fall of 1968, the board lacked a quorum for six consecutive regular board meetings, with absentees most notable among persons associated with PAAC, including the board chairman. Attendance at committee meetings was also lagging. In January, 1969, a new board election was held. This time PAAC did not organize a slate and now has no formal representation except its one appointed member. Following the election, a training program was instituted for new board members.

By and large, relationships with the school board have been smooth. The school board has served mainly as a fiduciary agent and as a go-between with federal agencies and has not attempted to interfere with programs or internal management. However, these duties were sufficiently demanding that the school board had to appoint a full-time person to work with the Hartranft Community Corporation.

As often happens with related federal programs, only about half the Hartranft area was included in the initial boundaries of the Model Cities area, which takes in a large portion of North Philadelphia. However, the Hartranft corporation was given the choice of having their section deleted from the Model Cities area or being a part of this new program, conceivably adding all of Hartranft. In December, 1968, they decided that all the Hartranft area should be part of the Model Cities Program.

COMMENTARY

How are these four community corporations under the Neighborhood Centers Pilot Program to be judged? One way is to consider how well they are achieving the objectives set forth by the Washington Interagency Review Committee, which has guided this program. A second way is to look at them as community corporations quite apart from the federal project.

When WIRC formally invited applications in April, 1967, it stressed the following:

> The [local] sponsor . . . commits itself to develop, to the fullest extent of its capability, a comprehensive and integrated program of services for people in the neighborhood.
>
> On the Federal side will be a commitment to work with and support, to the fullest extent of its capability, the development of the Neighborhood Services Program. This includes priority consideration and expediting of project funding applications submitted to Federal agencies as components of the project.[3]

It takes quite a while to develop an integrated service delivery system, and it is too soon to judge how well the four community corporations are achieving this objective. However, efforts in that direction so far are neither remarkable nor unique. Of the four, the Hunts Point Multi-Service Center Corporation is making the greatest advance compared to what previously existed in its service, but what it is doing is not particularly different from what other community corporations in New York City are doing.

In St. Louis, the Yeatman District Community Corporation is proceeding along lines it probably would have followed without the demonstration. The Hartranft Community Corporation in Philadelphia has had to struggle with other local agencies every step of the way, and its sponsor, the school board, is not in a good position to lend support; neighborhood service is divergent from its main mission of public education. The People's Involvement Corporation in Washington is not particularly interested in developing a service delivery system, and to the extent that it is, it is in competition with other service centers funded by its sponsor, the United Planning Organization.

There is sufficient experience in the United States in this decade to indicate that an integrated

---

[3]Washington Interagency Review Committee, <u>Neighborhood Centers Pilot Program--Information and Instruction for Applicant Sponsors</u>, April 28, 1967, p. 1 (Mimeographed.)

service delivery system at the neighborhood level depends upon at least three factors: technical competence of the administrative staff, cooperation of a wide array of participating agencies, and sufficient sanctions to command effective coordination. All four of the corporations have now, or at least have the potential for, sufficient staff competence to coordinate an integrated delivery system. The ones in St. Louis and Hunts Point seem to be getting better cooperation from local agencies than those in Philadelphia and Washington. However, none of them is in a position to command and to exercise sanctions over component programs except where it has control of funds, and this does not cover a very broad segment of the service spectrum.

This brings us to the federal role, for the Federal Interagency Committee was supposed to help with the mobilization of resources, many of which are derived from federal programs. As pointed out earlier, this was not the first venture of this type. In fact, there were three similar attempts between 1962 and 1965. The President's Committee on Juvenile Delinquency tried to achieve joint federal funding of youth development programs, and even though the President's brother was committee chairman, only the Office of Manpower, Automation and Training, the research and development arm of the Labor Department, participated. The Concerted Services Program, sponsored by HEW and the Public Housing Administration, talked piously of coordination, but all funds made available had to follow tortuous routine review procedures and then had to be handled by the traditional agencies, not by a new neighborhood-based agency. The Economic Opportunity Act required federal agencies to give preference to local applications that were components of the Community Action Program, but OEO was never able to enforce this preference for the programs delegated to other federal agencies, much less for programs authorized by other federal statutes.

Thus, WIRC was challenged to succeed where previous efforts had failed. In the four pilot cities I visited, it was not very successful. OEO was the most cooperative in providing funds for planning and core services and then block grants with considerable flexibility, but its price was to reshape the program to provide more community control. Moreover, two special units within OEO--Head Start's parent-child centers and Comprehensive Health Services--insisted on their own arrangements in spite of neighborhood preferences. HUD was willing to earmark funds for the construction of new neighborhood facilities, but because the local use of these funds was controlled by City Hall, HUD could not keep them from being diverted elsewhere, as in St. Louis. The Labor Department committed "resources," not funds, which turned out to be personnel from the State Employment Service and referral to training programs, handled in traditional ways. HEW provided very little, except for a few state welfare workers stationed in the centers but not controlled by corporation staff, until finally in 1969 the Yeatman District Community Corporation got a grant for health services. Some of the other ten centers have received HEW funds also. Of the Federal Review Teams, which are assigned to support each center, the greatest assistance seems to have been provided in New York where the Hunts Point center was supported in its struggle with the cumbersome City Hall bureaucracy. In the Economic Opportunity Amendments of 1967, Congress gave the President the authority to arrange for joint funding of these kinds of programs, allowing a single federal agency to handle money drawn from two or more federal programs, but this authority has not been used to support this project. Apparently, President Johnson and his White House staff long ago forgot the promise of the Syracuse speech. In sum, the federal interagency approach has probably been somewhat helpful, but not remarkably so.

As to the value of the Neighborhood Centers Pilot Program in developing new community corporations, those organized are not particularly unique, but they do give us further experience with this type of organizational mechanism. Like the ones in New York City (see Chapter 2), these four community corporations have needed technical assistance as they organized and developed programs. In St. Louis, the community action agency has been helpful, and so was the one in Washington initially, but in New York and Philadelphia the local sponsor made no staff available. OSTI has worked under an OEO contract to provide technical assistance, and all four groups have praise for the help received. However, they also complain that during the first year OSTI consultants flew in and out of town so quickly that their assistance was not sustained, although in recent months OSTI changed its approach so that the consultants now give longer blocks of time. OSTI has also had too many roles to play--technical assistance, broker for OEO, and evaluator--which has compromised its technical assistance capacity somewhat. In Philadelphia, the Hartranft Community Corporation hired independent consultants, called advocates, and this was helpful. Gradually, the corporations are building staff capability so that their need for outside help is lessening, but considerable technical assistance seems to be highly desirable in the early stages and continues to be useful on certain specialized matters even after a good staff is hired.

Board training is a common need so that board members can better understand the full potential of what a community corporation can do and what programs can be carried out. They also need guidance on how to keep their focus on key policy issues and not become overly involved in administration. However, in a poor neighborhood, who gets the new jobs is often regarded as a policy matter, not an operating detail. The corporations that have made the greatest attempt to get poor people and youth on the board, such as those in Washington and Philadelphia, have the greatest need for board training, for these persons have less experience in the dynamics of committee work.

All four of the community corporations have had problems in obtaining and defending their "territory." In St. Louis, the Yeatman corporation, sponsored by the community action agency seemed to be working things out with its neighborhood rival, Jeff-Vander-Lou, Inc., when the Model Cities Agency reopened the division. The Hunts Point Multi-Service Center Corporation had to struggle with the community corporation for the whole Hunts Point area and with the city's Community Development Agency, but it finally established its jurisdiction and then was able to come to terms with the Bronx Model Cities Program. The Hartranft Community Corporation, sponsored by the school board, has been in a perpetual contest with the Philadelphia Anti-Poverty Action Committee, Temple University's neighborhood health center, and the Concentrated Employment Program. The People's Involvement Corporation has had to compete with MICCO, funded with urban renewal funds; with the Model Cities Program, operating under a different kind of HUD planning grant; and with three neighborhood programs funded by UPO, its own sponsor. As they gain strength and neighborhood support, the community corporations are able to work out jurisdiction problems, but the proliferation of separate federal grants makes this problem more difficult.

Indeed, one thing shown by the four community corporations participating in the Neighborhood Centers Pilot Program is the importance of neighborhood unity. When the neighborhood is united, its community corporation is in a much better position to deal with the separatism of the various local, state, and federal agencies which make funds available for neighborhood improvement. The corporation can demand and negotiate from strength and can begin to make programs operate on its own terms and not by the exclusive mandate of a distant funding agency.

Another key lesson is that the attitude of the local sponsor toward decentralized community corporations can make a lot of difference. In St. Louis, the city-wide Human Development Corporation was moving toward greater community control when the pilot program came along, and this made things much easier for the Yeatman District Community Corporation. In Washington, UPO previously had turned four of its ten neighborhood development programs over to community corporations, but its position on whether this should be done in the case of PIC, and if so, when and how, has been very ambivalent; this uncertainty has made PIC's organizational task much more difficult.

It is clear that federal agencies by themselves cannot achieve neighborhood unity or force city-wide agencies to favor neighborhood control. These are matters which must be worked out locally. However, federal agencies, singly and together, can remove obstacles that make it harder for community corporations to operate. They can refrain from funding competitive groups with overlapping functions in the same neighborhoods. They can alter their patterns of grants so that more funds flow to neighborhood-controlled agencies. They might even provide financial incentives to places that develop integrated service delivery systems with significant neighborhood participation (the Model Cities Program has this potential). However, it is clear that the limited powers given to the Washington Interagency Review Committee on the Neighborhood Centers Pilot Program are vastly insufficient to provide the federal support needed by community corporations.

CHAPTER **8** CITIZEN PARTICIPATION IN URBAN RENEWAL

Since 1954, the urban renewal program has required that before receiving federal assistance a city must provide for citizen participation. Most cities have met this requirement by a city-wide citizens advisory committee appointed by the mayor, with places for members of minority groups but usually not with specific representation for the neighborhoods affected by the renewal program. A few places, though, have gone beyond this minimum requirement and have tried to involve residents of renewal areas in project planning. I have had firsthand experience in two such cities, Philadelphia (1952 to 1958) and New Haven (1959 to 1965). To provide some historical perspective, their approaches are reviewed before the more recent experiences in Washington, D.C., and San Francisco, where residents have had even larger roles in urban renewal projects--though less than full community control.

LIMITED RESIDENT INVOLVEMENT: PHILADELPHIA (1952-58)

In Philadelphia, the first effort at neighborhood involvement in city planning after World War II occurred in 1946 and 1947 in the Southeast Central area. There a neighborhood planning conference was organized, built around delegates from school and local welfare organizations and then expanded to include representatives from block groups and other neighborhood residents. The chairman of the conference was the director of a settlement house. After many neighborhood meetings, a plan was formulated and presented to the City Planning Commission. As a result, the area was designated for redevelopment, but the professional planners, concluding that the people were unable to do the planning by themselves, rejected most of the recommendations as unsound.

The second attempt, in the East Poplar area, took the opposite tack, with the planners going ahead on their own. When their plan was ready, they got the district office of the Health and Welfare Council to call a meeting of neighborhood leaders, to whom the plan was explained. Before there could be a larger neighborhood meeting, the plan was published in the newspapers, which is how most residents were made aware of it. In other words, there was virtually no resident participation.

The third attempt, which occurred in 1949 and 1950, took a middle ground. The Planning Commission did the planning but regularly consulted with a committee from the neighborhood and took into consideration the members' ideas. This committee was set up by the director of the Health and Welfare Council's district office, and it consisted mainly of business and professional leaders, most of whom worked but did not live in the area.

In 1952, this third approach was the one generally in use. However, there was some dissatisfaction with this method, particularly the fact that city officials were the dominating force. A partial response was the establishment of housing committees in West Philadelphia and North Philadelphia by the Philadelphia Housing Association and the Health and Welfare Council, two United Fund agencies. The other main thrust came from the settlement houses, and one in Germantown in particular succeeded in achieving substantial resident participation in neighborhood planning, thereby affecting the city's renewal plan.

In the mid-1950's discussion of how best to achieve neighborhood involvement came to the fore at the Area Planning Conference, a body formed by 13 public and city-wide civic agencies to share information on their mutual acitivites. After a year's discussion, drafting, and redrafting, the Conference issued its conclusions:

> Whatever [form of urban renewal] treatment is decided upon, the approach to citizen involvement should be based upon

> a carefully developed community organization program. Ideally, there should exist citizen organization within all neighborhoods of the community. . . . Although experimentation is needed, it would seem that the private agency which is skilled in the field of community organization would be best equipped to do this job, providing there is adequate financial support, whether from government or private sources. . . . Preferably, the public agency staff would not engage in community organization, but rather in public information and technical assistance.[1]

The United Fund was unwilling to cut back on services to individuals in order to put more money into community organization, and the only alternative was for public funds to be channeled to private agencies, which would hire professional community organizers (usually social workers). This staff would work under the direction of the typical social agency board consisting of concerned citizens, most of whom did not live in the neighborhoods served.

However, the public agencies chose not to turn over significant funds to private agencies, and for the most part they reserved for themselves whatever community organization work was to be undertaken related to renewal projects. The one exception was a contract that the Redevelopment Land Agency made with the Citizens Council on City Planning to assist in working with residents of Eastwick, a sprawling partially developed area not far from International Airport.

In a study of educational efforts related to urban renewal, I took a look at the resident involvement process and found that two years after the Area Planning Conference had recommended independent community organization, scarcely none was being performed

---

[1] Philadelphia Area Planning Conference, <u>Citizen Participation in Urban Renewal</u>, 1957, p. 3

in connection with the urban renewal program. In a city of 2 million, there were less than 30 privately paid community organizers working with neighborhood groups, and most of them were not active in renewal areas. The Redevelopment Agency had assigned workers to conservation neighborhoods to do a combination of community organization and community relations, the latter being more a matter of selling residents on the agency's program rather than informing citizens about what they could do.

But even with these limitations, Philadelphia was ahead of most other cities, for the vast majority of planning directors and renewal chiefs around the country preferred not to get involved at all with neighborhood residents. One exception, though, was New Haven.

EXTENSIVE RESIDENT INVOLVEMENT: NEW HAVEN (1959-65)

When Richard Lee became mayor of New Haven in 1954, he embarked upon an ambitious urban renewal program. He hired Edward Logue as development administrator and organized the city's most influential leaders into the Citizens Action Commission (CAC), which met in his office.

The previous mayor had established a Redevelopment Agency, which had initiated a clearance project in the Oak Street area, the worst of New Haven's slums, but the planning was slow and unimaginative. Lee and Logue accelerated this process and expanded the project by tying in a major highway connector with the Connecticut Turnpike. As these pieces fell into place, they embarked upon an even bigger effort, the Church Street project, which eventually was to clear four blocks in the very heart of the central business district. Working in characteristic secrecy, Logue and his staff developed a plan and lined up tentative federal support before Lee presented the program publicly, first to the executive committee of the Citizens Action Commission and then at a public luncheon sponsored by CAC.

The third project to be initiated, and the first to achieve resident participation, was Wooster Square, named after an open space in what had been New Haven's first suburb, circa 1820. The fine old homes near and around the square were still structurally sound, but the eastern part of the neighborhood was badly blighted with a mixture of loft factories and tenement houses dating from the post-Civil War period when industrialization came to New Haven. Italian-Americans were the dominant ethnic group in the vicinity of the square, and they tended to be older people; the younger generation had been attracted to the suburbs. In the eastern section, the people were poorer; the ethnic groups, more varied, including a Negro segment. Already the city planning commission and the state highway department had agreed upon an expressway to bisect the Wooster Square neighborhood, and this, combined with the deteriorated conditions, practically foreordained total clearance east of the highway.

A group of residents of the western section had been organized into an improvement committee by a Catholic priest and had succeeded with somewhat superficial clean-up activities. Eventually, Mayor Lee explained to the improvement committee the possibilities of using the rehabilitation provisions of the Housing Act of 1954. Acting under this stimulus, they petitioned the city to initiate a renewal program and renamed themselves the Wooster Square Neighborhood Renewal Committee. All of the members were Italian except a neighborhood Episcopalian minister; no residents of the future clearance area were involved.

As plans began to be drawn for the renewal of Wooster Square, Logue hired Mary Small, who had been employed by Philadelphia's Citizens Council on City Planning, and assigned her to work with the Wooster Square committee. In this process, the planners gathered facts and prepared tentative plans, and the citizens committee reacted to these proposals. They also registered complaints about various aspects of municipal services, with Miss Small serving as liaison with the appropriate departments. By the time the plan was ready for public unveiling in mid-1958, the Wooster Square committee had met 62 times over the course of three years, and at the public hearing, they gave enthusiastic support. When federal funds became available, the chairman of the committee, a former alderman, was hired by the Redevelopment Agency as a "neighborhood representative."

The Dixwell Project was the next renewal program initiated. The planning process was similar to that followed in Wooster Square, with the planners proposing and the residents' committee disposing. Dixwell is the oldest center of black population in New Haven, and although a number of neighborhood organizations were available, none seemed suitable to the needs of the Redevelopment Agency, and a new committee was formed by city staff. This time funds were available from the beginning to hire a neighborhood resident for liaison work, and he and the project director proceeded to meet with the committee to review the planners' proposals. Throughout, control of this process was in the hands of City Hall.

After Community Progress, Inc. was organized in 1962 (see Chapter 1), the Redevelopment Agency contracted with it to provide neighborhood workers in urban renewal areas to assist with neighborhood organization activities and to help provide social services. CPI began to provide staff assistance to the rudimentary organizations in three "middle ground" neighborhoods. One of these, the Dwight Neighborhood Improvement Association, eventually participated in the planning of an urban renewal project by responding to plans prepared by the Redevelopment Agency and City Planning Commission. Although CPI had staff in Wooster Square and Dixwell, the Redevelopment Agency continued to play the dominant role in dealing with neighborhood renewal committees. Thus, the addition of CPI broadened the base of staff assistance to neighborhood groups, but it did not alter the fundamental style of city officials proposing and citizens reacting. Nonetheless, at that time neighborhood residents had a larger role in renewal planning in New Haven than in almost any other city in the country.

HUNTERS POINT, SAN FRANCISCO

During the 1960's San Francisco was engaged in an urban renewal program noted for the professional competence of its staff and the excellence of building design and choice of sites of redevelopment areas. In the early 1960's, the approach to citizen participation by the San Francisco Redevelopment Agency was fairly ordinary, relying mainly on advisory relationships with existing organizations in renewal areas. But beginning in 1966, it entered into what its staff calls a "collaborative planning" relationship with residents of one urban renewal project. Simultaneously, another group in the same area, assisted by OEO funds, was engaged in what its consultant refers to as "advocacy planning," which is quite a different style. These two approaches were carried out in a section called Hunters Point.

Located four miles south of downtown San Francisco, Hunters Point is a hilly peninsula projecting into the bay. The lower flatland has long been developed in houses, industry, and a naval shipyard. When the shipyard expanded during World War II, "temporary" housing for war workers was built up the hillsides and along the ridge of the peninsula. In 1948, the San Francisco Housing Authority took possession of the housing project, described at the time as "almost unlivable,"[2] with the understanding that the units would be demolished within six years. However, the Federal Government gave one extension in 1954 and another in 1961, even though deterioration continued. By the 1960's, some buildings were so bad that demolition could no longer be avoided, and by 1967 only 800 units remained of the original 1,850.

For many years, the Hunters Point project was racially integrated. In the early 1960's, however, poor black families were displaced from the Western Addition urban renewal project, which is near the central business district, at a time when the city was providing no new low-income housing. Many moved to Hunters Point, and project occupancy became almost all black.

Over the years, the citizens of Hunters Point have formed numerous organizations. For example, the Crispus Attucks Club, named after the first black man to die in the American Revolution, was started in the late 1940's to combat de facto segregation. This club in turn founded the Bayview Community Center in 1956 as a locus for community activity. In 1961, the Bayview Citizens Committee was organized to resist evictions by the housing authority, which wanted to begin demolition, on the grounds that alternative housing was not being provided. In 1968, there were more than 50 civic and social organizations in the area.

---

[2]San Francisco Redevelopment Agency, <u>1967-68 Annual Report</u>, p. 12.

During the past two decades, the Hunters Point-Bayview area has had the social characteristics of other low-income areas, with high rates of unemployment, juvenile delinquency, and dependency. In 1961, the Ford Foundation gave a grant to the San Francisco Committee on Youth, a body appointed by the mayor and chaired by the YMCA director, to conduct a youth development program in the housing project: two years later, the California State Employment Service opened a youth opportunity center there. When the "war on poverty" came to San Francisco, Hunters Point-Bayview was one of five "target" areas selected by the local Economic Opportunity Council. After a power struggle in which residents of the poor neighborhoods wrested control of the community action program away from City Hall, the target area boards, including the Hunters Point-Bayview Area Planning Board, gained the authority to determine program priorities for their neighborhoods and to control the hiring of neighborhood staff (who were, however, on the central payroll). This arrangement was put into effect in September, 1965.

Collaborative Planning

There had been serious discussion about making Hunters Point into an urban renewal project since 1962, when the Board of Supervisors of the city and county of San Francisco passed a resolution instructing the Redevelopment Agency to explore "the possibility of the use of the Hunters Point area for housing substantially in the moderate-priced private housing brackets."[3] Fearing the displacement of occupants without an enlarged supply of low-income housing and wanting to avoid the lack of effective citizen participation that had characterized the first part of the Western Addition project, the Hunters Point-Bayview Area Planning Board on December 28, 1965, designated itself

> as the official body to deal with the Redevelopment Agency in the planning and execution of all projects proposed for this area; reserving the right to designate

---

[3]Resolution 236-62, adopted by Board of Supervisors of the City and County of San Francisco at meeting of April 23, 1962.

> another body for that purpose
> should the Area Board see this as
> the most feasible plan.[4]

The board wrote to the Redevelopment Agency asking it to endorse this self-designation, and two weeks later the Agency gave an affirmative response. After further discussion and local organizing efforts, the Bayview-Hunters Point Joint Housing Committee was formed in July, 1966, to be the official vehicle for resident participation. This new committee started with 15 members, drawn mainly from the area board; a year later, it claimed 125 members, representing 43 local organizations.

One of the first tasks undertaken by the Joint Housing Committee was to review a survey questionnaire developed by a research firm hired by the Redevelopment Agency; 12 residents were hired by the firm to do house-to-house interviewing. In the fall, the Redevelopment Agency brought the committee into the process of selecting the prime consultant, who would prepare the master plan for the entire project. Committee members and agency staff jointly interviewed representatives of the 16 firms that applied for consideration and together narrowed the number to 6. After further give-and-take between the residents and staff, the Redevelopment Agency hired Aaron G. Green, a San Francisco architect and one-time associate of Frank Lloyd Wright. Subsequently, committee members have participated in picking sub-contractors to prepare special technical studies, such as engineering, social studies, housing feasibility, land economics, and landscape architecture, and also in selecting architects for the first phase of housing construction.

During the next year and a half, members of the Joint Housing Committee met frequently, usually once a week, with the planning consultant, often working through an executive committee and subcommittees on education, health, housing, contract review, and other neighborhood concerns. Attendance at these meetings ranged from poor to good, being largest when some key issue reached a crisis stage. All

---

[4]Letter from Mrs. Bertha Freeman, acting chairman, Hunters Point-Bayview Area Planning Board, to Mr. Justin Herman, executive director, San Francisco Redevelopment Agency, December 30, 1965.

staff work for the committee and subcommittees was handled by the Redevelopment Agency; the committee had no staff of its own. The meetings were held in a neighborhood office established by the Redevelopment Agency, but the consultant did most of his work in a downtown office. As the plan emerged and began to be translated into an application for federal funds, committee members reviewed the various items that were to be included in the application. When the plan was completed and the application ready, the Joint Housing Committee gave its support at public hearings and in a letter to the Department of Housing and Urban Development.

During this same period, planning was initiated for a nearby industrial redevelopment project in an area known as Butchertown. The Joint Housing Committee joined the Chamber of Commerce in supporting the request for federal planning funds and in advising the planners. When completed, this project will provide new employment opportunities, a major need of the Hunters Point-Bayview community.

The planning process itself created several new jobs. The Redevelopment Agency hired four persons from the project area for its site office, an engineering consultant employed a neighborhood youth as a draftsman trainee, and other residents were hired by consultants to do part-time survey work. However, most of the residents who spent long hours at committee meetings were not paid. Finally in April, 1968, the San Francisco Foundation put up $10,000 to be used by the Joint Housing Committee to reimburse members for carfare, babysitters, and incidental expenses and to permit them to go to conferences. However, the funds were not administered by the committee directly, but by the San Francisco Planning and Urban Renewal Association, a city-wide civic agency.

M. Justin Herman, executive director of the San Francisco Redevelopment Agency, refers to the process that occurred in Hunters Point-Bayview as "collaborative planning." In his view, "the most important feature of the relationship is an attitude of trust on both sides."[5] Some local critics say that he has

---

[5]M. Justin Herman, "Citizen Partnership with Renewal Bureaucrats is the Order of the Day," Journal of Housing, No. 1, 1968, p. 28.

the Joint Housing Committee "in his pocket," but individuals who have provided civic leadership in the project area over many years are generally satisfied with the relationship and believe that they have had an honest and important role in shaping the plan. It happened that the goals of the Redevelopment Agency and the goals of the citizen leaders were similar, so details could be worked out within a mutual framework.

Advocacy Planning

Interestingly, another style of citizen participation planning was occurring at the same time and place. Known as "advocacy planning," it is a style proposed by some of the younger generation of professional city planners. It is founded upon the premise that many planning decisions are the expression of values and interests of certain groups and that therefore planning policy is never wholly objective. Therefore, each interest group should have its own planning advocate to give it the necessary technical competence to participate in the decision-making process. One view of advocacy planning was stated by Paul Davidoff:

> The planner as advocate would plead for his own and his client's view of the good society. The advocate planner would be more than a provider of information, an analyst of current trends, a simulator of future conditions, and a detailer of means. In addition to carrying out these necessary parts of planning, he would be a proponent of specific substantive solutions.[6]

Another view has been expressed by Marshall Kaplan, who described the role of the planning advocate as follows:

> His role is to defend or prosecute the interests of his clients when he and they together think that

---

[6] Paul Davidoff, "Advocacy and Pluralism in Planning," Journal of the American Institute of Planners, Vol. XXXI, No. 4 (November, 1965), p. 333.

> they need prosecution and/or defense. Rather than linking the law to objectives, the planning advocate links resource and strategy alternatives to objectives. He joins issues at the request of his client when the facts interpreted by others overlook, minimize, and/or negatively affect his client's interests.[7]

Kaplan wrote this description in 1968 after he had served as a professional planning advocate with another neighborhood group in Hunters Point, the Community Non-Profit Development Corporation. This group was created in August, 1965, by the Hunters Point-Bayview Area Planning Board, which later also organized the Joint Housing Committee. The fundamental purpose of the corporation, as stated in its articles of incorporation, was to provide low- and moderate-income housing for rent and sale. As a membership corporation ($1 a year dues), it signed up nearly 600 residents during its first year. These members elect the 15-man board of directors. It has had mostly male leadership in contrast to the predominantly matriarchal Joint Housing Committee.

In August, 1966, the corporation received a $98,000 grant from the San Francisco Economic Opportunity Council to pay for a small staff and to hire planning consultants. This occurred as the Joint Housing Committee was helping to screen applicants to be the Redevelopment Agency's prime consultant. Consultants for both would be paid from federal funds, those of the Redevelopment Agency coming from HUD and those of the Non-Profit Development Corporation from OEO.

In the next few months, the corporation hired and discharged two planning consultants (both black), apparently because of inharmonious relations. Then in February, 1967, it contracted with the firm of Marshall Kaplan, Gans and Kahn to conduct surveys, to analyze plans developed by the Redevelopment Agency and its consultants, and to propose alternative

---

[7]Marshall Kaplan, "Advocacy and Urban Planning," <u>The Social Welfare Forum, 1968,</u> ed. by National Conference on Social Welfare Staff (New York: Columbia University Press, 1968), p. 64.

courses of action. This firm had entered the competition to be the prime consultant to the Redevelopment Agency for the Hunters Point-Bayview urban renewal project and had been among the six finalists, but it lost out when the contract was awarded to Aaron Green in November, 1966.

Kaplan's staff conducted several surveys, using residents as volunteers in some instances. One of the first reports produced related to the desire of area residents to get improvements in some housing units owned and operated by the Housing Authority, and likely to remain so. This report provided back-up support for a campaign being led by the Tenants Union, another local group, and helped get a commitment of $500,000 from the Housing Authority for housing rehabilitation.

In August, 1967, Kaplan submitted a report calling for immediate construction of new housing on ten acres of mostly vacant land that would be split off from the 125-acre urban renewal project. This was a direct challenge to the Redevelopment Agency, whose plan was not yet ready. Soon a public verbal battle raged between the corporation and the Redevelopment Agency and more directly between Marshall Kaplan and Justin Herman.

In rebuttal, the Redevelopment Agency issued a comparison between the Kaplan proposal and its own uncompleted plan. The Agency stressed the need for a master plan of development so that street layout and sewer locations in the entire ridge area could be redesigned as a whole. Moreover, the Agency argued that splitting off ten acres from the urban renewal project would mean that the housing development would have to absorb the cost of streets, utilities, lighting, drainage, and other site improvements (leading to higher rents) instead of having them paid for as part of the federally aided renewal project.

Nonetheless, Kaplan's proposal was endorsed by the Joint Housing Committee, which was the Redevelopment Agency's collaborative planning partner. It was also supported by black leaders in San Francisco and by the major black newspaper. Finally, as a compromise the Redevelopment Agency agreed to provide five to ten acres of land to the Non-Profit Development Corporation as soon as feasible, so that it could become a housing sponsor.

During the heated debate on the merits of the alternative proposals, Kaplan, as a planning advocate, tended to become a public spokesman for the residents, not merely their professional advisor. As his advocacy took this form, some of the corporation board became dissatisfied with his role, and after a while he was discharged.

When I visited Hunter Point-Bayview in the fall of 1968, the Community Non-Profit Development Corporation was by then a fairly weak organization, unstable internally and quite uncertain as to its future. In contrast, the Joint Housing Committee was stronger and more vigorous. Yet, while the members of the latter had criticisms of the corporation, they felt that at least it belonged to the community and that with its own funds for consultants it had a kind of independence which they lacked. They did not want a professional advocate, but they could see the advantage of having funds of their own to hire staff and consultants and thereby enhance their role in collaborative planning.

Collaborative planning in San Francisco is reminiscent of the style of neighborhood participation used in New Haven. The main difference is that San Francisco used planning consultants and let the residents help select them, whereas New Haven relied upon staff planners, whom residents did not choose. But the fundamental relationship is the same in both cities: the agency planners originating most of the proposals, the residents responding. In neither place have residents had the technical capacity to take the initiative.

EQUAL-BARGAINING PLANNING IN WASHINGTON, D.C.

While the two styles of collaborative planning and advocacy planning were competing at Hunters Point, San Francisco, a third approach to neighborhood participation in urban renewal planning was under way in the nation's capital. For lack of a better name, it will be called "equal-bargaining planning." The residents had a measure of equality with the official agencies because they had political influence and independent professional competence--in other words, power and knowledge.

Actually, this was not the first time this style was used in urban renewal planning, for this has been the way institutions and business interest in a number of cities have dealt with redevelopment agencies. For example, Michael Reese Hospital in Chicago, Case Institute and Western Reserve University in Cleveland, and Downtown Progress, a businessmen's organization in Washington have hired their own planners to provide technical support for the political influence they already possessed. But in Washington, for the first time, residents of a poor area adopted this approach and received federal financial assistance for their endeavor.

In Washington, equal-bargaining planning occurred in the Shaw urban renewal area. The project got its name from an archaic junior high school in the area, which citizens and school officials have long tried to have replaced, only to be thwarted by the Congress of the United States, which has ultimate control over the internal affairs of the District of Columbia. The area also has thousands of deteriorating housing units badly in need of rehabilitation and quite a number of dwellings beyond repair. Indeed, the housing conditions provided the impetus for the project.

The principal initiator of the Shaw project was Rev. Walter Fauntroy, who was born in the neighborhood in 1933 and whose parents were natives of Washington. When he graduated from the Yale Divinity School, he became pastor of the New Bethel Baptist Church in the Shaw area and has served there ever since. He is the director of the D.C. branch of the Southern Christian Leadership Conference, served for 18 months as vice-chairman of the City Council, is active in the Black United Front, and is one of the few black leaders in the city who has the respect of militant blacks as well as establishment whites.

As new housing laws emerged from Congress during the 1960's, Fauntroy began to examine how his church and other civic groups might sponsor new and rehabilitated low-rent housing. Early exploration found that speculators were keeping housing and land prices so high that civic groups could not carry out an economically feasible housing project without some form of public assistance.

In 1966, Fauntroy approached John Duncan, one of the three District Commissioners (and the only black one). Duncan in turn referred him to Walter Washington, executive director of the Housing Authority. Although Washington had no applicable program, he arranged a meeting with Thomas Appleby, executive director of the Redevelopment Land Agency, and they discussed the possibility of an urban renewal project, which could provide assembled land at a reduced price and would allow a tie-in with special financing arrangements of the Federal Housing Administration (FHA). At first, Fauntroy was reluctant; urban renewal had a bad name in Washington because of the Southwest Project, which had displaced thousands of poor black families without providing a single unit of low-rent housing in the redevelopment area. Nonetheless, he entered into discussions with RLA staff.

Appleby's first major tasks as director of the RLA had been to speed the development of the still uncompleted Southwest Project and move the Northwest 1 project into execution with a schedule that would minimize dislocation while new housing was being built in the project area. After spending about a year to get on top of these two projects, he was ready to expand the renewal program; the next logical area was adjacent to Northwest 1, that is, the Shaw area. He was trying to figure out how to get citizen support when Fauntroy came along.

Fauntroy's group included several professional and business leaders from the black community, and they used their know-how and influence to gain support for a Shaw project from the District Commissioners, the RLA board, and the National Capital Planning Commission (NCPC), the three agencies whose assent is required. As this was happening, the citizen leaders formed a new private nonprofit corporation called the Model Inner City Community Organization, Inc. When the local and federal agencies completed their review and gave approval to the Shaw project early in 1967, MICCO negotiated a contract with the RLA to obtain a formal role in project planning and to get a share of the planning funds.

This contract, signed in March, 1967, gave MICCO $276,000 to serve as a broad-based and representative organization for citizen participation in renewal planning, to participate in developing physical planning concepts and proposals, and to be involved in social and economic studies and in other surveys required by federal urban renewal procedures. At the same time, the RLA entered into an $88,000 contract with an organization called Uptown Progress to achieve business participation in urban renewal planning.

The MICCO leaders, though, had not waited for the contract to move into action. They could not afford to, for the Board of Education was proceeding to select a site for the new Shaw junior high school, and the choice would be a key feature of the renewal plan. With a school board hearing scheduled for the end of March, MICCO stimulated neighborhood discussion of proposed sites and in the six weeks before the hearing held 25 meetings with Shaw area organizations and citizens. When the school board held its hearing, about 700 citizens were in the audience and 40 testified. This was followed by three months of negotiations and more neighborhood meetings, which by the end of June led to the adoption of a modified school site and a commitment to build relocation housing before the site was cleared. As these steps were taken MICCO played the principal public role, but in the background the RLA staff were deeply involved, providing technical assistance and feeding in their own planning ideas.

In mobilizing the neighborhood for the school site discussions, MICCO had identified about 300 organizations in the Shaw area. Upon approval of the RLA contract, MICCO went about signing up these organizations, and within four months 150 had affiliated with MICCO. This was important, for MICCO had been set up by a fairly small group of community leaders, mostly middle-class professionals. As they were negotiating the contract with RLA, other groups in the Shaw area, such as some of the citizens advisory committees of UPO, Washington's community action agency, contested its claim to speak for the neighborhood. As a result, the RLA wanted assurance that MICCO had a broad base of support and participation. The board was enlarged from 12 to 49, with seats assigned to the following interests: UPO neighborhood committees (10), civic associations (9), community service organizations (5), parent-teacher associations (5), business and professional groups (5), churches and church alliances (5), fraternal organizations (5), resource people (3), and labor organizations (2). A year later, six more board members were added to provide representation for youth groups (5) and unaffiliated organizations (1). However, much of MICCO's conducted by a 17-man executive committee consisting of the officers and chairmen of ten standing committees.

Besides the question of the school site, one of the first tasks MICCO had to undertake under the RLA contract was to prepare a program development report, which would set forth the general concepts to be followed in preparing a Shaw urban renewal plan. This was done in consultation with other organizations and submitted to the RLA in midsummer of 1967. Then MICCO moved into planning analysis along with the RLA and NCPC planning staffs, for this was a joint venture, not the solo work of a single agency. Together the agencies performed the standard surveys of land use, building type, housing conditions, transportation, community facilites, and social conditions. For the field surveys, neighborhood residents were hired by the agencies and their consultants.

In the fall of 1967, when the District government was reorganized by presidential decree with a mayor (Walter Washington) and City Council appointed by the President, Rev. Fauntroy was chosen to be vice-chairman of the Council. Until that time he had been serving both as president and executive director of MICCO, but his new councilmanic duties made it necessary for him to drop his executive role. MICCO then hired a full-time executive director. Other staff were, of course, already at work, and by the end of the first year under the RLA contract, MICCO had 31 employees: 6 in administration, 13 in planning, and 12 in community organization.

During the last half of 1967, MICCO continued to be involved with the site of the new Shaw junior high school, which had to be approved by the RLA for early land acquisition, by the NCPC and the new City Council, and finally by the Department of Housing and Urban Development. As a result of this significant citizen input, part of the package was a complex staging plan for site clearance, school construction, and the erection of relocation housing. The school site and the planning surveys took most of MICCO's time the first year of its planning contract.

Then on April 5 and 6, 1968, civil disorders raged in the Shaw area and in other sections of Washington following the assassination of Dr. Martin Luther King; business structures in particular were heavily damaged. When the smoke cleared, the District government moved into action. Mayor Washington announced a crash program to have rebuilding plans completed in 100 days. Two or three new groups were formed to ensure that rebuilding would be controlled by blacks. But in the black community, only MICCO had the capacity to develop plans quickly, and immediately its planning work was accelerated.

When half the mayor's 100 days had elapsed, MICCO had ready the draft of a "concept plan" and launched a series of meetings to present it to residents and get their reactions. The proposal called for a mixture of housing types (townhouses, high-rise and garden apartments), employment and business centers (black owned and operated), multipurpose community centers, community schools and an educational park, changes in the planned D.C. subway (a different route and three stops instead of two in the Shaw area), and activity centers at the most popular gathering spots (an entertainment and business center, a cultural center, a medical and education center). Many of these ideas had been proposed by residents at previous meetings, and the concept plan, which put them together, was well received. The package was presented to the mayor in late August.

During the 18 months that MICCO had been engaged in planning, staffs of the RLA and the NCPC had also been working on plans for the Shaw area. Although the three sets of planners were in regular communication with each other, they worked in different offices and had somewhat different ideas. Thus, in the fall of 1968, it was necessary to combine their work into a unified plan. There were a number of bargaining sessions attended by Appleby of the RLA; Charles Conrad, executive director of NCPC; Fauntroy and Reginald Griffith, the chief planner for MICCO; and other members of the agencies' staffs. There was give-and-take on details, but MICCO's basic concepts were substantially retained in the final Shaw urban renewal plan.

In January, 1969, the plan was ready for submission to the three boards that must approve it: RLA, NCPC, and the City Council. The City Council held two nights of public hearings, one in the District Building and one in the old Shaw junior high school. There was some objection to a few details, but for the most part the plan gained wide support from neighborhood organizations and citizens. Two days after the City Council gave its endorsement, HUD--pushed by President Nixon who wanted to make a quick impact on the capital--approved the plan and authorized funds for the first year of its implementation.

Was the plan different because of the process through which it was prepared? The answer can be only speculative. MICCO employed professional planners, as did the RLA and NCPC, all trained in the same general tradition and all working within the framework of the same federal program, and the product of their thinking was not sharply different. However, MICCO's questionnaires, neighborhood meetings, and office location within the project area sharpened its planners' sensitivity to residents' needs and wishes and the pattern of community life. Among other matters, this heightened perception was expressed in the proposals for rerouting the subway and for establishing activity centers. Competent planners working downtown might have come up with the same ideas, but neighborhood involvement ensured that such features would be developed.

Perhaps the most important result is that an urban renewal plan was widely accepted in a black neighborhood which two years earlier was highly suspicious of the program. In this case, residents perceived the Shaw renewal plan as their own, not as one developed by others and sold to them through a public relations effort. Even if an outside plan had all the same features and displaced no more people, it might have been resisted merely because it was prepared on the outside. In other words, attitudes as well as plan substances are ingredients in neighborhood acceptance.

MICCO had concentrated on physical planning, and in the neighborhood there has been basic support for its work in that field. It has also had a secondary interest in social problems, but on that topic the same harmony has not prevailed. From the beginning, there has been friction between MICCO and UPO with its Neighborhood Development Centers 1 and 2, located in the Shaw area. Giving the UPO groups spots on the MICCO board helped some, but board membership has not always stopped public criticism. Then UPO established the People's Involvement Corporation to operate a pilot neighborhood center in the same area, and (as related in Chapter 7) from the beginning PIC and MICCO have perceived one another as rivals. Then Model Cities came along with the possibility of developing programs of both physical and social improvement, and this has confused matters further.

Similar confusion exists in the field of economic development. Since its inception, MICCO has had an interest in economic development. It joined with Fairchild-Hiller (an industrial corporation) to form Fairmicco, Inc., which manufactures ammunition boxes, wooden platforms, and radio cables under government contract and employs about 60 persons, drawn mostly from the hard-core unemployed. It has also organized a subsidiary, called the Model Inner City Development Corporation, to undertake various projects. But Mayor Washington has also set up a development corporation, and other black groups in the Shaw area are pushing economic development schemes. Although a pluralistic approach is clearly desirable, there seems to be a surplus of economic development proposals in this part of Washington. Nevertheless, having looked at several of the organizations in the Shaw area, I sense that a sorting out of responsibilities is beginning to occur.

On the matter of physical planning, which has been MICCO's greatest strength, success has occurred for several reasons. First, Rev. Fauntroy and his associates have had considerable political influence throughout the proceedings. They were a force the RLA and NCPC had to reckon with, and Fauntroy's position as vice-chairman of the City Council, while not misused, certainly helped. Second, MICCO was able to sustain sufficient breadth of participation to present a united front and to prevent any sizable opposition bloc within the neighborhood. Third, MICCO had the technical competence to come up with creditable ideas which could not be destroyed by professionals from the public agencies. Fourth, the heads of these agencies, such as Appleby at the RLA, were sympathetic to what MICCO was doing and cooperated willingly rather than erecting obstacles. With these factors present, equal-bargaining planning has worked in Washington's Shaw urban renewal project.

At the beginning of the next round of renewal planning in Washington, however, all of these elements were not present, and heated competition quickly developed among several groups. Rev. Fauntroy was not reappointed to the City Council by President Nixon. When he left his councilmanic post in mid-February, 1969, he announced that he, Reginald Griffith (MICCO's chief planner), and two other black leaders were forming a new consulting firm called Inner City Planning Associates, Inc. Soon the word was out that this firm was to receive a $428,000 contract to put together urban renewal plans in two other business areas damaged by the 1968 riot. As a first step, "community fellows" would be hired from the two areas to conduct neighborhood surveys. The contract would be with the Reconstruction and Development Corporation, which had been set up by Mayor Washington in August, 1968, to spearhead and coordinate reconstruction and to administer a $600,000 grant from the Ford Foundation. RDC had established an office in a trailer in the Shaw area, but it had no full-time staff until December. Consequently, it was slow in getting serious planning under way.

After the new Nixon Administration had approved the Shaw renewal proposal, the White House put pressure on District agencies to speed planning and rebuilding for two other riot-damaged sections, 14th Street, N.W., in Upper Cardozo, and H Street, N.E. In response, RDC staff talked to Fauntroy about undertaking the planning for these two areas.

However, when organizations in these two sections learned what was happening, they protested that residents and established neighborhood agencies were being bypassed. Particularly vocal was CHANGE, Inc., in Upper Cardozo, which was already developing a plan for rebuilding 14th Street, N.W. (see Chapter 3). Other black leaders seemed to be concerned that Fauntroy was getting too big a piece of the action.

Faced with this opposition, RDC backed off, even though a verbal commitment had been made to Fauntroy and a contract was ready to be signed. Instead, RDC took on the planning task itself and hired some of Fauntroy's planners and community fellows to carry it out.

In the Shaw area, MICCO was set up by a few neighborhood leaders, expanded its base of participation when it got the renewal planning contract, and then developed technical competence. In anticipation of planning for Upper Cardozo and the Near Northeast, Inner City Planning Associates had professional

CITIZEN PARTICIPATION IN URBAN RENEWAL 185

ability but not a strong neighborhood base for resident participation, and they immediately ran into difficulties with existing organizations. Know-how coming in this manner proved to be a source of disunity. In this study, we have already seen that know-how and unity must be combined if neighborhood-operated programs are to succeed.

COMMENTARY

None of the cases cited in this chapter represent community control of an urban renewal project. The one that goes the farthest in that direction is the Shaw project in Washington, where MICCO, the residents' corporation, entered into a contract to receive federal renewal planning funds and was able to bargain as an equal partner in making planning decisions.

The HUD officials who run the federal renewal program are not disposed toward repeating the experience of the Shaw project by encouraging other cities to channel planning funds to neighborhood corporations. However, in June, 1968, HUD made a tiny step toward greater resident participation by requiring for the first time that in every new renewal project involving housing rehabilitation there must be a "project area committee" made up of residents of the project area. The new regulation permits the local redevelopment agency to spend project funds so that the agency's staff can provide technical assistance and clerical help to the project area committee, but it does not authorize funds to go to that committee along the lines of the MICCO model. The urban renewal segment of HUD seems to prefer the collaborative planning arrangements of San Francisco and New Haven.

However, collaborative planning is not always possible. It worked out fairly well in the Hunters Point-Bayview project in San Francisco because residents and city officials were in fundamental agreement on the goals for the area: low- and moderate-income housing. But nearer downtown San Francisco, in the Western Addition project, this kind of resident participation is not possible because the residents and the city planners have basically different goals. The residents want to prevent mass dislocation and to preserve the neighborhood as a residential area for lower-income groups, whereas the city planners want some of the land redeveloped for nonresidential uses and conceivably used to construct new housing for upper-income groups.

In New Haven, residents have been brought into the planning process only in rehabilitation areas, not where total clearance and change from residential land use would occur. In fact, I know of no city where residents have had a planning role when the planners and redevelopment officials anticipated substantial displacement. Mayors, civic leaders, planners, and redevelopment executives argue for a city's right to renew itself, while neighborhood leaders, such as those in the Western Addition, insist upon neighborhood determination. This is a difference of values as well as a matter of power. And so far in most cities, overwhelming power has been on the side of city government in determining urban renewal projects. In these cases, the equal-bargaining model is more relevant.

CHAPTER **9** NEIGHBORHOOD CONTROL IN TWO MODEL CITIES

In November, 1966, President Johnson signed a law that created a new form of federal assistance intended

> to assist comprehensive city demonstration programs for rebuilding slum and blighted areas and for providing the public facilities and services necessary to improve the general welfare of the people who live in those areas.[1]

Here was an urban program broader than any ever passed before, in many ways urban renewal and community action wrapped up in one package, plus the potential for education, health, manpower, transportation, and anti-crime programs. If carried out as intended, it would pull together other existing federal programs already serving demonstration neighborhoods. It would do this by giving "supplemental" grants usable for a broad range of activities and awarded partly on the basis of how many other federal aid programs were tied into the package.

The origin of the Demonstration Cities Program seems to have been a thought that massive resources should be poured into one city, or at most three or four, on a trial basis, but political realities prevented such a bonanza for so few places. Thus, the program concept was expanded so that 60 to 70 cities could begin planning demonstration programs the first year, with others to follow later.

---

[1] Demonstration Cities and Metropolitan Development Act of 1966, P.L. 89-754.

It was also conceived in part to provide the new Department of Housing and Urban Development, created the year before, with a major new program for cities. HUD was formed mostly from the Housing and Home Finance Agency, which had been concerned almost exclusively with physical development and housing finance. The Demonstration Cities Program would give HUD a "soft-goods" component.

The Demonstration Cities Program could also be seen as a second-generation Community Action Program, building upon the experience of that controversial program and avoiding some of OEO's mistakes. In as much as demonstration projects would be in the same neighborhoods as CAP, with the possibility of the same program activities, some even thought that the Demonstration Cities Program might take the place of CAP, which was then losing favor at the White House and in Congress. A presidential task force had recommended the transfer of the Community Action Program from OEO to HUD and although President Johnson rejected the idea at the time, Demonstration Cities might prepare HUD to absorb CAP eventually. If this happened, then perhaps the pattern of private nonprofit community action agencies might be replaced by city agencies under the control of the mayor and city council. For under the new law, a city demonstration agency had to be designated by the local governing body of the city or county and had to be a public agency.

By the time the bill passed Congress, the White House had decided that "demonstration cities" sounded too much like social protest. At the bill-signing ceremony the President referred to the program as "model cities," a name that has been used ever since.

HUD had its guidelines ready by January, 1967, and gave cities until May 1 to submit applications for planning funds. Altogether 193 cities responded. HUD was ready to announce the successful applicants in June before the fiscal year ended, but the White House did not allow this on the grounds that Congressmen from districts with rejected applicants might vote against the still-pending Model Cities appropriation for the supplemental grants of the action phase. It was not until November that the first 63 cities were awarded planning grants. Along with a notice of selection, each city was given a "discussion paper," which outlined matters that must be attended to before planning funds would be released. In most cases, the city was required, among other things, to improve its plans for citizen participation.

The Demonstration Cities Act requires that localities provide for "widespread citizen participation." When called upon by Congress to explain what that meant, HUD Secretary Robert Weaver had said:

> The requirement means that the city will be expected to involve area residents in the demonstration in a meaningful way. Since the cooperation and assistance of residents of the program area will be essential to the success of the demonstration program, the city should insure that the needs and desires of local residents are given a hearing, and some workable mechanism for communications between citizens of the area and the demonstration agency is developed. No precise formula for citizen involvement will be imposed. It will be up to the cities themselves to devise appropriate ways in which citizens will participate.[2]

HUD's first guidelines, which came out a few months after the Act was passed, also stressed communications between residents and the official agency and stated that the city demonstration agency "should provide a meaningful role in policy-making to area residents and to the major agencies expected to contribute projects and activities to the program."[3]

In the longer than expected interval between receipt of applications and the announcement of the

---

[2] U.S. Congress, Senate, Committee on Banking and Currency, Subcommittee on Housing, Hearings on Housing Legislation of 1966, 89th Cong., 2nd Sess., Pt. 1, p. 100.

[3] Department of Housing and Urban Development, Improving the Quality of Urban Life, A Program Guide to Model Neighborhoods in Demonstration Cities, December, 1966, p. 11.

planning grants, internal argument broke out within HUD's Model Cities Administration on the means of achieving resident participation. From this debate emerged new guidelines for cities. Among other things, they stated that there must be some form of organizational structure for citizen involvement, that the "leadership of that structure must consist of persons whom neighborhood residents accept as representing their interests," that the structure must have sufficient time to react to proposals and "must have the technical capacity for making knowledgeable decisions," including "some form of professional technical assistance, in a manner agreed to by neighborhood residents."[4] Between these guidelines and the discussion papers, enough questions were raised so that most cities had to revise their policy-making structures and arrange for other ways to enlarge the role of residents of model neighborhoods.

The pattern of City Demonstration Agencies (CDA) that emerged from this revisionary process was described by HUD as follows:

> Most CDA structures include a coalition policy-making group, a central planning group, a central residents' advisory or coordinating group, a technical group, CDA staff, and anywhere from 8 to 15 planning committees or task forces. In most cities, planning task forces (or planning committees) are deliberately heavily weighted with neighborhood people . . . . Most task forces are chaired by city officials, but some are chaired by elected or selected neighborhood residents and others have a neighborhood resident as co-chairman of each task force.[5]

---

[4]Department of Housing and Urban Development, *Citizen Participation,* CDA Letter No. 3, November 30, 1967.

[5]Department of Housing and Urban Development, *Citizen Participation in Model Cities,* Technical Assistance Bulletin No. 3, December, 1968, p. 4.

In my own review, I have found that representatives of the model neighborhood constitute a minority on most CDA boards, and of course the city council has final say on the application for federal funds. In many cases, the CDA provides staff assistance to residents' committees, and in a number of cities OEO has made funds available to community action agencies to provide a somewhat independent source of technical assistance.

However, in about one-sixth of the first-round model cities, residents have gained a much more significant role in planning and determining priorities for the model neighborhood. They have achieved this by obtaining a veto over all program proposals before submission to the city council and by controlling a sizable portion of planning funds so that they can hire their own planners.

Because this is another variation on the theme of community control, I selected two cities--Dayton and Oakland--where this has happened. This chapter relates how neighborhood residents in these cities won major roles in their local Model Cities Programs and what they are doing with the power they gained.

"EQUAL PARTNERSHIP" IN DAYTON, OHIO

Dayton, Ohio, is a city that keeps up with new programs developing in Washington and is prepared to reap new benefits as soon as they are available. In the summer and fall of 1966, Dayton's city manager's office followed closely the progress of the Demonstration Cities Act through Congress, and when passage seemed likely, it began preparations to apply for funds. In order to get an application ready, the City Commission made $5,000 available to the Special Committee on Urban Renewal (SCOUR), a private organization that was the city's official vehicle for resident participation in urban renewal. SCOUR obtained a matching sum from two local foundations and hired a consultant to draft the application. In carrying out his assignment, the consultant worked with city officials and private city-wide agencies.

To the consultant, the most logical section of the city for the Model Cities Program was West Dayton, a predominantly black neighborhood of 42,500 people. When residents of West Dayton learned of this preparatory work, one of their organizations, Moving Ahead Together (MAT), protested the lack of neighborhood involvement and wrote to HUD Secretary Weaver, but apparently was not able to change the drafting process. In January, 1967, the city manager asked the Supporting Council on Preventive Effort (SCOPE), Dayton's community action agency, to endorse the city's application for Model Cities planning funds, as required by federal regulations, but SCOPE refused on the grounds that it had not seen the application and that neighborhood residents were not properly involved. For the next three months, there were other exchanges but no mutual planning that could bring together the city manager's office, SCOPE, and West Dayton residents. However, when the application was submitted to HUD, it contained a proposal that West Dayton residents have three out of nine seats on the Model Cities Planning Committee, with the other six going to representatives from the City Commission, the County, Board of Education, Housing Authority, Chamber of Commerce, and Health and Welfare Planning Council. As further preparation, a City Demonstration Agency was established within the office of city manager, and William Schmidt, as assistant city manager, was appointed director.

By then, it was clear to Schmidt that much more attention must be given to the question of resident involvement. It was also apparent to West Dayton residents that they needed to devise a means for achieving a united front to deal with the Model Cities Program. During the spring, summer, and fall of 1967, numerous meetings were held in West Dayton. Many of these were held by neighborhood residents alone, and Schmidt participated in others. In October, even before HUD approved Dayton's application, Schmidt established the CDA office in West Dayton, the first municipal unit to be located there.

For their part, the residents decided that they needed a new organization as their vehicle for participation in the Model Cities Program. A decade earlier, the West Dayton Area Council had been the most vital neighborhood group, and although it was sponsoring a multiservice center under the Community Action Program, it had become too middle-class and staid to represent the neighborhood in Model Cities planning. MAT, the militant organization that had challenged the city's initial Model Cities application, had gone out of existence. Consequently, the West Dayton residents first formed an ad hoc committee and then decided to incorporate as the Model Cities Planning Council. They began preparing for an election in March, 1968, to choose the first governing board of the new corporation.

At the same time, HUD notified Dayton that it had been awarded a Model Cities planning grant and sent along the discussion paper on matters to be resolved before the planning funds would be released. One of these items was the need to clarify the role of neighborhood residents. The ad hoc committee and Schmidt had, of course, been working on this issue. They seemed to have established a close working relationship and were moving toward a joint approach to Model Cities planning.

Then, early in March, the city manager submitted an application to the U.S. Department of Labor for funds to plan a Concentrated Employment Program, which would also encompass West Dayton. He did not formally clear this in advance with the ad hoc committee, and when they learned of it they charged the city with breach of faith. The next day a prolonged meeting was held between the City Commission and the leaders of the ad hoc committee. They hammered out an agreement, enacted five days later by the Commission in the form of a resolution, which declared that the Model Cities Planning Council "shall be a full partner in all programs, decisions and planning related to the target area and the decisions of the Planning Council shall at all times be given full consideration in all decisions made by the Commission affecting the welfare of the target area residents."[6]

With this matter resolved, the Planning Council held its election with 24 per cent of the 13,000 eligible voters in the Model Cities area participating--one of the largest turnouts in neighborhood elections under the Model Cities and Community Action Programs. For the election, the half of West Dayton under the Model Cities Program was divided into 27

---

[6]Quoted in Model Cities: Dayton (Dayton, Ohio: Model Cities Planning Council, March, 1968), unpaged.

sub-areas, and one representative was elected from each of these. The newly elected council members chose Roger Prear, former head of the ad hoc committee, as chairman.

The resolution of the issue of resident participation also led to the release of planning funds by HUD. Thereupon, the city of Dayton made $50,000 of these funds available to the Planning Council (and later an additional $19,000), and SCOPE, the local community action agency, provided $23,000 more from OEO funds. With these funds, the Planning Council hired a staff headed by Floyd Johnson, who had been a leading initiator of negotiations with the city a year earlier. Other staff included technical specialists and neighborhood aides. In addition, the residents were able to benefit from the services of several consultants hired by the CDA and staff assigned by other public and private agencies. Altogether, the Planning Council controlled, or was a major influence on, the spending of about 40 per cent of the planning funds.

The Planning Council divided into seven subcommittees to help develop the Model Cities plan: education, employment, crime and juvenile delinquency, health, parks and recreation, physical development, and social services and income maintenance. The subcommittees had the services of the council's consultants and technical staff, along with those from the CDA and other public and private agencies. In several instances, the city gave Model Cities planning funds to an agency, which hired a consultant, who in turn worked with (and almost for) the residents' committee. For example, the Board of Education designated as an education consultant a militant black who was vice-principal of a neighborhood school and assigned him to the neighborhood, and the Health and Welfare Planning Council did the same with a health consultant.

Model Cities planning funds were also used to enlarge the city's CDA staff working under Schmidt. This staff worked closely with the Planning Council and helped to develop a Dayton Model Cities plan. As it turned out, major city-wide agencies and metropolitan civic leaders played a relatively small role in planning (contrary to what usually happens), for the Planning Council insisted upon being the dominant citizen force. In fact, the council members acted as the exclusive representative of the neighborhood and once elected tended to provide relatively little involvement of other residents in the planning process.

This planning activity produced three documents required by HUD: Part I--statement of problems and goals; Part II--five-year plan; Part III--first-year program and request for Model Cities supplemental grant. Starting in November, 1968, each part was approved first by the Model Cities Planning Council and then by the City Commission. All three were ready for submission to HUD in February, 1969.

The difference made by this extensive resident participation in the planning process is evident on the very first page of the Part I submission:

> The over-riding problem of racial discrimination, with its many specific manifestations, is the dominant restrictive theme throughout all aspects of community life in the Model Neighborhood. Consequently, it serves to provide the focus from which the Planning Council subcommittees examined and expressed the problems of their specific component areas.[7]

It is highly unlikely that such a statement would have emerged in the conventional planning process dominated by city officials, city-wide agencies, and civic leaders.

The report points to five ways in which racial discrimination is manifested: exclusion, inadequate services, inadequate income, lack of access to services, and lack of choice. Programs were then designed to respond to these expressions of the problem. Most of the proposed new services are familiar: community schools, youth leadership training, manpower, "jobs not jail," housing development, pre-school program, comprehensive health center, mass transportation study. The difference is more in the administrative structure.

---

[7] Dayton City Demonstration Agency, Model Cities Application, Part I, February, 1969, p. 1.

For the first year of the action program, Dayton plans to continue the "equal partnership" arrangement, which was negotiated in the spring of 1968. The City Commission will have "final program responsibility" (this is required by federal law) and will approve and monitor all programs. The Model City Planning Council will also approve all programs and through its committees will monitor operations. The City Commission will be assisted by the staff of CDA (part of the city manager's office), which will be the "administrative and coordinative body." The resident-controlled Planning Council will also have a small staff but will not operate programs directly.

Program operations will be carried out either by existing public and private agencies, such as the Board of Education, the Health Department, and so on, or by new satellite corporations, including one to run a multiservice community center and another to be organized as a not-for-profit housing corporation. These new corporations will provide broader participation for neighborhood residents. For example, the proposed board of directors of the community center will have 36 members: 10 from participating agencies, 2 appointed by the city manager, 12 from the Planning Council, and 12 residents or citizens at large from Greater Dayton, who will be designated by the Planning Council. The housing development corporation, according to the proposal, will be run by members of the Planning Council and the "black community in general." Each community school will have an advisory council consisting of six parents, the principal, the community school director, two teachers, and, in the case of the high school, one student.

In other words, broader and more diverse resident participation will be used in Dayton to overcome the problem of exclusion, and a broad array of programs will deal with inadequate services, income, and choice.

POWER STRUGGLE IN OAKLAND, CALIFORNIA

Oakland, California, like Dayton, made an early start to obtain Model Cities planning funds, but in Oakland it took the city government and the citizens of the model neighborhood much longer to resolve the battle for control, and the struggle was much more intense.

Oakland was the first city to receive a grant under the Ford Foundation's Gray Area Program in December, 1961. Known as the Interagency Project, it was hatched by the city manager, who presided over an executive committee composed of agency officials. There were five advisory committees, one composed of citizens and four of technicians (research, program directors, and so on). Funds were placed in a special trust fund, ultimately under the control of the City Council.

When the Economic Opportunity Act was passed in 1964, the Oakland Interagency Project was transformed into the local version of the Community Action Program. The staff was reconstituted as the Department of Human Resources within the city government, which controlled the funds, and the citizens advisory committee was the nucleus for forming the Oakland Economic Development Council (OEDC), the CAP governing board. At first, five Target Area Advisory Committees (TAAC) chose 10 members of the 36-man council and the mayor appointed the other 26, but after prolonged contention the TAAC's in January, 1967, forced a change that gave them 20 seats on a 39-man board. Although neighborhood residents thus gained control of OEDC, the staff remained on the city payroll, and this bifurcated structure became a source of further tension. During 1967, OEDC incorporated; in January, 1968, the staff transferred to the new private non-profit agency, and the community action program was no longer controlled by City Hall. When the Green Amendment came along, the neighborhoods retained their 20 seats, the mayor's appointees were reduced to 13 (the required one-third), and private city-wide interests were given the other 6.

About halfway through this struggle for control of the Oakland community action program, the Model Cities Program was conceived. In February, 1966, the Oakland Redevelopment Agency had contracted with planning consultant Marshall Kaplan to examine the various federal programs operating in the city. The study quickly showed a proliferation of programs and the need for better coordination. By mid-year, the Model Cities legislation was moving through Congress, and the Kaplan study became the basis for advance

preparations for an Oakland application. After the
new legislation was signed by the President in November, the city manager appointed a task force of
12 public officials and retained Kaplan's consultative services. Although the task force included the
head of the Department of Human Resources, who served
as executive director of OEDC, it had no citizen
representation. This was a sore point, because just
as the neighborhoods were about to gain control of
OEDC, the city was starting another new program without <u>any</u> citizen involvement. Not until the application for planning funds was almost ready for
submission (April, 1967) were two citizens added to
the task force--one each from North Oakland and West
Oakland--the two areas then under consideration for
Model Cities.

While the citizens had no meaningful involvement in its preparation, the application did propose
a means for citizen participation in subsequent Model
Cities planning. Funds would go through OEDC to the
West Oakland Target Area Advisory Committee and then
to a model neighborhood committee, which would hire
it own staff and consultants--somewhat on the order
of the advocacy planning arrangement that Kaplan was
then engaged in at Hunters Point, San Francisco (see
Chapter 8). However, real control would be in the
hands of the city manager, who would decide which
program proposals would go to the City Council for
its approval, which is the customary operating procedure in Oakland municipal government. The citizens
of West Oakland were not satisfied with this proposed
structural arrangement, and, at about the same time
that the city submitted its request for planning
funds to HUD, West Oakland residents sent letters to
HUD protesting their lack of participation.

Six months later, HUD informed Oakland that its
application had been approved and sent the discussion
paper of items, including resident participation,
that must be clarified before planning funds would be
released. By then, West Oakland had been picked for
the site of the Model Cities Program, and a few days
after Thanksgiving, 1967, city officials and West
Oakland residents had the first of many meetings on
the role of citizens in the planning process. The
next day, a mass meeting was held in West Oakland
under the aegis of OEDC. At this meeting, the residents' demands came into focus--the Model Cities Program should be controlled by black people for the

benefit of black people, and there should be a neighborhood planning committee answerable only to the City Council. A week later, the West Oakland Planning Committee (WOPC) was formed, consisting of persons elected by delegates from about 70 neighborhood groups which attended the organizational meeting. A decision was made not to use the West Oakland TAAC, the existing neighborhood committee of OEDC, as the vehicle, apparently because it was too ingrown and unrepresentative. But Ralph Williams, who had been chairman of the TAAC, became the chairman of WOPC. By then, OEDC had assigned one of its staff, Paul Cobb, to work full-time on this issue, and OEDC's executive director, Percy Moore, was active in West Oakland as well as on the city manager's task force.

By the end of December, it was clear to the mayor and city manager that WOPC was demanding not merely participation but full control, subject only to the action of the City Council, for which federal law provides no alternative. In January, 1968, the city manager offered to give West Oakland residents majority membership on a "Model Cities steering committee" and equal representation on a committee to select the Model Cities director, who would be a city employee. But he was unwilling to relinquish his traditional role of being the sole channel for transmitting proposals to the City Council. WOPC rejected this because they wanted to deal directly with the City Council.

More meetings, more exchanges followed until, on March 15, HUD gave Oakland a third and "final" extension of a deadline to answer the discussion paper within 30 days or lose its eligibility to receive first-round planning funds. About that time, two points were settled--the neighborhood would have a 51 per cent majority on all committees involving neighborhood residents, city officials, and representatives of city-wide organizations; and the neighborhood could veto any unacceptable project proposals. For a while, it seemed that WOPC and the city's task force had agreed to assign $92,000 of the $201,000 planning grant to WOPC to hire staff and consultants, but the city manager balked on the grounds that although $92,000 had been listed in the original application, the total had then been $480,000; therefore, unless other federal funds could be obtained, WOPC's share should be scaled down to reflect the smaller total approved by HUD.

When WOPC refused to accept a reduction in its share of planning funds, it also formally raised a brand new issue--that it should have a veto not only over projects funded as "supplemental" Model Cities grants but also over all other federal projects in model neighborhoods, regardless of the source of funding. This matter was discussed at a WOPC-City Council negotiating session held just before HUD's April 15 deadline. Although that issue was not resolved then, the meeting did produce an agreement to provide a neighborhood majority on joint committees, to have the city and WOPC each appoint three members to the committee to select the Model Cities director, to give WOPC the $92,000 demanded, and to have WOPC's proposals go directly to the City Council.

WOPC had won a large measure of control. There would be various study committees on which West Oakland residents would have a 51 per cent majority. Proposals from these committees would then go to a Model Cities Policy Committee, also with a West Oakland majority. This committee's recommendations would then be subject to veto by WOPC, which would have its own staff. Only what WOPC approved would be submitted to the City Council, which could veto anything but could not make additions without the approval of WOPC.

But the issue of the broader veto still remained unresolved. Representatives of major federal agencies appeared to concur by saying that they would go along with a neighborhood veto to the extent permitted by law, but this hedging excluded, among others, most of the HEW programs which go through the states. The largest stumbling block, however, was whether WOPC should have a veto over redevelopment projects. This was acceptable to the Redevelopment Agency in the West Oakland residential area, but not in adjacent blocks in downtown Oakland. Earlier the city had included part of the central business district within the boundaries of the West Oakland Model Cities area, and now the City Council, the mayor, and the city manager were adamant that WOPC should not have a veto over a central city project. This dispute lasted into the summer, so Oakland did not get its planning funds with the other first-round cities. WOPC finally yielded on this issue in August and agreed to exclude the center city from the Model Cities area, and a final adjustment took out a few blocks of nearby Chinatown. With this settled, the City Council ratified the response to the discussion paper and Oakland's revised application was submitted to HUD.

By this time, the West Oakland Planning Committee had become a strong and effective instrument for neighborhood action. Its basic membership consisted of delegates from 125 organizations, who elect the executive committee. At the height of the struggle for control, between 200 and 300 attended meetings at least once a month and sometimes biweekly; the executive committee met every week.

There were byproducts of this neighborhood mobilization. For example, while the battle for control of the Model Cities Program was raging, the residents organized a West Oakland Health Council, which obtained a grant from the Economic Development Administration to construct a neighborhood health center and got a commitment from HEW to provide operating funds.

In another bit of fallout from the Model Cities dispute, the West Oakland Planning Committee began negotiating with the Port of Oakland Authority to secure a voice in how nearby port land would be used and to obtain a commitment of jobs for neighborhood residents. This arose because 40 acres of port land were originally included within the model neighborhood boundaries. Because the land is not under the jurisdiction of the City Council, it was not part of the basic dispute between WOPC and the city. But once the issue was raised, it gave West Oakland leaders an entree into negotiations with the Port Authority.

When I visited Oakland in the fall of 1968, the city was awaiting release of Model Cities planning funds from HUD, so I cannot report on the nature of the program being developed. This was my fourth trip to the city since 1962, and I was struck by the changes that had taken place. At the time of my first visit, the Interagency Project was well kept (like City Hall and other public facilities) and tightly controlled by the city manager and his appointees, but not very exciting in program substance. Six years, two city managers, two mayors, and three community action directors later, the organizational arrangements were anything but neat, yet the potential now exists for much greater program depth and far more significant results. In the interim, city control over the community action program had gradually broken down. For a while, Norvel Smith (now president of Merritt College), as head of the Department of Human Resources and executive director of OEDC, had straddled the two horses and yet managed to achieve some results, but finally the two forces were too strong to hold under one set of reins. From 1966 through the middle of 1968, struggle for control arose first in the community action program and then in Model Cities, and in both cases residents of poverty areas gained greater authority. The structure of power is now much more pluralistic in Oakland than it had been.

Whether the arrangement developed for Model Cities will work remains to be seen. The first test will be whether WOPC and the City Council can agree on a program. The second test will occur when action funds are provided by HUD and substantive programs get under way, perhaps in the second half of 1969. All sides have emerged from the struggle in a position to work together for a program that will benefit the citizens of West Oakland and the city as a whole. Only time will tell.

COMMENTARY

Of the cities in the first round of the Model Cities Program, Oakland and Dayton are not typical in the extent of control gained by residents of the model neighborhood. By far the more common pattern is for the neighborhood to have an advisory committee without its own planning funds and to have residents select a minority of the over-all policy board. The prevailing attitude of HUD is that Model Cities belongs basically to the mayor and city government with neighborhood residents associated in a somewhat junior partnership. But faced with a statutory requirement for widespread citizen participation, HUD has required that new cities should provide area residents with a meaningful role in policy-making and then has allowed each community to work out its own solution to this requirement.

Nonetheless, when the federal agency sent out its discussion papers along with the notification of the award of planning funds and issued guidelines on resident involvement, in Dayton and Oakland enough questions were raised about the structure of citizen participation to give neighborhood residents an opening wedge. Thereupon, West Dayton's ad hoc committee and the West Oakland Planning Committee mobilized residents of the proposed model neighborhood. HUD would not release planning funds until the matter of citizen participation was settled. In this situation, these two groups were in a strong bargaining position in that City Hall would either have to work something out or drop the whole program, and it is a rare city that will forgo a new pot of federal funds. The two organizations maintained a united front for their neighborhoods and in the end made the city government make major concessions.

After initial resistance, Dayton's city manager and City Council were more responsive to the residents' demands than similar municipal officials in Oakland. The result was less polarization and fewer hard feelings in Dayton, and this led to faster planning conducted as "equal partners," rather than as contending parties, as in Oakland.

In both cities, the Community Action Program provided background assistance to the neighborhoods. SCOPE, the community action agency in Dayton, refused to sign-off the first draft of the city's application for Model Cities planning funds because residents were not involved: later it channeled funds to the resident-controlled Model Cities Planning Council. The Oakland Economic Development Council supplied full-time staff to the fledgling West Oakland Planning Committee and used its influence as a member of the city manager's task force on behalf of neighborhood residents. In both cities, many of the neighborhood spokesmen had gained leadership experience in the Community Action Program.

Though similar in some respects, the Model Cities citizen planning organizations of the two cities differ in their organizational setup. WOPC is composed of delegates from neighborhood groups, whereas the members of the Planning Council in West Dayton were chosen in an election in which one-fourth of the neighborhood participated. The mode of indirect selection used in Oakland has made the WOPC subject to charges of being self-selected and unrepresentative. Yet, because of its delegate body, the West Oakland committee has had a ready-made constituency for mass meetings and for reporting on the progress of negotiations. In that sense, it has a better means of accountability to the residents than West Dayton, where members of the Planning Council have no structured form of communications with those who elected them in the 27 sub-areas. However, as the action program gets under way in Dayton, broader resident participation is being provided in the satellite corporations being established to operate specific programs.

In both cities, neighborhood unity was forged by a commitment to black pride. Both organizations have succeeded in obtaining support and participation from a fairly broad range of the conservative-militant spectrum. This has meant that the rhetoric has often been strong, and sometimes the presence of hostile-looking youths and young adults at public meetings has seemed intimidating, but militancy has so far been expressed only verbally, not through direct action. In contrast, the Black Panthers, headquartered in another section of Oakland, have been more violent in expression and action but have not developed the organized strength necessary to claim and win neighborhood control of public programs. It is the strong organization, not militant verbosity, that is the key to gaining community control.

What has neighborhood control accomplished? In Dayton, the first-year action plan was clearly different, because racial discrimination was used as the framework for developing program proposals. Oakland's planning is not far enough along to report on. The verdict on whether the new programs will make the neighborhoods better places to live will have to wait another year or two. But already the organizational struggle has paid dividends in West Dayton and West Oakland in raising neighborhood morale and self-pride. And that is worth a lot.

CHAPTER **10** CONCLUSION

This report has reviewed nearly 30 different examples of resident participation in public service programs, showing a variety of forms and styles of community control. Is community control working? Does it make a difference? If so, what kind of difference? Answers to these questions depend to a considerable extent upon the values that underlie the measures of success.

STANDARDS OF JUDGMENT

Efficiency has long been a central criterion in judging the effectiveness of public programs. The term has many usages, but generally definitions relate to the allocation and control of government resources; "the accomplishment of the work at hand with the least expenditure of man-power and materials" is how an influential authority on public administration expressed it in 1937.[1] To be sure, in the last 20 years books on administrative theory have given more attention to "human relations," that is, the social and psychological processes that occur within organizations, but they ultimately do not abandon efficiency as the foundation stone of good administration. For example, the latest fad to sweep public administration was presented in the following manner by a director of the U.S. Bureau of the Budget: "The new planning-programming-budgeting system will be capable of making a major contribution to greater efficiency in the allocation of resources, and thus will increase

---

[1] Luther Gulick, "Science, Values and Public Administration," Papers on the Science of Administration, ed. by Luther Gulick and L. Urwick (New York: Institute of Public Administration, 1937), p. 191.

the benefits derived from the Government's many activities."[2]

Efficiency stresses rationality and thus deals with one part of man's nature. But man is also an emotional being, a creature with feelings, and this side of human nature also needs to be taken into account in judging the effectiveness of a public program. Positive feelings of personal self-worth, identity, belonging, and self-pride (yes, black pride too) should be recognized, along with such negative feelings as alienation, hopelessness, powerlessness, and rage. Thus, how people feel must join with efficiency in measuring the success of public programs.

This does not mean that wasting scarce resources can be automatically justified if it makes some persons feel better. But it does mean that the dollar sign in itself is not sufficient for judging program effectiveness. Human feelings should be considered as well.

EVALUATION SUMMARY

Let me now review the various community-controlled programs described in the previous chapters in terms of the dual test of efficiency and feelings. My judgments are, of course, subjective, but they are based upon direct observation conditioned by years of involvement with community programs.

On the whole, the network of community corporations in New York City is not remarkably efficient. There is much slippage in the system, a lot of wheel-spinning, and the end product of new opportunities and better services for poor people seems to be relatively small in proportion to expenditures and efforts made. Yet the present arrangement is accomplishing more in concrete program results than the more centralized system of municipal control that previously existed. Furthermore, some of the individual

---

[2]Charles L. Schultze in an introduction to <u>Program Budgeting . . . Program Analysis and the Federal Budget,</u> ed. by David Novick (Washington, D.C.: Government Printing Office, 1964), p. iii.

CONCLUSION

community corporations rank in the top quartile of community action programs around the country.

As to feelings, New York's community corporations and the central Council Against Poverty represent a distinct gain for the city's poor. There have been heated intra-community struggles for power, a lot of contention for position, some dissatisfaction with the end result, and wonderment of whether it was worth the effort. But through all of this, community residents are beginning to have a little more control over programs that serve them. Alienation has not disappeared nor has powerlessness been dissipated, but positive steps are being taken to enable black people and Puerto Ricans to feel they are more a part of their community and that they have a worthwhile place in this giant of cities.

The ten neighborhood programs in Washington, D.C., are conducted by three different types of organizations: community corporations, conventional social welfare agencies, and branch offices of UPO, the community action agency. There is no clear indication that one form is superior or inferior to the others. The two community corporations described in this report represent a contrast in effectiveness: one struggling, the other performing well.

But apart from organizational form, the entire neighborhood program in Washington constitutes a significant broadening of civic participation in a city that has been blocked from the usual kinds of political activities by Congress, which does not permit citizens to elect their own mayor and city council. The citizen's advisory committees and their representatives on the board of UPO have given several hundred citizens a role in public life for the first time. Persons so engaged are moving on to other civic activities.

In Newark, the United Community Corporation made a promising start with eight area boards, which formed a strong foundation for resident participation, the basis for selection of representatives of the poor to the central board, and a source of representation for subsidiary corporations. The area boards went into an eclipse as a result of ineffective staff leadership for a year, conflict between City Hall and the black community, and requirements by OEO that UCC headquarters take stronger control of the community action program. Only now are some of the area boards moving toward incorporation, but altogether they have less than 10 per cent of the UCC budget.

ECCO in Columbus has shown that a neighborhood center governed by neighborhood residents can be as effective as the usual settlement house with a non-resident majority on its board (the case with 80 per cent of the settlements in the United States). These traditional settlements argue that having board members from both within and outside the neighborhoods helps to overcome the separation in an increasingly polarized society (although this could be done with a resident majority). They have also justified outside control on the basis that it helps in fundraising and gives assurance to the United Fund that the settlement will be well managed. Since ECCO has received funds from Washington, it has escaped the need for sponsorship by the local "establishment." But once the federal demonstration money runs out, ECCO will face a day of reckoning, and to survive it will have to develop stronger ties with those who control program funds in Columbus.

The rural areas discussed in this report have lesser developed institutional structures than the cities, and therefore there are very few established agencies with which to compare the rudimentary efforts in which the rural poor have a voice. Where they have programs in common with other parts of the country, such as Head Start, the rural programs with significant resident participation seem to be doing as well as those operated by more experienced agencies in cities.

However, it is in reaching out to the rural poor and involving them in civic activities for the first time that these programs are performing particularly noteworthy work, for there is probably no more isolated group in American society than the rural poor. In Mississippi, of course, the scene is superimposed on a racist social system so that community control is inextricably involved in the movement for racial liberation. Mexican-Americans in the Arizona and California communities discussed also feel the adversity of discrimination and separation, and resident control also provides an opportunity for them to move into the mainstream of American life.

CONCLUSION

As Indian tribes conduct their own community action programs, they gain a kind of freedom rarely permitted before by the paternalistic Bureau of Indian Affairs. For the first year or two, some of the tribes (though not the ones discussed in this report) performed poorly with the new responsibility, but on the whole the programs have been well run. This demonstrated capacity to manage their own affairs has strengthened tribal morale, and it has stimulated the BIA to adopt measures that enlarge the role of tribal councils, such as contracts to perform specific services.

From an efficiency standard, the pilot neighborhood centers operated by community corporations do not rate very high. The difficulties of organizing the corporations vastly complicated the task of establishing an interagency approach, which was at the heart of the pilot program. In two of the cities, Washington and Philadelphia, the precarious position of the corporations in the institutional structure has made them weak instruments for coordinating the work of other agencies. But where their role is more certain, such as in St. Louis and Hunts Point, New York, the resident-controlled neighborhood centers have helped to pull together services at the neighborhood level better than previous efforts.

A coordinating mechanism masterminded downtown at City Hall or at the headquarters of the health and welfare council may be able to muster more force over various service agencies, but these central agencies, even with the use of branch offices and neighborhood advisory committees, can probably never develop as much neighborhood support as a community corporation can. Perhaps a workable combination of central leadership and neighborhood operations would be one in which the central authorities set up the ground rules for coordination and then delegate substantial coordinating powers to the corporation board and to the staff executive of the neighborhood center. But none of the four pilot cities surveyed has gone very far in that direction.

In the field of urban renewal, MICCO in Washington's Shaw area illustrates significant neighborhood participation in equal-bargaining planning to the extent of determining many features of the redevelopment plan. In a more controlled fashion, the Bayview-Hunters Point Joint Housing Committee and the San

Francisco Redevelopment Agency engaged in collaborative planning to the general satisfaction of both sides. But advocacy planning in the same project broke down when the outside planning consultant tried to be the spokesman for the neighborhood rather than an expert adviser to the Non-Profit Development Corporation. The Shaw area plan was probably better because of neighborhood involvement; the Hunters Point physical plan likely would have been about the same without citizen participation, but a social program element was added in Hunters Point and probably would not have been included otherwise. Moreover, in both cases, black neighborhoods came to support a program which previously had been called "Negro removal."

The emergence of neighborhood councils as dominant forces in Model Cities planning in Dayton and Oakland constituted a whole new approach to the relationship between muncipal government and black neighborhoods in those cities. In Dayton, the residents call it "equal partnership;" and in Oakland, neighborhood control is even stronger. The plan produced in Dayton starts with racial discrimination as the general background problem and develops solutions accordingly. This study terminated before the Oakland plan was ready, so the results in that city cannot be related here. In both places, important gains have been registered in the feelings of residents.

In sum, various forms and styles of community control of public service programs are making differences in a number of cities. Unmistakably, on the feelings side of my standard for judgment, significant results have been achieved. On the efficiency side, a number of the community corporations are performing well, and with one or two exceptions all those surveyed are doing no worse than related decentralized operations without resident control.

The community control approach is not an easy one to carry out, and progress is not inevitable. The movement toward community control should, however, be viewed developmentally; that is, it should be seen in a time perspective. We are only in about the fourth year of a significant change in the way of organizing social programs, and the promise in this change may take a couple of decades to be fulfilled.

CONCLUSION

It might be useful to recall that in 1786, ten years after the 13 American colonies declared their independence from Great Britain, there were many signs of failure of this new approach to self-government. But in three more years, a new Constitution was in effect and George Washington was installed as the first President in a government that has since endured. Yet even then, local government in many of the new states struggled another decade or two before achieving a reasonable level of effectiveness as newly franchised citizens gradually developed experience in self-government. This is the time perspective needed for the emerging forms of community control.

UNITY, KNOW-HOW, AND LEADERSHIP

Even though the development of greater community control is in its infancy, there is already enough experience to draw upon for some preliminary conclusions and to extract some tentative generalizations. The common ingredients in the most successful community corporations are neighborhood unity and technical know-how, which is expressed by and through effective leadership. These intangibles are far more important than any particular form of organization or operating procedures.

By neighborhood unity I do not mean uniform opinion or monolithic organization. Rather, the crucial factor of unity is a willingness to work together regardless of potentially divisive influences. This is particularly a challenge in neighborhoods with two or more ethnic and racial groups and where residents cover a wide range of the conservative-militant spectrum. But the Brownsville Community Corporation (New York City) has achieved united action among blacks and Puerto Ricans, the Guadalupe Organization (Arizona) has enabled Mexican-Americans and Yaqui Indians to work together, and MICCO (Washington, D.C.) and the West Oakland Planning Committee have had the support of militant blacks as well as less activist middle-class residents.

Know-how is required in order to deal effectively with the many laws and regulations that surround most social programs, financed as they are by government funds. Moreover, in many fields of service--education, health, city planning, manpower training, and so on--there is an established body of knowledge which, even though it need not be accepted as the final word, should be comprehended in the design of new programs. Although some central agencies provide technical assistance to community corporations, the best corporations have independent sources of knowledge through staff, board members, and consultants.

Effective leadership is the other crucial element in the success story of the best community corporations. Let there be no mistake; decentralization and grass-roots democracy do not lessen the need for leaders. What community control does is broaden the basis for leadership selection, to eliminate issues of social class, wealth, formal education, and occupation which have wrongly narrowed the choice of community leaders in the past. Every one of these communities has leaders, already recognized by their fellow citizens, waiting for an opportunity and a better structural arrangement through which it can be more effectively expressed. But the leaders need technical know-how and a setting of reasonable unity so that the leadership element is not engaged in factional struggles, thereby preventing achievement of community goals.

But more leadership training is needed if community-controlled programs are to be successful. This has been recognized belatedly by the Community Development Agency which oversees community corporations in New York City and by the Neighborhood Centers Pilot Program. In both instances, corporations were formed and thrust into business without new board members knowing enough about the purpose and potential of their new organizations and without having the experience or training to understand their role as policymakers, not administrators. A university consortium has helped Indian tribal councils with leadership development, but most other places have not had a training program for leaders.

Although more systematic leadership training is needed, there is ultimately no substitute for actual experience. This takes time. Leaders in Guadalupe, Hunter Point, West Oakland, and East Central Columbus have had a number of years of apprenticeship. In Mississippi, leadership development has occurred in the face of strong opposition from a hostile

CONCLUSION

"establishment," and from this experience have come some of the most effective grass-roots leaders in the United States.

Staffs need training, too--the executive directors as well as other members. The chief executive of a community corporation needs the administrative abilities of a city manager and the political sensitivity of a mayor. Finding such well-qualified administrative generalists who can be effective community leaders is an extremely difficult task. Indeed, the shortage of persons of this caliber is one of the major problems of virtually all of the "Great Society" programs started during the last five years.

Technical assistance is another need of the fledgling community corporations. OSTI has helped the neighborhood center corporations, the university consortium has assisted the Indian tribes, and some of the community action agencies have helped neighborhood corporations. But on the whole, this resource has been vastly inadequate in quality and quantity. The necessary technical assistance can and should come in a variety of ways. Corporations should have funds to hire their own consultants; the local agency delegating program responsibility should have technical assistance units, and so should federal and state agencies; perhaps there should also be a number of independent regional organizations specializing in helping community corporations.

As for unity, most of what must be done to keep a neighborhood united depends upon the action of resident leaders. But outside agencies can help. For one thing, now that community control is gaining in popularity, it seems that each federal agency wants to fund its own community corporation; as a result, the traditional division among the federal bureaucracies is being duplicated in inner-city neighborhoods. The worst example is in Washington, D.C., where in one section of the city the following federal agencies fund independent corporations or quasi-independent operations: OEO (four different ones); HUD/Model Cities; HUD/Urban Renewal; Labor Department (two); and District government (two). I do not believe that a single all-encompassing community corporation should be a mandatory requirement for each neighborhood--for instance, economic development and social services require significantly different skills and approaches and therefore need not be handled by the same agency--but I am convinced that the present proliferation is intended more to serve the bureaucratic needs of federal agencies than the interests of neighborhood residents.

REPRESENTATIVENESS AND ACCOUNTABILITY

If federal, state, and local government agencies are going to fund community corporations, they are faced with the need to know who truly speaks for the community. And if a community corporation is to gain legitimacy as an authentic instrument for decentralized operations controlled by residents, it must demonstrate that it is governed by a board that is representative of and accountable to the community.

Long experience in the United States has shown that to gain a representative governing body there is no adequate substitute for the use of democratic procedures that achieve widespread citizen participation. But as to what procedures work best with community corporations, there is no clear answer from the experience of the last few years.

A number of corporations have used direct elections in which all neighborhood residents over a certain age (usually 16) have been eligible to participate. Of the corporations examined in this study, 5 to 10 per cent participation has been typical; the best record was 25 per cent in West Dayton.[3] The latter seems to have produced a reasonably representative governing board, and so have some of the others with lesser turnouts. But in some of the New York City community corporations, it was found that choosing all board members by direct election tended in some instances to produce ethnic imbalance and in

---

[3] A survey of municipal elections held independently of other elections in 1962 found the following median turnout of adults: partisan elections--for mayor, 43 per cent; for councilman, 37 per cent; nonpartisan elections--for mayor, 32 per cent; for councilman, 23 per cent. <u>The Municipal Year Book, 1963</u> (Washington, D.C.: International City Managers' Association, 1963), pp. 80-83.

other cases to exclude experienced middle-class neighborhood leaders who, although perhaps representing a small constituency, could contribute to the running of corporation affairs.

The membership corporation used a variation of the direct election approach. Any resident may join the corporation, but only members may vote. This is the case with the Guadalupe Organization (Arizona), the Hunters Point-Bayview Non-Profit Development Corporation (San Francisco), and CHANGE, Inc. (Washington). With these, also, there has been a range of voter turnout.

Indirect election, such as having organizational delegates choose the governing board, seems to have worked well in some cities, for example, with the West Oakland Planning Committee. Yet, in an earlier period in New York City, this method produced community committees composed mostly of middle-class persons to the exclusion of the poor.

In some places, a proportion of the seats, ranging from one-third to two-thirds, are reserved for poor persons, on the grounds that they would not otherwise be adequately represented. Other communities let the residents choose whom they think best represents their interests. Even without reserved seats, most of the boards have a considerable number of poor members.

There are a few boards of community-controlled programs whose members are co-opted, that is, selected by a small leadership group to be representative. The Bedford-Stuyvesant Restoration Corporation, an economic development group, is of this variety, and it has a fairly broad range of the conservative-militant spectrum. MICCO in Washington started with a small co-opted group, and when its board expanded, specific organizations were chosen and allowed to elect representatives. These two organizations have delivered effective programs and are supported in their communities, but self-selected boards that are not very productive are more likely to be challenged as not truly representing the community. Usually it helps to have the legitimacy that democratic selection procedures provide.

A number of places have combined selection methods, electing some members directly and having others appointed either by those elected or by a body of delegates. At first, the executive council of ECCO in Columbus had 13 members chosen by the general assembly and 8 by neighborhood clubs; later, this was changed to have the assembly elect 14 and the clubs 16. Twenty members of the board of the Hartranft Community Corporation in Philadelphia are elected, and public officials appoint four. In the second round of selecting board members in New York's community corporations, two-thirds were elected and the rest appointed.

In rural areas, a pyramid of representation seems to be the most common pattern, with community action committees (chosen by direct election) selecting representatives to the district, county, and multi-county boards. For instance, Friends of the Children of Mississippi is governed by a board selected by county councils, which in turn are made up of persons chosen by the center committees, which are elected by ballot. In Tulare County, California, a new county-wide corporation has been formed and will be governed by delegates from community action committees whose members are elected directly by residents of small settlements.

There is no clear evidence that one selection method is superior to another in all places at all times, but whatever procedures are used, the mandate of the electorate should be renewed regularly. In a number of cities, there are neighborhood advisory committees that were chosen during the first year of the "war on poverty" and have become self-perpetuating, and they have then been bypassed by the next program seeking a representative neighborhood group. This happened, for example, in both Dayton and Oakland when the new Model Cities groups were set up because the old CAP neighborhood committees were no longer representative. To provide for regular "consent of the people," most corporations have annual elections of the whole board, although some provide for two-year (or three-year) overlapping terms so that one-half (or one-third) of the board is up for election each year.

To get a representative board, some persons associated with community corporations, community action agencies, and OEO believe that large numbers are needed. This may or may not be true, depending upon the circumstances. When many members are added to a board of directors, it begins to take on the character of an assembly. Because many persons may want to speak on each topic, relatively few items are placed on the agenda for significant discussion and more matters are referred to committees for detailed consideration by a few individuals. This is the way Congress and state legislatures work, and the will of the small committee is almost always respected. In contrast, when a board is not excessively large, the entire board membership can consider more issues, which means that discussion can reflect a broader range of views than the assembly and committees system.

While it may be useful to back the work of a community corporation with a larger delegate assembly, general membership, or open "town meeting," a board of about 21 members and probably no larger than 30 can provide a reasonable balance between representativeness and effectiveness. Moreover, if the membership is not too large, the chance of paying a stipend to board members is greater--and this might be appropriate, particularly in low-income neighborhoods.

Another major concern is whether the corporation boards are accountable. Do they have methods for continuously consulting neighborhood opinion, for obtaining views on proposed programs, for reporting on action taken? The answer for many of the corporations is "no," and most do not make enough effort to be accountable. They operate without the kind of hearings customarily conducted by city councils, state legislatures, and Congress. Corporation board members who are directly elected have no organized constituency to consult with; those chosen by organizations do have specific groups to report to. The membership corporations, such as ECCO and the Guadalupe Organization, have assemblies that convene periodically, and other corporations organize neighborhood meetings or send representatives to other groups. Most of the corporations have a newsletter, which reports on program activities. But not enough is being done along those lines.

Although community corporations have been organized specifically to achieve greater resident participation, they themselves need to increase the prospects for citizen involvement in their own affairs. The larger the community served, the greater is the need. Some of the big-city corporations, serving areas of

25,000 to 100,000 (and up to 300,000 in New York City) probably should decentralize and turn certain operations over to neighborhood boards serving small areas. All corporations should have a conscious strategy of citizen involvement.

More resident participation and better means of accountability are matters that deserve more attention if this new form of organization for community control is to become a vital new instrument of American democracy.

THE CENTRAL AGENCY

Each of the community corporations studied in this volume serves as a decentralized operation of a program funded by a central agency. All receive and spend federal funds. The majority get these funds through a local agency, such as the community action agency, the Model Cities agency, the redevelopment agency, or the school board. The only ones funded directly from Washington are the Indian tribes, two Head Start agencies and the Delta Opportunities Corporation in Mississippi, and in part, ECCO in Columbus. Therefore, the relationship with the local central agency is a crucial factor in the life of community corporations.

In almost all cases, this relationship has been troublesome at some time or other. In New York, certain agencies within the Human Resources Administration resisted for a while the plan to work with and through community corporations; the Community Development Agency, which was supposed to help them, was long ill-equipped to do so; and the Council Against Poverty has not always respected local determination. Also in New York, the Hunts Point Multi-Service Center Corporation had to fight against these agencies and the local community corporation as well. ECCO has been engaged in a continuous battle with the Columbus Metropolitan Area Community Action Organization, from which it gets part of its operating funds. In Newark, the United Community Corporation pulled back on the trend toward greater control by area boards. UPO in Washington has been ambivalent in its commitment to community corporations, particularly with the People's Involvement Corporation set up to run the pilot neighborhood center. The Association

CONCLUSION 219

of Communities of Bolivar County (Mississippi) had a hard struggle to get Head Start funds from the county community action agency and is always uncertain whether its funds will continue. In St. Louis, the Yeatman District Corporation has gotten along well with its primary sponsor, the Human Development Corporation, but its relationship with the Model Cities Agency, a secondary sponsor, has been touch and go. The Hartranft Community Corporation has had fairly smooth relations with the school board, its sponsor, but not with the Philadelphia Anti-Poverty Action Council. The Bayview-Hunters Point Community Non-Profit Development Corporation, funded through the community action agency, got into a public dispute with the San Francisco Redevelopment Agency. The citizens in West Dayton and West Oakland gained control over the Model Cities Program only after a long fight with City Hall.

Interestingly, these struggles have not been so noticeable in the rural community action programs in West Virginia, Kentucky, and Tulare County, California. The reason seems to be that the community action groups and district councils are much more creatures of the community action agency and are much more clearly a part of the agency's strategy. However, both the central agencies and the community action groups have engaged in fights with county governments. In the cities, even where the central agency seems to be encouraging community corporations, it is caught in the midst of greater counter-pressures, so that its commitment to decentralization becomes compromised.

Some of the urban cases, though, present general harmonious relations. MICCO was in a strong enough position to engage in equal bargaining with the Redevelopment Land Agency of the District of Columbia. Although it lacked final decision-making power, MICCO relied upon the public pressures it could mobilize, which were considerable. The Bayview-Hunters Point Joint Housing Committee participated in collaborative planning with the San Francisco Redevelopment Agency, although it had no direct control of urban renewal planning funds.

The Guadalupe Organization was in existence when the "war on poverty" began and got its first grant directly from OEO before a county community action program was organized. Thereafter, the

Maricopa County Community Action Agency has treated GO as a delegate agency, not as one of its own decentralized area councils. This has meant fewer of the "parent-child" relations that are the hallmark of the relationship between a number of community action agencies and community corporations.

It is not too surprising that the relations between central agencies and corporations have been difficult in most places. After all, the process of decentralization and community control means that the central body is losing some of its power. And power is not like a Thanksgiving basket, which can be given as an act of charity; it must be demanded and claimed. No matter how committed the central agency is to the idea of decentralized control, the community corporation has to press in order to gain the measure of control the residents want. The boundaries of what belongs to the community and what belongs to the central agency are nearly always unclear, and this makes contention virtually inevitable.

Transition can be much smoother, though, if the central body makes up its mind that decentralization and community control is beneficial for both the neighborhood and the larger community. Then that commitment must be backed up by varied measures of technical assistance and training programs so that community leaders and staff will be able to perform well under their new responsibilities. Indeed, the most difficult situations have been those in which the agency could not decide whether it really wanted decentralization and consequently adopted halfway measures.

This does not mean that decentralization requires the central agency to abrogate all responsibility for the program. The community action agency, the Model Cities agency, and redevelopment authority, the school board, or whichever agency delegates programs and money to community corporations is accountable for how these public funds are expended. Therefore, it needs to set and enforce standards for fiscal management and personnel administration. It should guarantee the rights of employees who have been operating the program from the central agency and who are transferred to the community-controlled agency. It should require the community corporation to adopt and carry out grievance procedures for its employees. If the corporation is to serve as an umbrella agency and assign funds to other neighborhood groups, it should be required to follow due process in making such determinations. Most staff and board members of community corporations to whom I have talked seem willing to accept such standards if clearly specified and fairly enforced.

A much touchier area is the control of program emphasis. The central agency wants to adopt a rational plan for achieving its objectives, such as the elimination of poverty, the improvement of living conditions, or the education of children; and the central planners and executives believe they know what programs are needed. But the corporation leaders also want a say in how their funds are spent. In the case of umbrella community corporations, this raises the question of which neighborhood groups should be funded. Here the central agency may have its favorites or may suspect the leaders of the community corporation of favoritism. The corporation rebuts that the selection of who should be funded in the neighborhood is at the heart of community control. The dispute then is a matter of power and a matter of trust.

One way to handle the problem is through quality controls, designed to be as self-enforcing as possible. Thus, the community corporation would be required to have a plan of action, precisely stating its objectives and whom it intends to serve. Then it would be required to present measures of success by reporting what it is accomplishing and whom it is actually serving. Within that framework, the corporation would have considerable freedom of action, but it would be held accountable for its actions.

NEED FOR A STRATEGY

What is needed is an over-all strategy on decentralization and community control. An agency can decentralize without providing community control, but if it does move toward community control, it is likely to find itself involved in a process of decentralization that is contrary to some of the established dogma of public administration. A thorough-going strategy of community control will require us to rethink some of the basic premises that have come to dominate administrative theory.

Much of our thinking in public administration is founded on a commitment to a hierarchical form of organization. In 1949, the Hoover Commission stated how this was supposed to work:

> Responsibility and accountability are impossible without authority--the power to direct. The exercise of authority is impossible without a clear line of command from the top to the bottom, and a return line of responsibility and accountability from the bottom to the top.[4]

There it is, clear and simple. The ones on top command, those below respond. This theory is reconciled with democracy by stating that the man at the top is elected by the people so that he, and even the lowest subordinate through the chain of command, is accountable to the electorate.

But community control, although not necessarily turning the pyramid completely upside down, alters significantly this traditional hierarchical relationship. It creates another system of representation alongside that of municipal government and empowers those new community representatives to undertake directly, without going to the top and then down the chain of command to get things done. Still, the public funds are controlled by the old system, and the administrators want the same relationship with the community corporation that they have previously had with their subordinate branches. But they cannot if there is to be community control.

Students of public administration realize that a strict hierarchical form of organization is more a conceptional model than a completely accurate desription of reality. Constitutional checks and balances prevent the executive branch from having unlimited power. Interest groups intrude from the outside, and interaction among employees and agency units work from within to modify the hierarchical relationship.

---

[4]U.S. Commission on Organization of the Executive Branch of the Government, <u>General Management of Executive Branch</u> (Washington, D.C.: Government Printing Office, 1949), p. 51.

Nevertheless, many administrative practices are designed to strengthen hierarchical control. For example, the planning-programming-budgeting system was instituted in the Defense Department by Secretary Robert McNamara to gain greater control over the divided policy planning of the armed services. The technique has been extended to the entire federal executive branch to increase central control as well as to achieve greater efficiency in the allocation of public funds.

In contrast, community control says that several thousand local corporations around the country will have the right to decide the priorities for spending a certain segment of public funds. This is bound to boggle the mind of the well-schooled administrator. But if feelings and citizen participation are valued as well as efficiency, then alteration of traditional administrative practices is inevitably required.

Changing some of our administrative practices and modifying administrative theory does not necessarily mean abandoning any and all forms of central control and hierarchical relationships. In my previous example, I believe that it was desirable for the civilian leadership of the Defense Department to have greater control over the planning done by the military. There are areas where stronger presidential leadership is needed, such as in truly mobilizing the nation's resources to eliminate poverty. Governors and mayors need better management tools to pull together the operations of state and local governments, for these chief executives are elected by the people, unlike the agency heads which operate without any direct popular control.

Thus, while in some cases more central control may be desirable, in other situations greater decentralization is needed. It is not a matter of either/or. It is a matter of degree. And what is appropriate in the balance between centralization and decentralization changes over time. But at this time in American history, decentralization should have greater emphasis, not merely from the national government to states and municipalities but also to neighborhoods and to small rural settlements.

NEIGHBORHOOD GOVERNMENT

If this is so, how far should we go with community control? Should we have neighborhood government, as some are starting to advocate? Does the experience thus far with community corporations indicate that they could become units of general government at the neighborhood level?

To answer the last question first, I would say that the corporations are too new for their potential and limitations to be fully understood. It appears that ECCO in Columbus, whose ideological father wanted it to become a neighborhood government, has little chance of gaining that status. In New York City, the Lindsay administration as a whole does not have enough faith in the community corporations to give them significant roles in other programs, such as in the Model Cities program, for which a new set of community agencies was created; and most of the New York corporations have been slow to demonstrate that they have the capacity to take on much more. Washington, D.C., also has a proliferation of competing community corporations in the same areas, and such division prevents a neighborhood from having a primary citizen-controlled agency which might take on added responsibilities.

Of the corporations examined in this study, the closest to neighborhood government are the two "second-generation" approaches--the West Dayton Model Cities Planning Council and the West Oakland Planning Committee. Building on the start made under the Community Action Program, these groups have claimed neighborhood control over the Model Cities Program and, through Model Cities, over a variety of programs financed from other sources. In the future, they will likely effect a merger with CAP in their neighborhoods and overcome the divisive competition fostered by the two federal agencies that run these programs nationally.

The arrangement in these two cities is a new twist to the old doctrine of the separation of powers. An early writer on this topic was James Harrington, the seventeenth-century English political theorist who described the fictitious Commonwealth of Oceana,

CONCLUSION

in which a small, essentially aristocratic body formulated policies and a larger, popularly elected group accepted or rejected these proposals but could not modify them. It is like two schoolgirls dividing a cake, he wrote; one cuts, the other chooses. In West Oakland and in West Dayton, the neighborhood agency formulated the program proposals, and the city council concurs, vetoes, but cannot adopt any modification unless it is agreed to by the community board. It is a promising blend of community control with the hierarchical system of fund distributions.

Even though the neighborhoods of West Dayton and West Oakland carry community control this one step further, they are still dealing mainly with programs paid by federal grants. So far, they are not demanding control over traditional municipal service functions, such as sanitation, housing inspection, streets, police, schools, libraries, and so one, although they may come to that. There are cities, though, where inner-city residents, particularly in black neighborhoods, are demanding control of some of these functions, especially schools and police. The reason invariably is that the residents are convinced that the personnel running these services are not properly attuned to the needs of their neighborhood and may even be hostile to their aspirations. In these instances, demand for community control tends to signal a breakdown in the service system and not merely the advocacy of a social theorist or a general drive for power. If the trash is collected and the streets are repaired, most citizens do not care who manages the services. But when the schools are not educating their children properly and the police are harassing but not protecting them, neighborhood leaders begin to wonder whether they might do better by running the services themselves.

In all likelihood, the broadening of community control will come about most often in response to local demands related to specific needs. To make this process as rational as possible, it would be helpful to have a careful analysis of which functions can be effectively performed at the neighborhood level, which ones need city-wide action, which require a metropolitan basis, and which can be handled in more than one way. For example, in the transportation field, mass rapid transit would require a metropolitan system, major boulevards could be handled by the city, and maintenance of local streets, alleys, and sidewalks could be a neighborhood function--if the neighborhood wanted to undertake this task. And likewise with other public service functions.

As helpful as such an analysis might be, it is even more important that we enter into the quest for community control with an open mind and a willingness to try new approaches. We should be pragmatic and experimental, letting community corporations evolve, testing their strengths, correcting their weaknesses, giving them new assignments, facilitating mergers of needlessly competing neighborhood agencies, not expecting every city to be alike or even every neighborhood in the same city, willing to accept variation, recognizing the merits of pluralism.

A FINAL WORD

Community control is in part a matter of power: who gets what, when, and how, as Harold Lasswell formulated the central issue of politics some 30 years ago.[5] Democratic selection procedures and pluralistic organization are methods long used in the United States to make officeholders responsible and to prevent misuse of power. In many ways, the community corporation is an extension of these practices, a fresh institutional development to deal with an age-old problem.

Community control is also a matter of freedom, the right of man to control the institutions that serve him and not be controlled by them. And freedom is one of the most precious commodities of our democratic heritage. Indeed, freedom is at the very heart of democracy.

In our system, government should be an instrument not to rule us but to serve as an organized means for obtaining the common good. Community corporations, perhaps leading to varied forms of neighborhood government, are in essence a new version of local democracy. As such they should be nurtured. If they are, I believe they will flourish and will serve us well.

---

[5]Harold D. Lasswell, <u>Politics: Who Gets What, When, How</u> (New York: McGraw-Hill, 1936).

ABOUT THE AUTHOR

Howard W. Hallman is President of the Center for Governmental Studies, a Washington, D.C. organization that does research into the workings of public programs and their aspects of citizen participation and decentralization. During the 1967 Congressional session, when he was director of the poverty program study of the Senate Subcommittee on Employment, Manpower and Poverty, he directed nationwide public hearings and assisted in drafting the Economic Opportunity Amendments of 1967 and the Emergency Employment bill.

From 1959 to 1965, Mr. Hallman was New Haven's Director of the Division of Neighborhood Improvement of the Redevelopment Agency, principal planner of the community action program, deputy director of Community Progress, Inc. (established to administer the community action program), and consultant to the President's Task Force on Poverty. Prior to his New Haven experiences, he spent seven years in Philadelphia with the Philadelphia Housing Association and as consultant to several citizens' groups.

Mr. Hallman has contributed numerous articles to such publications as the Journal of Housing, Housing Yearbook, Land Economics, and the Journal of the American Institute of Planners, and has written many reports to the U.S. Senate.

Howard Hallman received B.A. and M.A. degrees in political science from the University of Kansas.